60 MORE Seasonal Homilies
by Fr. Bill Bausch

TWENTY-THIRD PUBLICATIONS

185 Willow Street • PO BOX 180 • MYSTIC, CT 06355
TEL: 1-800-321-0411 • FAX: 1-800-572-0788
E-MAIL: ttpubs@aol.com • www.twentythirdpublications.com

Second printing 2003

Twenty-Third Publications
A Division of Bayard
185 Willow Street
P.O. Box 180
Mystic, CT 06355
(860) 536-2611
(800) 321-0411
www.twentythirdpublications.com

ISBN:1-58595-198-6
Library of Congress Catalog Card Number: 2001135979
Printed in the U.S.A.

Dedication

To Father Bill Anderson
on his fiftieth anniversary of ordination.
In many ways, priest, prophet, and king.

Contents

Holidays

September 11, 2001

Introduction

What I often hear from different folks around the country gives me a good feeling. One priest from the Virgin Islands, for example, presided at the funeral of a young man who died by his own hand. He didn't know what to say for the homily. But someone gave him one of my homily books and he gave one of my homilies verbatim and it was very well-received. Others have told me gratefully how often they use the homilies, either verbatim or modified, with great effect. Many deacons tell me they rely on them. Why do I mention this? To boast? No, to confess. For the truth of the matter is that I in turn have drawn on the insights and gifts of others, and all my homilies—all of them—reflect my earnest debt to them.

And that's how it should be. "No man is an island." So goes the saying; and the same is certainly true about the homilist. Thus this new collection of homilies reflects this fact. Most, if not all of the homilies herein, are sparked by a fetching thought or insight from another with more talent and insight than I have. At times I will copy substantially from others, adding my own twist here and there. At other times, I will simply borrow an idea or a story or a paragraph and spin my own words around them. In either case, I am acutely aware that I am standing on the shoulders of others and if others are standing on my shoulders, they should know that the shoulders go all the way down. And so, I take for granted, and indeed desire, that others, if they so wish, continue to use, copy, change, borrow freely what they find here.

In the notes at the end I acknowledge those remembered sources, while being aware that there may be others I have either forgotten or so absorbed that I think they are my own. If anyone from whom I have borrowed sees no reference, call my publisher for a correction and please accept my apologies.

One decision I have made with these homilies is not to change local references or dated allusions. I think keeping them gives a better sense of immediacy. If I mention an article naming my local newspa-

1

per as its source, for example, I give the reader enough common sense to know that he or she can change that paper to their own local paper. If I allude to a religious or political or social event now past I credit the reader with enough intelligence to keep the dynamics of the thought and update the reference.

After a kind of introductory homily on spirituality, the homilies generally follow the liturgical year from Advent to Pentecost and through Ordinary Time, ending with some homilies for other specific occasions. At the beginning of each homily I list the liturgical season, the Scripture reference, and the theme I am trying to develop (except where the theme is obvious from the title itself).

One final comment. This book deals with passion. You have in this volume sixty homilies. Within that number there will inevitably be some unevenness, some homilies being more powerful and attractive than others. Whatever the case, you are reading words written down that once were spoken, preached, and proclaimed, often with great subtlety but always with passion. And there is no way I can convey this spoken passion on paper. So it is good to remember that the feeling, intonation, cadence, and pathos that come from a spoken presentation are missing. As such, it might be a good idea, rather than just to read the words silently, to say them out loud; even better, to stand up and preach them. It does make a difference.

For now, here they are.

1

Spirituality

No special liturgical time or theme here. Just a general introduction to the series on a timely topic.

I want to tell you up front that my topic for today's homily—a bit challenging for summertime—is spirituality. I say that so you can be prepared to be bored. And why not? Spirituality is one of those chameleon words that can mean almost anything. And, besides, it sounds so "theological," so esoteric, something from la-la land where those other-worldly saints and mystics dwell. So, catch your nap, and while you're taking forty winks, I'll come at spirituality from a different angle. But, first, some necessary preliminary background.

More than one observer has commented that in our age there is a virtual conspiracy against the interior life. What they mean is not that there is a conscious conspiracy against proper values and true spirituality. What they mean is that today, a number of historical circumstances are blindly flowing together and accidentally conspiring to produce a climate within which it is difficult not just to think about God or to pray, but simply to have any inner depth whatsoever. We must admit that the air we breathe today is generally not conducive to the interior life.

Why? What factors are accidentally conspiring to cause this situation? Well, among the many things that work against the interior life today, four can be singled out as particularly powerful: narcissism, pragmatism, unbridled restlessness, and speed. These are like the Four Horsemen running roughshod over our spiritual lives.

Defined simply, narcissism means excessive self-preoccupation; *my* world, *my* career, *my* image, *my* wants, *my* needs, *my* happiness. This excessive self-absorption is a major feature of MTV—if you can stand to watch it.

3

Pragmatism means an excessive focus on work, achievement, and the practical concerns of life. You see this in the career folk who pass by human relationships in the night.

Restlessness means an excessive greed for experience, overeating, as it were, not in terms of food but in trying to drink in too much of life. Note the popularity of extreme sports and extreme reality programs on TV.

Speed means an excessive pace that simply doesn't allow time for contemplation. Today, for example, we just don't do one thing anymore: we multi-task. In the car we drink coffee, listen to self-improvement tapes, talk on the cell phone, and floss. We use shampoo that cuts down drying time by thirty percent. Politicians are coached to speak in ten-second soundbites, and a three-minute television news segment is considered long. Smell the roses? Fine, if you order them on the Web and ship them overnight.

Narcissism accounts for our heartaches, pragmatism accounts for our headaches, restlessness accounts for our insomnia, and speed accounts for our shallowness. And the combination of all four together accounts for the fact that we rarely find the time and space to be in touch with the deeper movements inside of and around us because they dissipate our energies. And that's the word that zeroes in our topic: energy.

If there is one thing you can say about spirituality it is that spirituality concerns energy; human desire, the fire in our bellies, a hunger, a gnawing nostalgia, the ache at the center of human existence. In short, spirituality is what we do with our energy, with our desire, with our longing; it's what we do with our yearnings, our hunger. Spirituality is how we channel our drives. That's it. "Every choice is a renunciation," as the medieval saying goes. So spirituality asks, What can we renounce for the higher good? What can we close off to find something better?

Spirituality is the way we struggle to make our energy constructive, not destructive. It's the way, for example, we desire drugs or crave alcohol but know that ultimately they will make us less human, and so we try to make that drive productive, not destructive. It's the way we want so badly to be loved and held, but struggle not to use that drive to be manipulative and smothering. It's the way we so badly want sex, but struggle not to let our sexual drives be exploitative. It's the way we want food, but struggle not to hoard when our neighbor is in want. It's the way we all crave adulation and recognition and acceptance, but struggle not to sell our souls for fifteen minutes of fame. When you come down to it, it's the way we deal with narcissism, restlessness, pragmatism, and speed, how we channel these energies and avoid their pitfalls.

Spirituality is all these here-and-now human drives—for food and drink and love and sex and recognition, self-fulfillment and achievement, drives that are good and noble and decent in themselves—and what we do with them. If you want to know if you are a spiritual person you should ask yourself: "How am I handling, channeling, my everyday, normal, human drives?" It's as basic as that.

Gandhi took his natural human drive to eat and turned it into the energy to sustain the hunger strikes that helped free India. Vincent de Paul took his drive to have sex and channeled it into his unending efforts to serve the poor; Francis of Assisi left behind his ardent drive to have material possessions, of which he was quite fond, and walked away naked in the public square to accompany Brother Sun and Sister Moon. Dorothy Day shook off her need for fame and adulation and went to live among the downtrodden and rejected.

That's spirituality.

All right. Now its time to wake up the kids. Here's their homily on spirituality. It's a take on the tale about how the robin's breast became red. Not the Christian version of the robin pulling out a thorn from the head of Christ on Calvary, but a Native American version that shows us how someone very small can use his or her passion to serve others.

Long ago in the Far North, where it is very cold, there was only one fire. A hunter and his little son took care of this fire and kept it burning day and night. They knew that if the fire went out the people would freeze and the Great White Bear would have the Northland all to himself. One day the hunter became ill and his son had to do all the work. For many days and nights he bravely took care of his father and kept the fire burning.

The Great White Bear was always hiding near, watching the fire. He longed to put it out, but he did not dare, for he feared the hunter's arrows. When he saw how tired and sleepy the little boy was, he came closer to the fire and laughed wickedly to himself. One night the poor boy grew so tired that he could keep awake no longer and fell fast asleep. Then the Great White Bear ran as fast as he could and jumped upon the fire with his wet feet, and rolled upon it until he thought it was all out. Then he trotted happily away to his cave among the icebergs.

But, a little gray robin had been flying near, and had seen what the Great White Bear was doing. She was greatly worried when she thought that the fire might be out, but she was so little that she could do nothing but wait until the bear was out of sight. Then she darted down swiftly and searched with her sharp little eyes until she found one tiny live coal. This she fanned patiently with her wings for a long, long, long time. In doing so her little breast was scorched red and hurt her, but she did not stop until a fine red flame blazed up from the ashes. Then she flew away to every hut in the Northland. Wherever she touched the ground a fire began to burn.

Soon, instead of one little fire, the whole north country was lighted up, so that people far to the south wondered at the beautiful flames of red and yellow light in the northern sky. But when the Great White Bear saw the fires, he went farther back into his cave among the icebergs and growled terribly. He knew that now there was no hope that he would ever have the Northland all to himself.

This is the reason that the people in the north country love the robin, and never tire of telling their children how its breast became red.

For you adults: that little bird, like all of us, had a passion to live. Spirituality is what it did with its passion.

Oh, yes, one parting word: the red breast reminds us that when we bend our drives for good, we do tend to get bloodied in the process.

Advent &
Christmas

2

The Last Times

Thirty-third Sunday in Ordinary Time, Cycle B
Mark 13:24–32

Theme: the meaning of the Advent warnings. I have used this homily during Advent, but it could also be used in its proper place in Ordinary Time (Thirty-third Sunday, Cycle B).

The sun will be darkened, and the moon will not give its light, and the stars will be falling from heaven, and the powers in the heavens will be shaken. Then they will see "the Son of Man coming in clouds" with great power and glory.

A darkened sun, a blank moon, crashing stars, planetary collapse, Jesus' fearful return on the clouds: you know when you hear this that you're in the exotic realm of apocalyptic literature. This struggle between a cosmic doomsday and the imminent return of Christ to rapture the good and nuke the bad is a variation of the age-old battle between good and evil, light and darkness. It is echoed in the stories of the battles between Arthur and Mordred, Holmes and Moriarty, Luke Skywalker and Darth Vader, Simba and Uncle Scar, Christ and the anti-Christ, where the underdog is ultimately triumphant.

We see it when Eliza Doolittle says "Just you wait, 'enry 'iggins, just you wait!" Someday things will be reversed, and we will be rewarded and you will be punished. Mary sang of this very theme in her Magnificat: "He has brought down the powerful from their thrones, and lifted up the lowly." And her Son inveighed: "But woe to you who are rich, for you have received your consolation. Woe to you who are laughing now, for you will mourn and weep." In apocalyptic litera-

9

ture, the underdogs even know when these reversals will happen, which the top dogs don't, because they, the underdogs, alone possess the key to the books—especially the Book of Daniel and the Book of Revelation—that unlock the signs and the timetable of the endtime.

It's an old story, isn't it? Predictions of the end of the world have been a staple of the ages, from the writings of the early Church Fathers; to the so-called prophecies of St. Malachi in the twelfth century; to Joachim of Fiore; to Nostradamus in the sixteenth century; to Archbishop James Usher, who predicted that the end of the world would occur in 1996; to the Jehovah Witnesses, who predicted the end with great regularity until they threw in the towel in 1994; to David Koresh and his end-of-the-world sect who perished in the Waco tragedy of 1993; to the millennial Japanese sect who released poisonous gas in a subway in 1995; to the 1997 Heaven's Gate disaster, whose members committed mass suicide in order to speed up the second coming; to the Jews who were elated over the birth of a red heifer in 1997, a sign to them of the imminent coming of the Messiah; to Jerry Falwell; to the Fatima secrets; to the mumbo jumbo nonsense of Hal Lindsey's *The Late Great Planet Earth*, a book that has sold over thirty-five million copies, and the bestselling, equally nonsensical endtime stories of Tim LeHaye. Obviously endtime scenarios have a hold on the public imagination.

Yes, end-of-the-world themes are as old as ancient Jewish and Greek literature. They are deeply embedded in the New Testament, from Jesus to St. Paul, and are enshrined in our liturgy. After all, today and every Sunday we all unthinkingly recite our creed, which says: "He will come again in glory to judge the living and the dead"; and our acclamation after the Consecration cries out, "Christ has died, Christ is risen, Christ will come again."

Besides, since there are always signs of disaster with us—the Holocaust, global warming, tornadoes and tidal waves, the Concorde crash—there will always be people reading signs of the last times and reversals of fortune in these events. These people, with their tortured arithmetic and imaginative fantasies, will always capture an audience, especially among society's have-nots who look forward to being on top and seeing Bill Gates on bottom. For the "haves," however, whose signs of the end are a dip in the Dow Jones or a dent in their Mercedes, it's a different story. They look on these sign-carrying prophets of doom and their long list of consistently failed predictions with benign indifference or patronizing smirks, as cartoon characters sidelined to the nut fringe. Alas, they sigh as they go about their business, they will always be with us.

But they should be. And listen up here: they should be because behind all the exaggerations and fanaticism, there lies a truth that we desperately need to be reminded of and cling to. The truth the crazies fervently proclaim is that God is God. We need to hear that because we, with our portfolios and insurance plans, our platinum credit cards and bonuses, our frequent flyer miles and second houses, generate a certain hubris, a certain pride that we are insulated from life's tragedies. We entertain the fantasy that we are in charge.

And yet all of the Fannie Maes, stock options, and self-made satisfactions plummet into insignificance when we leave the doctor's office stunned with the news that we have breast or prostate cancer; when we learn that our marriage has grown cold and that our spouse is divorcing us; when we find out that our son is on drugs; when death has snatched away a husband or wife, or child in his or her prime like the 170 youths whose ski train suddenly turned into an oven; when we have been downsized; or when all our toys have become boring and empty.

And all these tragic interruptions to our complacency pale into nothing when, like lightning out of the blue, grace strikes and Saul, breathing the fire of persecution, finds himself as Paul breathing the Spirit of the Risen Lord; and the libertine, out-of-wedlock father Augustine blubbers his first confession to St. Ambrose; and the rich merchant's son, Francis, shocks his parents as he embraces Lady Poverty; and the slave dealer and womanizer, John Newton, sings of amazing grace and gives us our unofficial national religious anthem; and ex-communist and unwed mother, Dorothy Day, astounds her bohemian friends by converting to Catholicism and shoving the poor in our faces; and Charles Colson, the second most powerful man in America, ministers to prisoners; and Tom Bloch leaves his position as CEO of H&R Block, the multibillion dollar finance business his father founded, to teach in St. Francis Xavier High School for substandard wages; and the late Cardinal O'Connor takes off his ermine and changes the bedpans of AIDS patients.

Remember, all of these people once had other plans and thought they were in charge.

The apocalyptic strain rightly says to all this, "What did you expect? Foolish ones, you were never in charge to begin with. *God* is in charge of times and seasons and lives. *God* will have the last word." Yes, *God is in charge, not us* is the apocalyptic truism. God will make all things new again. God will lift up the lowly and free the captives and turn your life upside down. Go ahead and live your lives. Just don't hug the illusion that you are in charge. Live piously, justly, and in the fear of the Lord, as the Scripture says. Do your best but be humble enough to give glory to God. Be open to the Spirit. Even learn to embrace your cross knowing that God can tease glory out of all that radiation and chemotherapy and fractured ribs and broken hearts. God is sovereign.

Thus evangelical fundamentalists and their weird apocalyptic messages have the virtue of putting human life and human experience and human history into the context of faith. There is a plan. We are going somewhere. Justice will triumph. Life has ultimate meaning. Even though we are a speck in the endless cosmos, we are a special, privileged, and beloved speck awaiting redemption and the fullness of love.

Timetables belong to God. Without any help from us, God will intervene and make all things new again. We indeed may take the howling of Scripture and the cosmic chaos it portrays in today's gospel, and place them smugly on the shelf with our Star Wars trilogy. But if we do, we will miss the point. The point is that "submit" and "obey" and "trust" and "open to the Spirit" are not favorite words in a culture that sees the self as the ultimate measure of all things, a self daily proclaimed to be the center of the universe. Apocalyptic language and thought simply remind us that this is the greatest illusion of all.

3

The Rising Son

First Sunday of Advent, Cycle C
Luke 21:25–28, 34–36

Theme: origins

The Christian church, as you know, has its own calendar, and in the church's calendar the new year begins today, on the first Sunday of Advent, which leads to Christmas. But what you also should know is that Christmas and Advent are wonderfully baptized pagan feasts, and so going back to pagan times when the celebrations started will give us spiritual insight into this season.

Here's the way it worked. The pagans saw the world as a great cosmic struggle between the powers of darkness and the powers of light. And they noticed, as they watched the battle in the skies, that at different times darkness seemed to be getting the better of the light. In fact, it seemed to them like they were watching two great cosmic wrestlers. Every once in a while they would see that the wrestler called darkness would pin down the wrestler called light and be ready to do it in. They surmised this because they could plainly see that the days were getting shorter. If they were getting shorter it meant that the light, or the sun, was fading. It meant that as darkness pinned the sun to its back and was ready to dispatch it, so to speak, the sun, the light, was getting weaker. Yes, it was obvious that those fearful dark days were getting stronger and longer. And the people were afraid that someday darkness would kill the sun and the light altogether. They shuddered in fear. That is, until December twenty-first.

Around December 21 the people noticed that the tables had begun to turn, that the sun was regaining its strength. Suddenly, the hero

13

who was pinned down on the ground with an adversary over him got a burst of strength. He flipped his adversary over, climbed on top of him, and started to pin him down. The people noticed that the sun had gotten a second wind and all of a sudden it began to push darkness off and against the wall. This meant that darkness was getting weaker and the sun was getting stronger. And so when this happened, the pagans celebrated the resurrection, the new birth of the sun. It was for them a sun feast, marking the transition from darkness to light. And they rejoiced.

When the Christians came along, they took over this fascinating pagan notion. They said, "We don't know the date on which Christ was born, but if we're going to have to choose one, this time of the year is perfect. After all, we know that the pagans are really talking about darkness and light, and we know that the only real darkness of this world is the darkness of sin and the darkness of death. And the only light in this world is Jesus. So we'll keep the concept and fix his birthday right after December 21st when the light is starting to return." The Christians settled on December 25th for the date of Jesus' birth. Then they took the word "sun," removed the middle letter, "u," and changed it to an "o." And the sun they were talking about who overcame the darkness was Jesus, the Son of God, and they made this time of year a celebration when we would get ready for the tables to be turned.

So, in the Christian scheme, within the great struggle between good and evil, light and darkness, this was the time when the darkness of sin and death would now be overcome by the light of the world, Jesus, the S-o-n of God. The Christians called this time Christmas, and they made Advent the beginning of the end of darkness, a time of looking forward to the coming light. And that's what it has meant to us Christians ever since.

Advent marks that time when darkness begins to grow weaker and the sun becomes stronger. Advent became, and still remains for us, a time signifying that the dark tide—that of hatred, racism, abuse, broken relationships, indifference to human suffering—will turn, and that we must turn it. In other words, Advent is an invitation to break through the darkness into light. It offers a challenge that comes to us very forcefully with a question: what darkness do you need to overcome? What darkness in your life and in your world would you like to see reversed? What breakthrough would you and I want for this new year? What tide would you like turned around? What sun, moon, and stars must fall before we can be free enough to sense our redemption?

I suggest that if you and I are looking for an Advent motif in order to roll back some of that darkness, it might be the motif of light-bearing. You and I realize the incredible fact that we contain within us— within our very look, our very hand, our very lips—the power to bring light. A gesture to make somebody feel better. A smile. Picking up the telephone. A courteous note. An apology given. A love spoken. A reach outward. A blow for justice. Very simple things; and yet with them we can heal hearts and souls—and often bodies. We have that power. That should be our goal for the new church year: to be light-bearers in the darkness.

There is a story of five people who froze to death around a camp-fire on a bitterly cold night. Each had a stick of wood they might have contributed to the fire, but for reasons satisfactory to themselves each person refused to give what they had. A woman would not give her stick of wood because there was a male in the circle. A homeless man would not give because there was a rich man there. The rich man would not give because his contribution would warm someone who was obviously shiftless and lazy. Another would not give his stick when he recognized one not of his particular religious faith. An African-American man withheld his piece of wood as a way of getting even with the whites for all they had done to him and his race. And the fire died as each person withheld their piece of fuel for reasons justifiable to them. This story was originally told in a poem that ends with these tragic lines:

> Six logs held fast in death's still hand
> was proof of human sin.
> They did not die from the cold without,
> they died from the cold within.

In the early part of the gospel, when Jesus is just starting his public ministry, two disciples of John the Baptist ask where Jesus lives. And Jesus simply says, "Come and see." How about that?

Jesus, where do you live today? I live within the darkness in people: come and see. I live within the dark hurt in you and in others: come and see. I live within the dark pain and dark grief and dark struggle of human beings everywhere: come and see, and bring your piece of wood to make light and warmth.

If this world, this nation, if you and I as a faith community are going to roll back the darkness, Advent is the time to begin. A new year, a new beginning, a time when darkness begins to slip. Then hopefully, in your life and mine and in the lives of those we touch, the Son, Jesus, will begin to rise.

We have the power to make it happen.

4

The Desert Fathers

Second Sunday of Advent, Cycle B
Mark 1:1–8

Theme: John the Baptist is the original desert father. Those who followed him
have much to teach us.

Most of you are familiar with one of the most dramatic discoveries of
our era. In 1947, a little Bedouin shepherd boy stumbled on some
hidden caves surrounding Qumran, an outpost in the Judean desert.
In these caves he found jars in which there were scrolls. They turned
out to be the famous Dead Sea Scrolls, which gave the world copies of
most of the Hebrew Scriptures. The find included a complete scroll of
Isaiah from the early part of the first century before Christ, making it
the oldest copy of Isaiah ever found.

The scrolls eventually revealed the existence of a sect called the
Essenes who had left Jerusalem and the Temple and civilization
behind to go into the desert to await a deliverer and get things straight
in their lives. That they went to the desert was significant because, you
recall, that's where religion began. They went back to the source, as it
were. After all, it was in the desert that God appeared to Moses. It was
in the desert that a small nomadic tribe, with no resources other than
what God provided—manna and quail—not only survived but flour-
ished and passed on its revelation and experience to the world. It was
in the vast loneliness and hot cauldron of the desert that a people of
God was forged.

The "desert experience" has come to mean going back to basics, back
to the source, back to utter dependency on one's Creator, going back to
reclaim one's true identity as son and daughter of God rather than the

ever changing celebrity image forced on us by a media that sees us as a consuming fire endlessly stoked by endless products. The desert experience means that one must pull away to gain perspective. It means letting go of what we think is so life-giving but which is, in reality, life-denying. It means entering a spiritually dry period, going apart, accepting vulnerability and a total dependence on God, for the desert is a harsh and unforgiving place where life is lived day-by-day on the edge and you come face to face with reality, with what really counts.

It is not without reason, therefore, that in today's gospel, John the Baptist was found in the desert and not in the city. Later on in Christian history, when the cities became corrupt and it was difficult to hold onto the faith amid such distraction, a whole group went to the desert—the Desert Fathers, we call them—and founded monasteries as havens of renewal and spiritual refreshment. People would flock to the monasteries like the crowds flocked to the desert to see John the Baptist, and they sat at the feet of the holy desert monk called the "abba," or abbot. The common refrain was, "Speak a word, Father, that we might live." And so they did. Their words, sparse and to the point, were, like those of John the Baptist, totally uncompromising when it came to seeking holiness.

The Desert Fathers, also like John, appeared decidedly eccentric at times. But there was a deep sense of purpose in what they did. If, for example, they went without sleep, it was because, Advent-like, they were watching for the Lord. If they did not speak often, it was because they were listening to God. If they fasted, it was because they were fed by God's word. It was God that mattered to them and their asceticism was only a means to that end. Eventually, their teachings, their sayings and stories, were passed around, collected, meditated on. Here are four of them: two on being balanced, a third on discipleship, and the fourth on pride.

John the Dwarf announced to his brother monk one day that he was going off deeper into the desert by himself to live as an angel. After several days the monk heard a knock on his door. "Who is it?" he asked. A voice, weakened by hunger, replied, "John!" The monk inside responded (with some satisfaction, I suspect), "John? it can't be, for John is now an angel and has no need of food or shelter." But, after a pause, he took the humbled John in and set him to work again in a more balanced life.

Once the great ascetic, St. Anthony, was relaxing with his disciples outside his hut when a hunter came by. The hunter was surprised and mildly shocked, and he rebuked Anthony for taking it easy. It was not his idea of what a monk should be doing. But Anthony said, "Bend your bow and shoot an arrow." And the hunter did so. "Bend it again and shoot another," said Anthony. And the hunter did, again and again. The hunter finally said, "Abba Anthony, if I keep my bow always stretched, it will break." "So it is with the monk," replied Anthony. "If we push ourselves beyond measure we will break; it is right from time to time to relax our efforts."

One day, some monks were proposing to go to the city of Thebaid to look for some flax, and they agreed that as long as they were in the area they would look in on the famous Abba Arsenius. So a messenger came one day to the Abba and announced, "Some brothers who have come all the way from Alexandria wish to see you." The old Abba shrewdly asked why they came and learned that they were here mainly to look for flax at Thebaid. So he told the messenger, "They will certainly not see the face of Arsenius for they have not come primarily on my account but because of their work. Make them rest and send them away in peace and tell them that the old man cannot receive them."

This tale, by the way, is cousin to the story of the disciple who came to an Abba seeking God. The Abba then took the young man down to the river and held him under the water to the point where the young man sprang up gasping for breath. He demanded to know why the Abba had done that, and so the Abba replied, "When you desire God with the same intensity you desire air, you will find him!"

Finally, this story on pride:

When the devil saw a seeker of truth on his way to the hut of the Abba, he was determined to do everything in his power to turn him back from his quest. So he subjected him to every form of temptation—wealth, lust, prestige—but the seeker was able to fight off these temptations quite easily.

When he reached the Master's house, however, the seeker was somewhat taken aback to see the Master sitting in an upholstered chair with his disciples at his feet. "That man certainly lacks humility, the principal virtue of saints," he thought to himself. Then he observed other things about the Master he did not like. For one thing, the Master took little notice of him. "I suppose that's because I do not fawn over him like the others do," he said to himself. He also disliked the kind of clothes the Master wore and the somewhat conceited way he spoke.

All this led him to the conclusion that he had come to the wrong place and must continue his quest elsewhere. As he walked out of the room, the Abba, who had seen the devil seated in the corner of the hut, said, "You need not have worried, tempter. He was yours from the very first, you know."

These are stories of wisdom acquired only in the desert where this morning we find John the Baptist, and soon we will find Jesus there when he receives his three temptations. The point of the gospel, the point of the stories of the Desert Fathers, is that if you want renewal and refreshment; if you want to shake off the barnacles of sin and selfishness that have accrued on your life; if you want to rise above humdrum consumer living and become a real person of depth and spirit, you must go back to the source. You must go to the desert.

Some take this literally, and they go to a monastery. Others go on a retreat or to a day of recollection. For others there is daily spiritual reading, playing spiritual tapes while they drive, and prayer time. For all of us, going to the desert means giving time and making space for God.

Where is John the Baptist? Where is Jesus? Where did it all begin? Where will you find God this Advent? In the desert of retreat, prayer, and spiritual reading.

5

What We Must Remember

Second Sunday of Advent, Cycle C
Luke 3:1–6

Theme: The reason for the season

About a hundred years ago a Russian scientist named Korsakoff identified a mental disorder that was eventually named after him. It's
called Korsakoff's psychosis. Korsakoff's psychosis is primarily the
result of long-term alcohol abuse, although the disease can be trig-
gered by an accident or a genetic factor. But most sufferers are chronic alcohol abusers. What happens is that their abuse leads to short-
term memory loss and an inability to maintain new memories. And
so to compensate, these people create new stories to fill in the gaps.
They come up with fantastic, wild, imaginary stories to fill the empty
memory tapes.

A practical case in point. Perhaps you remember reading about a
civil rights murder from the 1960s that was finally cleared up a couple of years ago. What happened was this: on January 10, 1966, civil
rights activist Vernon Dahmer was murdered by the Ku Klux Klan in
Laurel, Mississippi. Dahmer had been encouraging local black resi-
dents to register for the vote, and this made the KKK chapter furious.
Four members of the local Klan were eventually convicted and went
to prison for the crime. But few people believed that justice had really been done. For over thirty years, the case sat in the police files, until
finally someone came forward.

In 1994, police officials received a call from a Bob Stringer, a middle-aged man who had once worked as an errand boy for the local
Klan. Stringer had eyewitness evidence that the Klan's then-leader,

21

Sam Bowers, had ordered the hit on Dahmer, along with a string of other murders and various crimes. For years, Stringer had lived with the guilt of knowing the truth and remaining silent, until he finally succumbed to Korsakoff's psychosis. He suppressed his memory of the murder and forgot it, and he went on to spin other weird stories. Eventually, a gambling addiction led Stringer into a twelve-step recovery group. There he put aside his fantasies and remembered the truth.

One of those steps in that program, as you may know, is to make amends with those you have hurt. Bob Stringer knew he had to make amends with the family of Vernon Dahmer. And so, just three years ago, on August 21, 1998, due primarily to Bob Stringer's testimony, Sam Bowers was convicted of Vernon Dahmer's murder. Dahmer's family finally felt that justice was done.

I thought of this story because it reminded me that we Christians have a type of cultural Korsakoff's psychosis. We have collectively lost our memory and so have invented or absorbed fantasy stories to fill in the gap. It's very, very common at this time of the year. A simple illustration: a priest friend of mine asked the second graders of his Catholic school last week, "Advent is the time of getting ready. Who is coming?" They all answered, "Santa Claus!" We smile at this, but it's a perfect example of Korsakoff's psychosis occurring at a young age.

We adults do no better. Without thinking we easily accept the current psychosis about Christmas. It roughly goes like this: a jolly guy in a red suit squeezes himself down the chimney. And he brings toys, and because he gives gifts, we all exchange gifts. And we hang stockings from the mantel with more gifts. And there are reindeer pulling a big sled. Oh, and one reindeer has a shiny red nose that doubles as a searchlight in the event of a nor'easter. And Frosty the Snowman comes alive and sounds just like Burl Ives. Oh, and sometimes we stick a plastic baby in a little manger scene and line up the shepherds and the wise men and the angels and the donkeys and the mother and the father. And everybody wears red and green clothes.

That's our fantasy story. So we shop, send Christmas cards with dogs or snowmen on them, decorate our homes with holly, and get ready for family time, for isn't family time together what Christmas is all about? This, as I said, is a mild form of Korsakoff's psychosis common throughout our culture. The secular trends and popular customs are harmless in moderation, of course, but a steady diet of Disney Christmas dulls the memory of why we Christians celebrate the feast at all.

But here's what we Christians might remember this season:

that in Bethlehem, God was in Christ Jesus;

that the child came to save us from our sins;

that his name is called Wonderful Counselor, Mighty God, Prince of Peace, the Everlasting Father;

that he will reign on David's throne forever and ever;

that this child was born to die;

that the Spirit of the Lord rested upon him, the spirit of wisdom and understanding, counsel and power, of knowledge and the fear of the Lord;

that his name, Jesus, means Savior;

that although born in an obscure village and to humble circumstances, and although he would write no books and live publicly in the company of men for a brief thirty-six months, no person has left such an indelible mark on human history as this man;

that the Bethlehem child makes the difference between a life of quiet desperation and a life of meaning and purpose.

What else can we Christians remember? We can remember that Advent is precisely the time to remember—which is why John the Baptist is trying to get our attention by proclaiming a baptism of repentance for the forgiveness of sins and urging us to practice those deeds that rebirth Christ all over again. Listen to the words of a lay-woman, a twentieth-century mystic, Caryll Houselander, who writes:

When a woman is carrying a child, she develops a certain instinct of self-defense It is not selfishness; it is not egoism. It is an absorption into the life within, a folding of self like a little tent around the child's frailty, a God-like instinct to cherish and some day to bring forth the life. A closing upon it like the petals of a flower closing upon the dew that shines in its heart. This is precisely the attitude we must have to Christ, the Life within us, in the Advent of our contemplation. We could scrub the floor for a tired friend, or dress a wound for a patient in a hospital, or lay the table and wash up for the family; but we shall not do it in martyr spirit or with that worse spirit of self-congratulation, of feeling that we are making ourselves more perfect, more unselfish, more positively kind.

We shall do it for just one thing, that our hands make Christ's hands in our life, that our service may let Christ serve through us, that our patience may bring Christ's patience back to the world. By his own will Christ was dependent on Mary during Advent: he was absolutely helpless; he could go nowhere but where she chose to take him; he could not speak; her breathing was his breath; his heart beat in the beating of her heart. Today Christ is dependent upon us. This dependence of Christ lays a great trust upon us. During this tender time of Advent we must carry him in our hearts to wherever he wants to go, and there are many places to which he may never go unless we take him.

That says it all. Advent is the time when we, like Mary, carry Christ who will not be there unless we take him. Advent is the time when we must pause and remember that Jesus, not Santa or Rudolph, is the main event; to recall that Christmas is not a holiday, that politically correct term, but a holy day, very holy. It is the coming of God in the flesh. God came once. We must practice how to make him come again, every day.

So the difference between Christians and all others during this time of the year should be that Christians remember, and give evidence of it.

6

Good Pope John

Third Sunday in Advent, Cycle C
Luke 3:10–18

Theme: Redeeming a name

The crowds asked John the Baptist, "What then should we do?"

In answer, John goes deep and demands justice. Then he points to Another who will clear his threshing floor by gathering the wheat into barns. But the chaff—those who fiddled with the surface but did not have a deeper change of heart—will go into the unquenchable fire.

Because John was so on the mark, a man of such integrity and stature, centuries of Christians named their children after him. He was held in high regard in the pantheon of saints although not in the past century, which finds him a tad much too demanding, too forthright a believer. We like our saints sanitized and compliant, and so today, except for the times he is mentioned in the gospel, John the Baptist has fallen into oblivion and his name carries no special honor.

Of course, it hasn't helped that some of the so-called "bad" popes of history bore his name. It's not that good popes eventually became bad, but rather that bad men became popes. In bygone, chaotic times when there was no central government in most of the countries of Europe, Mafia-like henchmen, with their bands of cutthroats, corrupted and murdered and terrorized their way to the top of local feudal kingdoms and petty provinces and even to the papacy itself. It was much like some of the bloody dictators in Africa do today. So, for example, you get a thug like Pope John VIII, who was hammered to death. John X was murdered. John XI, the illegitimate son of Pope

25

Sergius III, witnessed the marriage of his mother to her brother-in-law. John XIII was not yet twenty when he became pope; he died while visiting his mistress. John XIX was a layman who in one day received all the ecclesiastical orders in order to ascend to the papal throne. The papacy in those times was run like a medieval Soprano family.

But on this third Sunday of Advent, I'd like to talk about a man who, this past September, was beatified by the Roman Catholic Church, a man whom we should not forget. This man was a pope and his name was John.

Yes, Angelo Roncalli, who became Pope John XXIII, is on his way to official sainthood. You may know him as the one who called the Second Vatican Council. And, in fact, the Council *was* his idea. But we may need a refresher course not only about the Council but about the life of this great man who can teach us much about how to be truly Christian, a follower of Jesus. A whole generation has been born since the Council, and so ignorance has settled in like a fog. In fact, one college teacher, who asked his students to identify Vatican II, got this for an answer: "It's where the Pope spends his summer vacation."

So who was John XXIII and how did he come to be known as "Good Pope John"? (I guess to distinguish him from the "bad" pope Johns!) Why did his death, after only five years as pope, bring people everywhere all over the world to tears? He was born in a village in northern Italy, the fourth of fourteen children. His parents were sharecroppers, who turned over half their crop to landlords and survived on what they could produce from the remaining acreage. The sharecroppers' houses all had names and the Roncalli house was called "the palazzo," the palace. But, as one biographer wrote, "there was nothing very grand about it. They shared the ground floor with their six cows."

The future pope was baptized on the same day as his birth, which was the usual custom. He never forgot his humble roots and said one time, amid the splendors of the Vatican, that he would like to go back and spend a single day working with his brothers in the field. Roncalli said he never remembered a time he did not want to be a parish priest. But he did not wind up in a parish as he had hoped. Instead, he became a teacher in a seminary, then secretary to a bishop, and then began a long career as an apostolic delegate in the diplomatic service of the church, spending twenty years in Bulgaria and Turkey. Then he was sent to Paris, where he finally be became a pastor by being named patriarch of Venice (and also a cardinal).

Still, how did this roly-poly man become pope? By accident. The long-reigning Pius XII had died and the curia was looking for an elderly prelate—Roncalli was seventy-eight at the time—to be an interim figure, one who would not make waves. When the votes began to move in his direction, he calmly made notes on his acceptance speech and on his choice of a name, which astounded them all. It was John. John? The cardinals exchanged embarrassed looks. Didn't the man know his history? It was like choosing the name Adolf after World War II. But Roncalli said later that he wanted to venerate two people who were so close to Jesus—John the Baptist and John the evangelist—and he wanted to restore honor to that name, for he knew that many of those who had used it in the past were hugely unworthy of the office.

Thirty members of his extended family came from their little mountain town for his coronation Mass. In a private audience they were overcome with emotion—but not the new pope who said, "Come now, no weeping. What they have done to me is not so bad!" At the coronation Mass, John XXIII declared his intent to be a pastor, a good shepherd. His first visits were to a hospital, an orphanage, and the main prison in Rome. His greatest surprise, of course, was calling an ecumenical council. It was and remains the greatest single religious event of the twentieth century, one that turned the direction of the Roman Catholic Church completely around, as we know and are experiencing today. In calling the Council, John XXIII said that he did not not think of the church as a museum in which to store beautiful things of antiquity, but as a garden of growth and life.

This Pope John kept his humility. Typical of his attitude was his reply to a letter he received from an eleven-year-old boy named Bruno. Bruno's letter said, "Dear Pope. I can't decide whether to become a pope or a fireman. What do you think?" And John replied, "Dear Bruno, Be a fireman. Anyone can become pope. Look at me." He never forget his humble origins and it influenced him to direct much of his attention to the poor. Listen to this passage from his book, *Journal of a Soul*:

We were poor but happy with our lot and confident with the help of Providence. There was never any bread on our table, only polenta; no wine for the children and young people, and only at Christmas and Easter did we have a slice of homemade cake. Clothes and shoes for going to church had to last for years and years....And when a beggar appeared at the door of our kitchen, when the children were waiting impatiently for their bowl of minestrone, there was always room for him, and my mother would hasten to seat this stranger alongside us.

Prophet John the Baptist, bad pope Johns, and the pope known as Good Pope John XXIII. Is there an Advent point to these comparisons? Yes; the point is that we have a lesson here. The name "Christian" hasn't been especially threatening or strong of late, nor has it carried any power of witness or evangelization or special identity. In fact, some Christians have never been known as such. Perhaps the message is that, like Good Pope John XXIII, it's time to reclaim and restore the name we carry, and make it mean something in our lives and in the lives of others.

After all, when is the last time someone said of us, "Now, there goes a good Christian?"

7
Home for Christmas

In one of his Lake Wobegon stories, Garrison Keillor pictures Christmas in his old hometown. All the "exiles" return, he says. That's what he calls them: exiles. All the people who left the little community to make it big in the world out there—like some of you here visiting your folks for the holidays. And some have made it big!

Corinne Ingqvist drives in from Minneapolis. She's a schoolteacher now. On the backseat of her car, she's got stack of essays to grade over the holidays. She's listening to a radio preacher along the way, and she gets so upset with his sermon, that she argues theology with him, and all the while her speed is rising with her anger…till she notices the flashing lights of a Minnesota highway trooper behind her!

Eddie, the jealous boy, comes home. He's so jealous about his good-looking wife that when he glances up from trying to put together a Christmas toy for his son and he can't find Eunice, he runs outside without a coat, thinking that she might be sitting in the warming house at the skating rink with her brother-in-law Fred.

Richard comes home. They called him Foxy in high school. Always out to make a buck. Always swaggering about how he was going to become rich some day. Always flashing a roll of bills to the girls. Well, he's a millionaire now. Drives home in his custom-made pink 1987 Ferlinghetti, telling tales of his houses and travels and conquests.

They all come home for Christmas. And some of them go to church with their aging parents, and some of them don't. And yet, somehow, as they're forced to face the old hometown, and as they're confronted again by who they are and what they've become, there's a sort of wistfulness that sets in. You see, says Keillor, they all believe. They all believe in themselves or in their looks or in their skills or in their luck. They all believe. But here's the crunch of Christmas. As they see the old farmhouses again, as they talk to their wrinkled grandparents, as they walk the streets that now seem so short and crude, they wonder to themselves. They wonder in their hearts if they've chosen the right gods.

There is a song by Billy Joel that sounds the same note. This was really the song that helped start his musical career big-time. It's called "Piano Man," and it describes life for Billy during those early days. He used to play the piano in a bar, and every night he would sing a few songs for the customers. It didn't take long before he got to know many of the customers personally. And in "Piano Man" he tells their stories. He tells about the waitress who's practicing politics, and he tells about Joe who plays amateur psychologist. And then he tells one more story. He tells about the man who comes up to him and says: "Son, can you play me a melody?/ I'm not really sure how it goes./ But it's sad and it's sweet, and it sounded complete/ When I wore a younger man's clothes."

We can picture this man, can't we? He's a man in his fifties. His suit is polished from wear, and his tie is a little out of fashion…he's a man like Willy Loman whose life hasn't turned out like he thought…like he had hoped…like he had dreamed. And every night he comes into this bar, and he gulps a few to take the edge off the day. And the hushed conversation keeps the loneliness from creeping in, and the soft lights and dark walls protect him from daytime's harsh glare. You see, the mirror in the morning reminds him he's not the man he used to be…the man he should have been.…the man his parents prayed he'd become. And when he hears the piano man, an old song hums up from his heart.

What is he saying? You know what he's saying, don't you? He's saying that he knew himself once. He knew himself once, because he knew the melody of his life. And he's saying that somehow he forgot that tune one day. And the only way he's ever going to find himself again is if someone helps him remember that song. "Son, can you play me a melody?/ I'm not really sure how it goes./ But it's sad and it's sweet, and it sounded complete/ When I wore a younger man's clothes."

The point of these stories is that everybody has faith. Everybody believes. The crisis in our lives comes when we find out that what we believe begins to shape us, begins to alter us, begins to change us. And then we look in the mirror and we say: "Is this the meaning of my life? What have I become? I remember I used to sing another song. What happened to me?" That, you might recall, was the question Mitch Albom asked himself in the bestselling book, *Tuesdays with Morrie*— Morrie being Morrie Schwartz, Albom's dying one-time professor whom he visits after sixteen years. Albom writes:

> Morrie's high, smoky voice took me back to my university years, when I thought rich people were evil, a shirt and tie were prison clothes, and life without freedom to get up and go, motorcycle beneath you, breeze in your face, down the streets of Paris, into the mountains of Tibet, was not a good life at all. What happened to me?
>
> The eighties happened. The nineties happened. Death and sickness and getting fat and going bald happened. I traded lots of dreams for a bigger paycheck, and I never even realized I was doing it.
>
> Yet here was Morrie talking with the wonder of our college years, as if I'd simply been on a long vacation. "Have you found someone to share your heart with?" he asked. "Are you giving to your community? Are you at peace with yourself? Are you trying to be as human as you can be?" I squirmed, wanting to show I had been grappling deeply with such questions. What happened to me?
>
> I once promised myself I would never work for money, that I would join the Peace Corps, that I would live in beautiful, inspirational places. Instead, I had been in Detroit for ten years now, at the same workplace, using the same bank, visiting the same barber.
>
> I was thirty-seven, more efficient than in college, tied to computers and modems and cell phones. I wrote articles about rich athletes who, for the most part, could not care less about people like me. I was no longer young for my peer group, nor did I walk around in gray sweatshirts with unlit cigarettes in my mouth. I did not have long discussions about the meaning of life. My days were full, yet I remained, much of the time, unsatisfied.
>
> What happened to me?

I think that is the power of Christmas, to bring us back "home"; not home in the sense of your street address, but home in the sense of who you really are, who you were called to be, a home that asks whether you have chosen the right gods. For Christmas asks not only "What happened to me?" but Christmas gives the answer: whatever happened, whatever you've become, whatever your motive for being here, there is a God so madly in love with you that this God could not tolerate any distancing but came and dwelt among us, took on our human condition and not only taught us how to live by being compassionate, forgiving, and self-sacrificing, but showed us the way.

This is the God who asks Morrie's questions—or, if you will, it is Morrie who asks God's questions: have you found someone to share your heart with? Are you giving to your community? Are you at peace with yourself? Are you trying to be a human as you can be? God in the flesh, Jesus, answers these questions. His answers are what Christmas is all about.

I love this Christmas season. I love seeing families come home. I love seeing the kids back from college. I love seeing the crowds at Mass. I love guessing what your stories are, what you were and what you have become. Most of all, I love to talk about Garrison Keillor, Billy Joel, Morrie Schwartz, and Jesus Christ all in the same breath because they all play the same melody, sad and sweet, and offer the same message, challenging and hopeful: Glory to God in the highest. And on earth? Peace to those on whom his favor rests.

And that's you. Merry Christmas.

8

The Family Album

Feast of the Holy Family, Cycle A
Matthew 2:13–15; 19–23

Theme: family likeness calls for family likeness

Picture this. It's Christmas. The family has gathered, pleasantries exchanged, a good meal shared, gifts opened and, then, sooner or later, as everyone knew would happen, Grandma starts the annual ritual. She goes to the dresser, opens the drawer, drags out the family album, and sits on the couch. Soon, as required by long custom, everyone surrounds her as she begins to intone the familiar litany of her favorite reminiscenses. She turns with anticipation to the first page. There they are. Babies, all babies. "Look, there's Joan; there's Alfred and Bobby. And look, there *you* are, such an adorable baby!" "How cute!" everyone chimes in. And, lingering over the sweet scenes, everyone oohs and ahhs over the darling infants.

Then, smiling to herself, grandma gleefully turns to the next pages. Are you ready for this? These pages couldn't be more of a contrast. But there they are in all of their graphic horror: there's a large, blown-up photo and several smaller ones at different angles of a young man sprawled out dead in an alley, the body all bloodied, hardly recognizable. It's easy to see that he was beaten to a pulp. "Ah," says Grandma wistfully, "your brother Stephen. So young to die. Some gang got to him. Look at all that blood. Look at that nasty gash on his forehead." And for a long while the family scrutinizes and studies each terrible detail.

Then she turns to the next page, where there are several pictures of uncle John on a slab. They all strain to get a look, their mouths open.

33

Uncle John had been boiled in oil. "So life-like," comments Grandma as they all gaze mesmerized at the pictures. After a while, she turns to the next page, and she chortles to herself as they all gasp, as they never fail to do. It's lots of pictures of their little cousins killed in a bus accident two years ago. Grandma finally turns to the last page, and there he is again: their sister's husband, Tom, who had had a sordid past, assassinated in the foyer of his own home. Mess everywhere. Blood everywhere. A mob hit. One last look and, satisfied, Grandma closes the album. Her annual ritual is over. Another holiday gathering; another year looking at the family album.

Now you're wondering. What in the world am I getting at? Is this some kind of ghoulish joke? This is something from the Addams' family, isn't it? Or the Munsters; that's *their* idea of family fun, of "home for Christmas!" Well, you're right to be puzzled, but you know that somewhere I have a point. And the point is this: I *wasn't*, I confess, talking about the Munster or Addams families, and in fact, that weird album really doesn't belong to them. The truth is, I'm afraid, I was setting you up. Fellow Christians, the album belongs to us. Yes, to us, the *Christian* family. And, don't you realize, we do this family album thing every year, every single year? It's an annual ritual.

Let me review it for you. There is, of course, as you know, Christmas Day, December 25, when we all gather and delight in the baby, that sweet Christ Child in the manger surrounded by loving parents, shepherds, angels, and exotic Wise Men. So far, so good. So far, so pleasing. So far, so sentimental. But then, without warning, on the very next day, December 26, like Grandma dramatically turning the page of the family album, the church shoves into our faces the feast of Stephen, the first Christian martyr, who was brutally stoned to death, beaten to a pulp. Blood all over the place.

Then, in rapid succession, on December 27, the church celebrates the feast of St, John, who was thrown into boiling oil for believing in Jesus. On the day after that, December 28, the church celebrates, if you want to call it that, the slaughter of the Holy Innocents, those tiny harmless babies killed on orders from a deranged King Herod. Finally, on December 29, the church celebrates the martyrdom of Thomas à Becket, one-time womanizer and crook who became an archbishop and a saint and was assassinated by a mob of soldiers in the foyer of his own cathedral in Canterbury, England, where even today you can see the mark on the floor where he fell.

Surrounding the Christ Child with all that blood, this Christian family album which starts off white and ends up red, is not much different than what we might expect from the Munster or Addams' families, you might say. But, listen up: unlike the stories of the Munster or Addams families, which are seeking laughs, the church has a serious point when it forces us to look at our family album each year during Christmas week. The point the church has in mind is as simple as it is common: *embrace the babe of Bethlehem and it will cost you.*

Embrace a spouse and it will cost you. Embrace a friend and it will cost you. Embrace a child and it will cost you. Embrace a country and it will cost you. Embrace a cause and it will cost you. Embrace Jesus Christ and it will cost you. Don't linger too long at the manger on Christmas Day, says the church, but move hastily on to the rest of the week to see what the manger implies. Look too at Stephen, John, the Holy Innocents, Thomas.

The week between the celebration of Christmas and the celebration of the feast of the Holy Family, then, is loyalty-test time. Are we part of the Holy Family? Have we earned membership? Have we moved beyond the sentimentality of Christmas? How much blood have we shed for Christ? Oh, I don't mean physically—although, Lord knows, in the Sudan, in China, in Africa, and in other parts of the world people are still being tortured and killed simply for being Christian—but I mean spiritually. How much has being a Christian cost us? A little? A great deal? Nothing? Can people tell from our wounds that we are Christian? Our speech, our honesty, our decisions? The church's Christmas card is not framed in red for nothing.

In his book, *Living Faith,* former President Jimmy Carter provides a simple test that tells us whether we might be included in the family album. He writes about a group of Christian laymen involved in missionary work who approached a small village near an Amish settlement. Seeking a possible convert, they confronted an Amish farmer and asked him, "Brother, are you a Christian?" The farmer thought for a moment and then said, "Wait just a few minutes." He wrote down a list of names on a tablet and handed it to the missionary. "Here is a list of people who know me best. Please ask them if I am a Christian."

Are we ready to make our list?

It's the feast of the Holy Family. Open up the family liturgical album. It's not just sweet Jesus, Mary, and Joseph there. It's the whole bloody clan: Stephen, John, the Holy Innocents, Thomas, and all those who, like ourselves, carry the same family name. They let it mean something to them. So should we.

9
Epiphany

This exotic feast is truly rich, full of symbol and meaning on many levels. Today, let's explore three facets of Epiphany symbolism by considering the Magi as outsiders, faith-seekers, and gift-givers.

First of all, the Magi are outsiders, heirs to a long-line of foreigners who figure dramatically in the Bible: think of Melchizedek, the king and high priest of Salem who blessed Abraham. Then there is Pharaoh's daughter, an Egyptian who saved Moses from the Nile; and Rahab, who let the Hebrew soldiers into her city to scout out its strength before the siege of Jericho; and Ruth, a Moabite who followed her mother-in-law back to Israel and became an ancestor of Jesus; the Samaritan leper who was cured and came back to give thanks; the Syrian woman who bantered for her daughter's health and got it; the Roman centurion who testified on Calvary that surely, this was God's Son. And joining all these remarkable biblical foreigners are the Magi.

What do they tell us, these foreigners in the history of salvation? They tell us, simply and profoundly, that no one is excluded from the love of God. We are all foreigners in a sense: divorced, different, out of the social loop, sinful, addicted, carrying shameful deeds and betrayals, unforgiving, vengeful. Alienated in a hundred different ways, we are moral outsiders. But the Magi story says there is room for us. That's it. Gay or straight, addicted or free, male or female, faithful or faithless, saint or sinner—think of James Joyce's phrase "Here comes everybody," because it is everybody, foreigners of all sorts, who is welcomed to the grace and love found in Jesus Christ.

Second, the Magi are faith-seekers. They don't have all the answers, but they don't give up. One modern wise man is Jimmy Carter. In his book, *Living Faith*, he describes his own faith journey which was not always an easy or simple one. He confesses his doubts about his faith but he writes, "doubt is an acceptable and necessary aspect of faith—faith implies a continuing search, not necessarily a final answer." Some, like the Magi, travel in the darkness but like them they must continually move toward the light. And the Magi story says that God will break through the darkness. We must live in such hope.

That's the theme, you recall, of the classic story, *The Other Wise Man*, by Henry Van Dyke, in which Artaban, a Persian astrologer and the fourth Wise Man, sets out to join his three brethren. They are waiting for him at the Temple of Seven Spheres so that together they can follow the star they have seen to the prophesied one. Artaban carries three precious stones to give the infant, but in the course of his journey he gives away two of them to help people in need. In doing so he is so delayed that he misses his three friends and ultimately, the child Jesus. And so, never finding him, Artaban returns downcast to Jerusalem to become a lifelong seeker of Jesus.

For thirty-three years Artaban looked for the Savior in vain. He was now an old man, weary and ready to die but still looking for the King.

It was now the season of the Passover, and there were many people in Jerusalem who had come for the great religious feast. Artaban asked some people the cause of the excitement in the city. They answered, "We are going to the place called Golgotha, just outside the walls of the city, to see two robbers and a man named Jesus of Nazareth hanged on the cross. The man calls himself the Son of God, and Pilate has sent him to be crucified because he says he is the King of the Jews." Artaban was astonished at these words, and thought, "At last I have found my King! The ways of God are stranger than the thoughts of men. It may be that I shall come in time to offer my pearl for his ransom before he dies!" So Artaban walked as quickly as he could to the gates of the city.

At the entrance he saw soldiers dragging a young girl down the street. Artaban felt great pity for the girl. But when she saw Artaban in his royal robes, she threw herself at his feet. "Have pity on me, save me!" she cried. So Artaban gave the girl his pearl, the last of the treasures he had saved for the King. "This, my daughter, is your ransom," he said. The story ends this way:

As Artaban spoke, darkness fell over the land, and the earth shook. The walls of the houses rocked, and great stones fell and crashed into the streets. A heavy stone fell upon Artaban and almost crushed his head. He lay dying in the arms of the girl he had helped. As she bent over him, there came a voice from heaven, and she heard Artaban saying, "Three and thirty years I looked for thee, Lord, but I have never seen thy face, nor ministered to thee." And the voice from heaven said, "Inasmuch as you did it to one of the least of my brethren, you did it to me." Artaban's face grew calm and peaceful. His long journey was ended. He had found his King!

The Magi story suggests that in every dark experience of life, God is not far from those who are faith seekers.

Third, the Magi are gift-givers, and it is here we find the essence of Christianity. God gave the gift of himself in the manger—the word was made flesh—and on Calvary. We are asked to follow suit and be gift givers of our time and talent and love—and ourselves.

A young woman went to teach for a couple of years in Fiji. When the time came for her to come back to the States, her students gave her gifts. One little boy brought her a spectacular cowrie shell. She knew full well that these shells were not found nearby and asked him where he had found it. He admitted that he had walked four miles to the beach where such shells are to be found, and then had walked four miles back after finding the shell. He then touched the teacher's heart by declaring, "Long walk part of gift."

Christianity is lots of long walks.

So this is our feast, this marvelous tale of the Magi who in reality are us: outsiders, faith-seekers, and gift-givers.They tell us that we are welcome, they show us how to proceed, and they encourage us on the journey. They are gifts to us as Christ was to them as we are to be to others.

May the Christ Child they came to seek be your companion on your long walks.

10

The Christophers from the East

Epiphany, Cycle A
Matthew 2:1–12

Theme: let your light shine

On this feast of the Epiphany with its theme of light, the focus is on the Magi, those mysterious figures whom tradition has given the wonderfully inventive names of Casper, Balthasar, and Melchior, declared their number to be three, designated them as men of different races to represent all humanity coming to the Lord, and even assigned exotic meanings to their gifts: gold for the sovereignty of Christ, incense for his divinity, and myrrh to foreshadow his suffering.

There is no way, of course, to disentangle all the legends and stories that have appeared throughout the ages about these mysterious folk who appear in Matthew's wonderful account. But through them all we should not, must not, miss the essential reason that Matthew introduced these figures. In effect, Matthew tells us that *the Magi were the first Christophers*. That is, having been guided by the light of the star and having encountered the Light of the World at Bethlehem, they were now commissioned to carry that light, be that light, for others. Thus, the Wise Men are presented to us as examples of living witnesses to the faith. They who came out of the darkness to follow the star's light to the Light of the World, were to go back to let their light shine before others. "Let your light shine" could well be their motto.

That's the meaning of this feast of the Epiphany: all who have encountered God must let their light shine. So let me bring you up to date and point out how this is done in our times. Let me introduce to you two modern wise men, separated by 2000 years from the Magi, but very much a part of them. As it happens, they come from the world of sports, and their stories were told in the *Wall Street Journal* in an article with the significant title, "You Can't Be a Beacon if Your Life Don't Shine."

Over thirty-five years ago, Sandy Koufax, a Jewish man who was a pitcher for the Los Angeles Dodgers, announced that he wouldn't pitch on Yom Kippur, the holiest day of the Jewish year—even though this game was the first of the 1965 World Series. The management was aghast. They coaxed him, pleaded with him, told him to pitch just a few of his fabulous pitches and then he could go to all the synagogues in Los Angeles, to his heart's content. Koufax refused. His religion came first. So Don Drysdale took his place and lost. Koufax pitched the second game and lost. But as you may remember, the Dodgers won the 1965 series 4–3, and Koufax pitched a shutout in games five and seven. But talk about being a Magi, letting your light shine! To pass up starting a World Series game for a matter of faith? Would you and I do that?

To come closer to our own time, there's Eli Herring, the six-foot, seven-inches tall, three-hundred-forty-pound offensive tackle for Brigham Young University. During his senior year, he sported a 3.5 grade point average and was judged to be the best offensive tackle in the draft. He is also a Mormon, a practicing one. A Christopher man, if you will. As a consequence, he turned down a multimillion dollar deal with the Oakland Raiders because he wouldn't play on Sunday— a holy day, and the day on which the Raiders always play. He also told the NFL that if he were drafted he would not serve. Since he was the third-ranked senior tackle in the country, he would have been drafted early on, but he turned them down. To think: he could have signed up with the NFL, played ball on Sunday, and filled his life with Rolls Royces, a suburban mansion, and Brooks Brothers suits'—or he could teach math for $25,000 a year and honor the sabbath.

And in fact, Eli now teaches math for $25,000 a year, instead of the $25 million he could have made. He coaches football at the high school level and wears chino pants and a nice Wal-Mart shirt. Talk about letting your light shine! It makes you think: ought we extend the list of wise folk? You know, Casper, Melchior, Balthasar, Sandy, and Eli? It makes us ask the big question, the big challenge: could our names be added to that list?

While we're pondering this, perhaps this little parable will sum up the point I'm trying to get across. It's called, "The Goat's Hair Monk," and bear with me as I share it. First of all, I must tell you that the Goat's Hair Monk wasn't a monk, and he didn't wear a goat's hair monk's robe. Actually he was only one of the poor street people who roam the shabby streets of the decaying inner city. He had been nick-named the Goat's Hair Monk because he went about mumbling to himself, "Goat's hair, goat's hair." The "monk" part came from his routine of going into old St. Martin of Tours Church several times a day to pray. Yet, the old eccentric *did* look the part of a monk as he made his daily rounds through the poor part of the city in his drab, ragged clothing.

But he was not your typical panhandler with his hand always out for charity; instead his hand was out giving away things to the poor. Reaching down deep into the old, battered canvas bag he carried everywhere he went, he would pull out a pair of socks for a street-walker who had none, a pair of warm gloves for a disoriented bum whose hands were blue from the cold, or a couple of sandwiches for a hungry old bag lady. With each gift, he would beam a big smile and mumble in his heavy German accent, "Goat's hair, goat's hair."

Now here's where it gets interesting. It so happened that the local street gang members were convinced the Goat's Hair Monk carried a big stash of money in that old bag of his. They had made up wild sto-ries about how he had once been a millionaire who got religion and went off the deep end, and about how he became one of the crazies who wander the city streets, carrying everything he owned in a bag.

Well, one day in church the Goat's Hair Monk was sitting with his eyes closed praying in front of a stand of flickering vigil candles beneath a statue depicting holy St. Martin giving half of his cloak to a beggar. Through the dark shadows of the dimly lit church a kid from the street gang snuck up behind him, confident that the old man had fallen asleep while praying, leaving his bag unguarded in the pew. As the kid reached to snatch the monk's bag, like a lightning bolt the old man's arm struck with a karate-like blow and his voice thundered out, "God's here!" The kid's face wrinkled in pain as the old man said, "Wise up, kid! You steal from me or from anyone else and all you'll get back in life is pain. Rob others and you yourself will be robbed of what's precious to you—that's the ancient law. Now, go, and remember: God's here."

As the kid ran out of the church, he began to realize that the old man *hadn't* been saying to everyone, "goat's hair," but rather "God's here!" Anyway, about half a block away from the church, the kid looked over his shoulder and saw that members of a rival gang were following him. Attempting to escape he ran down an alley, only to find it was a dead end. Turning around in fear, he faced several gang members coming toward him armed with baseball bats and knives. Then he remembered and said, "God's here." Two or three drew back as the rest hesitated. So he said it again, louder, "God's here!" Suddenly, the alley was empty.

After that, whenever the kid saw the Goat's Hair Monk going into St. Martin of Tours to pray, he too would go in and kneel beside him. Before long, he asked the old man to teach him how to pray. Soon, he quit the gang and became the old man's bodyguard and disciple, helping him care for the poor. Years later, when the old Goat's Hair Monk lay dying, he gave his old battered bag to the young man, saying, "Remember, son, God's here."

That little parable sums up the story of the Magi. "God's here." God, the Great Manifestation, the Light of the World, is here deep within you, around you, above you, below you. God's here, and how could you not reveal that startling fact by your life, your witness? How could you not bring your light to illumine your corner of the world? These are the questions implied by Matthew in today's gospel. These are the questions at the heart of this great feast of Epiphany.

"God's here." Let your life announce it. Let your light shine. Or, as Matthew might phrase it today, "Be a Christopher!"

Lent &
Easter

11
Jesus Among the Beasts

First Sunday of Lent, Cycle B
Mark 1:12–15

Theme: a lenten challenge to the culture

He was among the wild beasts....

When the two democratic candidates for the highest office in the land were falling all over themselves to proclaim who is more pro-abortion than the other...

when money buys elections, candidates' souls, and citizens' lives and campaign financial reform resolutely and cynically goes nowhere because those who could make the reform are awash in soft money...

when sports teams, the Olympic committee, higher education, and schools have all sold their birthrights to the marketplace...

when children who watch five and a half hours of TV daily are conditioned not only to watch greed but to absorb it as a way of life...

when administrators, teachers, and students engage in widespread cheating on high-stakes standardized tests...

when marriage is trivialized by millionaires who wed on TV shows, and when marriage becomes less common than couples simply living together...

when daily, children are scarred by the routine divorces of their parents...

when the National Institutes of Health says that twenty-five percent of our children are affected by alcoholism...

when we, the world's richest nation, have the highest rate of poverty for young children in the Western industrialized world...

when a baseball player is offered 250 million dollars, while health-care aides—those who are willing to bathe, dress, feed, clean, and care for the elderly in their homes or in nursing homes—are in critical short supply because they are paid only nine dollars an hour...

when violence and racism so pervade our society that they become common, acceptable staples of life...

when it is documented that more than 50,000 women and children are sold to the United States by foreign criminals as forced domestic servants, sweatshop laborers, and prostitutes...

when in our own country 40,000 new people are infected with AIDS each year and it rages as an epidemic in Africa; and the sexually transmitted disease chlamydia has become so common among teenage girls that doctors recommend sexually active girls be tested twice a year for the disease rather than once a year, as called for by current medical guidelines...

when even Orthodox Jewish communities, who pride themselves on disciplined detachment from modern secular life, have their own children dying from drug overdose...

when genocides in Rwanda no longer catch our attention...

when websites offer beautiful models selling their eggs for $150,000 so parents can have beautiful—not noble or moral—children...

when the governor of Illinois has to call a stop to executions because so many innocent people are landing on death row...

when America at last count has 170 billionaires—many of whom are in their 30s and 40s—in contrast to thirteen billionaires in 1982; and the top four percent of the rich have more money than all of the bottom forty percent of the poor put together...

when scandals of sexual predation and financial mismanagement in our own church shame and traumatize us...

when our precious schools are no longer considered safe, and six year olds from drug infested homes put their soft little fingers around a gun found in their own homes and kill other six year olds...

when, finally, we have become so jaded that we are no longer capable of moral outrage...

then we know that Jesus once more is sitting among the wild beasts. And, newly baptized and called beloved by his Father, he must again stand up and face the beasts with his inaugural words, "This is the time of fulfillment. The kingdom of God is at hand. Repent, repent, and for God's sake—literally—believe in the gospel!" And Jesus stands before us in this church, during Lent of this new millennium, of the year 2000, this year of Jubilee which the Holy Father has called a time of forgiveness and reconciliation, a time of fulfillment—and he cries out more than ever, "Repent! Believe in the gospel."

How can we, newly signed with ashes, heed Jesus' words? How can we, also baptized and called beloved, living among the terrible beasts of our time, get people to believe in the gospel? The answer, our agenda for Lent, is to *be* the gospel, to *be* good news. How, in practice, do we do this?

I'm not going to suggest something complicated and obtuse. What I'm going to suggest are two simple things that we can all try our hand at no matter whether we're children, teenagers, or adults. The first is this. Every day of Lent, look to do the noble thing no matter how small. You know what I mean. Do the better thing, the nice thing, the small but kindly thing. Here is an example:

Jimmy Carter was not such a great president, but he is a great man. He is a Christian, and, as you know, he takes his faith very seriously. Well, when former vice president Hubert Humphrey died, Carter was president. There was a large memorial service. Hundreds of people gathered for the service, among them, former president Richard Nixon. It was not long after Nixon had been forced to resign in disgrace because of the Watergate scandal, and the memory of that scandal was fresh in people's minds.

At the memorial service, people mixed freely, greeting old friends. Nixon, however, stood alone isolated, shunned. It was then that something very wonderful happened. President Carter came into the room and saw Nixon standing by himself at the edge of the crowd. Carter walked over to Nixon, smiling his big smile. Then he surprised everyone by greeting Nixon with these words: "Welcome home, Mr. President! Welcome back home again!"

That's it. That's it. Embracing the sinner. A time of fulfillment. A small, simple, noble, gospel deed that announces the kingdom of God is at hand.

A few years ago, a priest friend of mine attended a church conference where he heard the well-known priest and author Henri Nouwen speak. Nouwen had dedicated much of his life to working with mentally handicapped people. He was a true servant in all he did. At this conference, Nouwen brought one of his mentally handicapped friends, Bill, up to the podium to help him with his speech. But Bill, in his nervousness, just laid his head on Nouwen's shoulder and began to cry. My priest friend commented that at that moment, all the conference attendees were reminded of the real purpose of being church. It was not about budgets, building programs, fancy sermons, or even devotions. He said, "Our work is to stand next to one another and provide a shoulder for weeping." That's what I mean. There's so much hated and competitiveness in this world—so many wild beasts we dwell among—that we must proclaim a different way of life. Maybe we could carry around a little card, like the kids do, that reads "What Would Jesus Do?"

Keep a journal. Not out of pride, but just as a record, a reminder of the good deed you did that day: speaking an encouraging word, giving a compliment, holding the door open for someone, visiting the sick, calling a friend—whatever. Do the daily noble deed.

Next, give alms, that time-honored, Bible-advised way of repentance. Put an empty coffee can on the dinner table and each day put your loose change in it. At the end of Lent, give the money to the poor.

The noble deed. Almsgiving. Will they tame the wild beasts we live among? I don't know. But they will in their own way announce that the kingdom of God is at hand. They will give hope to the hopeless and a sign to the perplexed. They will keep the presence of Christ alive in the world. They will be remembered. Let me end with a personal story.

Old Johnny Donovan was a bachelor who never did much as far as I could see but putter around in his little garage next to his dilapidated house. A bum we kids called him behind our parents' backs. But every day Old John would happen to drop in the back of my father's bakery shop. "Hi, Charlie!" he'd always say and my Dad, looking up from his work would greet him back. Old John always managed to look as if he just "happened" to be passing by—at lunch time—and was intending to go on further but my dad would always say, "John, we just happen to have some left-over buns. Would you stay and have some with us?"

And Old John's standard response was, "Well, Charlie, I've had plenty to eat already but, like yourself, I hate to see good food go to waste." Then he'd stay and have some buns and coffee with my dad, passing along the local gossip.Even as a kid I was awed by this little daily drama and that they were both conning one another. I often wanted to protest and say, "Hey, Dad, I heard you say you were putting aside some buns and bread for Old John 'cause he would be coming by soon"—but I always held my tongue.

But one summer day after Old John had left, I finally asked my dad why he just didn't come out and say, "Hello, John, looking for a free lunch again? I have it ready for you." I have never forgotten my father's response. He said, "Well, son, it might hurt John's feelings to say that. And then I could begin to think that he's in my debt. The poor are their own gift to us and we owe them!" He said no more.

Do people talk like that anymore? I couldn't verbalize it then but even as a kid I knew that the kingdom of God was at hand.

12

The Transfiguration

Third Sunday of Lent, Cycle C
Luke 13:1–9

Many years ago I was walking in a shopping mall—the Cherry Hill Mall as I recall—when I noticed a group of people staring at something in a display window. Curious, I walked over to see what was happening. They were staring at a strange poster sitting on an easel. The poster was brightly colored and had what seemed to be meaningless symbols and patterns. "Must be new age art," someone mumbled behind me. "Never did understand that stuff."

Suddenly, someone in the crowd exclaimed, "I see him! I see him!" pointing at the poster. "See what? See who?" everyone asked together. "Well, I'm not sure who it is and I don't want to spoil it for you," she said. I thought to myself, "Yeah, right. You don't see anything." But then another person said, "I see him too!" We all looked at the poster with greater concentration. But after a few minutes, many walked away, shaking their heads.

"Uh, can you tell me what's going on?" I asked one of the persons who said she had seen him. "This is a hologram or 3-D picture," she explained. "If you look at it in just the right light and just the right angle, you will see an image hidden there." "Really?" I replied, still doubtful.

"Well, it's not easy. It takes time. But there he is. Don't you see him?" she said. I stared until my head ached. "I don't see anything," I replied adding, "There's not a Candid Camera crew set up around here, is there?" She smiled and said, "Don't give up." She walked away and I stood there. I must have looked at that poster a dozen times that day with the same result. I left.

But it intrigued me and so, later, on the way out of the mall, I decided to give it one last try. As I looked at it, bending my head to the side, the symbols started to fade and, sure enough, a face began to form. "I see him! I see him!" I said right out loud, grinning at the complete strangers behind me. I realized whose face it was I was seeing for the first time. It was Jesus. And there were three crosses in the background. I spent an hour after that trying to convince and help others see the face there. It was fun seeing their faces light up when they saw him too.

Sometimes I think that maybe that's what happened at the Transfiguration. Maybe everything was just in place, the light was just right, the angle was perfect and then, suddenly, the apostles saw. Beyond and behind and within the man they had known for three years, beyond the symbols and patterns of everyday life, there was something else. And, in a brief moment of revelation, they saw it. The gospel of the Transfiguration celebrates what they saw, their moment of insight.

But the question is, what took so long? Why didn't they see Jesus that way before this? The answer is to be found in that rather vivid sentence in the gospel that explains why. The sentence says of the three apostles, "Peter and his companions had been overcome by sleep but becoming fully awake they saw his glory." They were overcome by sleep and not fully awake. This is a good symbol, and a lesson that explains why we don't see God's glory. We miss so much because *our* minds are asleep. And, in fact, there are certain things that are designed to keep our minds asleep like, say, prejudice that makes us so set in our ideas that our minds are shut. Or overload from the incessant images, commercials, and noise that assault and distract us every day and dull our perceptions. You really have to go apart, seek out some solitude, like the disciples, to see behind things.

But mostly, I think, we are not fully awake, we don't see, because society puts such enormous pressure on us to focus our vision, our energy, our drive solely on the pursuit of a career or fame or celebrity status as *the* apex of living. And so we wind up giving these things such total devotion and priority that we become insensitive to deeper realities, blind to the human, and indifferent to the lives, joys, journeys, and needs of others.

Here is a sad case in point. In 1993, a white South African photojournalist named Kevin Carter began snapping photos of famine victims at a UN feeding center in drought-stricken Sudan. Then, one day, seeking relief from the sight of such misery, he wandered into the open bush. There he heard a soft, high-pitched whimpering and found a tiny, frail little girl crouched, head bowed, struggling to make her way to the feeding center.

Carter instantly got his camera ready, for here was a powerful picture. He started to photograph her when dramatically, a well-fed vulture, taller by far than the child, landed just a few feet behind her waiting to claim the child when she died. This was the picture of a lifetime! Careful not to disturb the bird, Carter repositioned himself for the best possible picture. He waited for about twenty minutes hoping the vulture would do something like spread its wings for an even more dramatic image. It didn't, and after Carter took his photographs, he chased the vulture away and watched as the little girl resumed her struggle alone.

Later in the day, when he had a chance to sit back and think about it all, he sat under a tree, chain-smoking, talking to God...and crying. He thought of his small daughter Meghan, and longed to hug her. The picture—you must remember it—first appeared in the New York *Times* in March of 1993. It proved controversial, and Carter was criticized for being so absorbed in his craft that he did not reach out to help the little girl. In 1994 his photograph won a Pulitzer Prize.

Two months later Kevin Carter committed suicide.

A sad and tragic event, but the whole incident becomes a parable about today's gospel of the Transfiguration. So many people get so sucked up into the tunnel vision of a totally demanding and absorbing job, the big career move, the spectacular deal, the salable moment, the fame-and-fortune project, the proper angle, the right advantage, the best position—they're so absorbed in what advances *them* that they become blind to the needs of others.

They simply don't see there are times that they should drop everything and go embrace their spouses, hug their children, help their friends, befriend the stranger, and carry the starving to the feeding center. Such insights, such transfigurations are not possible because, so focused on the immediate, the here and now, they, like Peter, James, and John, are not fully awake to see the glory of God where it is.

Lent was designed precisely as a time to wake up and examine our priorities. This gospel is suggesting that we too might be missing some transfiguring moments because we're not fully awake, that we are blinded by the wrong things, Not bad things—just things that are important but simply don't deserve *that much* dedication and devotion at the expense of relationships, reaching out to others, and discovering the splendor of what might be there if we took the time to look.

13

The Prodigal Son's Brother

Fourth Sunday of Lent, Cycle C
Luke 15:1–3, 11–32

The high schooler was assigned to read a Shakespeare play. To his immense surprise he discovered that he actually *liked* it except, he complained, "it was full of trite sayings." Indeed it is, like "every dog has its day" and so on. Of course the lad missed the point. Shakespeare is the *originator* of these sayings, not the one the who made them trite.

We have the same problem with today's parable. It has become trite because we have heard it so often and its phrases, such as "the prodigal son" or "the fattened calf," have fallen into common lore. Still, there are always riches to be explored in this story, and so today I want to take you to a different vantage point. I want to talk about the three sinners in the story, but especially about the sinner who got a bum rap. That's the elder son. He justifiably complained, "Look, all these years I served you and not once did I disobey your orders; yet you never gave me even a young goat to fast on with my friends." And the father admitted, "Yes, son, you *are* here with me always; everything I have is yours." But that wasn't enough.

Let's hear it for the elder son. He's steady and obedient and faithful and has served well. He's there when you need him. He works hard behind the scenes. You don't have to follow after him or remind him. He's dependable. He's a rock. He's loyal. He's the kind of son parents dream of. And all this means that his wonderfully forgiving father is not without sin and has something to answer for. That something is that obviously, he *has* taken the elder son for granted. When was the last time he praised him, told him how much he meant to him, that things around here would be in a pretty sorry mess without him, that he is grateful? More, that he's proud of him? Even more, that he loves him and thanks God every day for him? Never.

So we can resonate with the elder son and our sympathies are with him. He is legion. He is the housewife or mother who keeps the family together emotionally and physically, but who is utterly taken for granted, like an unpaid servant. He is the father who works hard to raise his family, putting in long hours, sacrificing his own wants and pleasures so his kids can go to a good school, but he is taken for granted. He is the loyal worker who is there every day, taking no phony sick leaves, giving her time and energy over and above what is required, and who is taken for granted. He is the teacher who stays longer than the bell, the crossing guard in the freezing weather, the little league coach rushing home from work to make the game, the mailman who delivers mail through the snow, the nurse on the midnight shift, the garbage man who simply comes and does his job, the friend you can count on, borrow from, and walk in on—all of these people taken for granted.

And, then, let someone else do one little thing out of the ordinary or let someone who is self-centered, manipulative, or uncaring do a good deed almost by accident or do something decent for the first time in their lives or fall into some good luck, and the whole world throws a party for them. And the elder sons and daughters of this world look on and shake their heads. It's not fair.

So, you see, there is sin all around in this parable. The sin of the younger son who insulted his father then fled, hurting his father deeply; the sin of the father, who graciously forgave this son but forgot to hug his other son and tell him what a right arm he was; and the decent elder son: what was his sin? His sin is one that plagues good people. It's the sin of the constricted heart, the ungenerous spirit.

Mary was upset with herself. Her sister was moving home. She should, after all, be happy, as happy as her mother was. But she wasn't. It just didn't make any sense. Since her father had died three years ago, Mary had taken care of her mother all by herself. She did everything for her mother. She talked to her on the telephone twice a day. She had her over for dinner two or three times a week. She bought her groceries, made her appointments and saw to it that she got to them, cleaned her apartment, and even handled her finances. Now that her sister was coming home she wouldn't have to do everything by herself. She should be happy that she was going to have help. But she wasn't. What was wrong with her?

What was wrong with her is understandable. Now she has to share. She is no longer in the limelight. Mary can no longer have her mom so exclusively. Besides, she, *not her sister*, has been there all the time like the elder son, day in and day out caring for mom and being a real support. And now this younger sister is returning home and displacing her, and people will forget all she did. Worst of all, her mother will probably throw a homecoming party for her sister.

You see, so often our identity is threatened, like Mary in our story. Our hope for appreciation evaporates as our steady, faithful deeds are forgotten; our place in the sun diminishes. Our dedication is taken for granted as another moves in. It's a deep and indelible sense we all have, that if someone else goes up on the seesaw of life we go down, and down there no one thanks us. So we feel a twinge of resentment, of hurt even as we try to smile.

But as we travel the spiritual path, we must resist this contraction of heart. Because sooner or later, if we don't, we will become like the elder brother who so let it get to him that, as noble as he was, he would not even come into the ancestral home, which was a grave insult in that culture; could not even bring himself to call his sibling "brother"—he used the oblique phrase, "*your* son"; and, worst of all, could not really be pleased that something truly wonderful had happened. He could not rejoice in the momentous gift of grace his brother received, and the generous outpouring of his father over a sinner who was redeemed.

Well, the truth is, none of us elder brothers and sisters ever really outgrows that constricting "if another goes up I must go down" syndrome. But we can go a long way toward peace and a truly generous spirit if, during Lent, we remember that God is in charge, that God sees what we do, that God is pleased with us, that God never takes us for granted. Rather, God invites us to laugh and rejoice wherever beauty, truth, and goodness reveal themselves, even in arrogant prodigal sons, because that is what makes us most like the One who sends rain on the just and the unjust alike.

So, a round of applause for the elder son. He just has to watch himself, resist the pouting and envious face, and forever remember his father's precious words. "My son, you are here with me *always*. Everything I have—*everything*—is yours."

14

Remember the Past, Look to the Future

Fifth Sunday in Lent, Cycle C
John 8:1–11

History is important; it is important to remember the past. How, for example, our country was born; how we gained hard-won freedoms; how God dealt with the Hebrews and the promises God made. Remembering tells you of your roots, where you came from, the people and events who formed you for better or for worse.

Nations set high store on memory, building shrines, erecting statues, and putting up museums and archives. The first thing invaders do is destroy the shrines of a people, erasing their memories so they will eventually lose their identity. The Hebrews set a high store on memory, which why the great Rabbi Abraham Joshua Heschel said that much of what the Bible demands can be summed up in a single word: remember! Elie Wiesel has said that for the Jews to forget the Holocaust is a crime against justice and memory. If you forget, he says, you become the executioner's accomplice. St. Paul openly remembers his past: "I persecuted the way of the church to death," he wrote. "I shut up many in prison. I persecuted them even to foreign cities"(Acts 26:10–11).

So, remembering the past tells us where we have been. But there is danger in staying in the past, and that is the topic of our gospel reflection this morning. St. Paul knew about this danger. After rehearsing his sinful past he nevertheless wrote, "One thing I do: *forgetting what lies behind and straining forward to what lies ahead,* I press on toward the goal for the prize of the upward call of God in Christ Jesus" (Phil 3:13–14). So, too, the adulteress in this morning's gospel. There is indeed a past for her, a shameful one, for she was caught in adultery. Jesus does not minimize it and calls it for what it is: a sin. He condemns the sin but not the sinner. But the past is past and notice that what concerns Jesus is the future, "From now on," he said, "avoid this sin."

The past is a part of our story and God's story, and we ought to know it because we live off it. Yet, as we said, there is the danger to be avoided, and that is to live in the past.

Well-known author and pastor Frederick Buechner writes sadly of his mother, who died a very lonely death as an old woman. Let me read his words about his mother:

> Being beautiful was her business, her art, her delight, and it took her a long way and earned her many dividends, but when, as she saw it, she lost her beauty...she was like a millionaire who runs out of money. She took her name out of the phone book and got an unlisted number....With her looks gone she felt she had nothing left to offer the world, to propitiate the world. So what she did was simply to check out of the world, that old, last rose of summer, the way Greta Garbo and Marlene Dietrich checked out of it, holing themselves up somewhere and never venturing forth except in disguise. My mother holed herself up in her apartment...then in just one room of that apartment, then in just one chair in that room, and finally, in the bed where one morning a few summers ago, perhaps in her sleep, she died at last.

How sad. After she lost her beauty and youth, Buechner's mother saw no other possibilities. She retired to the past, retreated from the present and missed the future.

You see, whether it's turning twenty-one or forty or sixty-five; whether it's an enfeebling illness or a crummy job or forced retirement; whether it's family problems or alcoholism or a nursing home; whatever the imprisoning situation, we can feel not only different but diminished, and the temptation therefore is to hark back to our glory days when things were better. Like Norma Desmond in *Sunset Boulevard*, we try to live forever in "Remember when?" But that is deadly.

One of my favorite films is *Come Back, Little Sheba*. The male lead, played by Burt Lancaster, is a reformed alcoholic. His wife, played by Shirley Booth, is a devoted woman with a big heart; but she bores him endlessly by ceaselessly recalling the good old days. Remember when...? Time and again she walks out on the porch calling for Little Sheba, the dog that has long ago disappeared, the dog that is a symbol of those bygone days, a symbol of dashed hopes. But for twenty years, these two good people live in that past, live what Thoreau called "lives of quiet desperation." But remember, faith tells us that the best days are ahead: life with Christ in glory. And so we must "strain forward" as St. Paul said, "and press on." In a word, tomorrow should be better in a different way than yesterday; for each day can be a new opportunity for grace.

But, alas, that's where guilt comes in. Guilt is basically being stuck in the past. For example, I think a risk for the adulteress may well have been her sense of guilt. I can imagine her asking herself, "How can a God who prizes fidelity ever forgive my infidelity? How can I expect my husband to forgive me? Above all, can I ever forgive myself? This strange, unique, compassionate man has told me that *he* doesn't condemn me, that no other Jew in the area dares to condemn me. But how can I live with their leering looks, live with my husband, live with myself?"

Many a Christian is like that. Many a Christian seems unable to accept Christ's forgiveness, goes through life wallowing in guilt, afraid of hell, tormented by past offenses, unable to make peace with his or her human frailty. But not for this did Jesus die for our sins. Christ "loved me," St. Paul insists, "and gave himself for me." That love persists through all our infidelities. So the trick is to fix our eyes not on yesterday's sin but on today's forgiveness and tomorrow's hope.

In his famous novel, *The Fall*, Albert Camus tells of a man tortured by guilt. Years have passed, but his memory haunts him. He has moved from one place to the next, but his guilt follows him. His terrible memories go back to a night in Paris when he was walking along the Seine River. He noticed a young woman dressed in black and standing on a bridge. He hesitated for a moment, and then walked on. Then he heard a splash and then cries for help and then silence. He convinced himself that he could not help, so he walked on. Years later, finally confessing his guilt to a stranger in a bar in Amsterdam, he concluded by saying, "O young woman, throw yourself into the water again so that I may a second time have the chance of saving both of us."

That's heavy stuff and maybe somebody here has something similar that they live with day after day and wish they could go back and undo it. But we cannot turn back the calendar and do what we should have done then. We cannot erase the past. However, we can make our lives count *in the days ahead*. Just like the woman caught in adultery. "*From now on*," Jesus encouraged her, "sin no more."

So, God will not only forgive us, God will not only provide us the opportunity to redeem the past, but God will and does call us every day to a glorious future.

What is the gospel message? Let Little Sheba go. Grace is beckoning.

15

Easter

Some people like to collect the more interesting tombstone epitaphs. Like the one in New Mexico that plays with names. It says:

Here lies Johnny Yeast.
Pardon me for not rising.

Another, obviously in memory of an accident:

Here lies the body of Jonathan Blake.
Stepped on the gas
Instead of the brake.

Another from Boot Hill, Arizona:

Here lies Lester Moore.
Four slugs from a 44
No Les no more.

Finally, another word play from Massachusetts:

Under the sod and under the trees
Lies the body of Jonathan Pease.
He is not here, there's only the pod
Pease shelled out and went to God.

This light gallows humor that disguises our innate fear of death—what does it have in common with the following true story?

A man was standing in line at the bank he overheard a commotion at the counter. A woman was quite distressed, exclaiming, "Where will I put my money?! Where will I put my money? I have all my money and my mortgage here!! What will happen to my mortgage?!" She was all upset. Well, it turned out that she had misunderstood a small sign on the counter. The sign read, WE WILL BE CLOSED FOR GOOD FRIDAY. I guess Easter was not uppermost in her thoughts, because she thought that the bank was going to close "for good" that coming Friday.

What do both episodes have to do with Easter? Two things. One is the fact that, at least in faith, we can laugh at death because Easter says it has lost its ultimate power. The other is that people, like the lady at the bank, continue to misunderstand Easter as well. But at least here, in this faith community, we can try to get some focus. So let me say three things about Easter and why Christians can laugh.

First, Easter is a testimony to the force of love. I know that sounds trite, but it is profoundly true. And that is not a novel idea to us.

In a cemetery in Hanover, Germany, there is a grave on which were placed huge slabs of granite and marble cemented together and fastened with heavy steel clasps. Why? Because it belongs to a woman who vehemently did not believe in the resurrection of the dead. So she directed in her will that her grave be made so secure that if there were a resurrection, it could not reach her. On the marker were inscribed these words: "This burial place must never be opened." Ah, but in time, you see, what happened was that an infinitesimal seed, covered over by the stones, began to grow. Slowly it pushed its way through the soil and out from beneath them. As it grew and its trunk enlarged, the great slabs were gradually shifted so that the steel clasps were wrenched from their sockets and, there it was, the grave was exposed. A tiny seed had pushed aside those enormous stones.

Easter says that if nature can move huge stones, God can move the huge stone at Jesus' grave. And ours as well. Such is the force of God's love.

Second, Easter is not only a validation of the life and horrible death of Jesus but a statement that goodness and beauty will endure. Jesus did his best. He washed the feet of the apostles and kissed Judas. He healed the ear of Malchus and answered Pilate's questions. He looked silently at Herod and admonished the women on his way to the cross. He thanked Simon of Cyrene. He forgave the soldiers and prayed for his murderers. He encouraged the robber on the cross next to him. But, finally, ugly and bruised, he bent his head and gave up his heart. Bleeding and disfigured, he fell and did not come up again. But God rescued him. Today we celebrate God's validation of his life and all that he stood for. Today Easter celebrates, not the ugliness of his suffering and death and what people did to him, but the enduring and compelling beauty of his life and love which surmounted it all.

The luminous paintings of the great artist Renoir are aglow with life and light and color. He seemed to put light inside the people he painted. Remarkably, as you may know, for the last twenty years or so of his life—his most productive years—Renoir was terribly crippled with arthritis. His hands were twisted and gnarled. His wrists, his arms, and his spine were ravaged by the disease. He couldn't even stand as he worked. He had to sit and be shifted about in his chair by assistants as he painted. At times the pain was so great as he worked that beads of perspiration would stand out on his face. On one occasion, one of his students (the great artist Matisse) asked him, "Why do you go on and torture yourself like this?" Renoir looked at the canvas on which he was working and replied, "The pain passes, but the beauty remains."

Easter is the celebration of the life-giving beauty of Jesus that remains beyond the pain—for Jesus and for us.

Third, Easter is hope. What I am about to say won't impress the young folks here today, but it will their parents and especially their grandparents and, in time, themselves. A celebrity of his time—playboy, wit, editor of the famous British publication *Punch*—Malcolm Muggeridge "got religion." Because he was so famous, the elite, who felt betrayed by him, couldn't ignore him. They gave him his fifteen minutes of fame and then dropped him. He had committed an unpardonable sin because not only did he get religion, he became a Catholic. And not only did he become a Catholic, but he did so because he was inspired by the presence and work of Mother Teresa. Already elderly when he converted, Muggeridge wrote many lovely things, including these words:

> As I approach my end, I find Jesus' outrageous claim ever more captivating and meaningful. Quite often, waking up in the night

as the old do, I feel myself to be half out of my body, hovering between life and death, with eternity rising in the distance. I see my ancient carcass, prone between the sheets, stained and worn like a scrap of paper dropped in the gutter and, hovering over it, myself, like a butterfly released from its chrysalis stage and ready to fly away.

Are caterpillars told of their impending resurrection? How in dying they will be transformed from poor earth crawlers into creatures of the air with exquisitely painted wings? If told, do they believe it? I imagine the wise old caterpillars shaking their heads—no, it can't be; it's a fantasy. Yet in the limbo between living and dying, as the night clocks tick remorselessly on, and the black sky implacably shows not one single scratch of gray, I hear those words: "I am the resurrection" and I feel myself carried along on a great tide of joy and peace.

Easter is such promise—for him and for us.

Easter, then, is a testimony to the power of love. Easter is a restoration of beauty, Jesus' and ours. Easter is promise of resurrection.

Let me end with a final epitaph, this one from England, a rather somber one you may have heard before:

Remember man, as you walk by
As you are now, so once was I.
As I am now, so shall you be,
Remember this and follow me.

To which some wag replied by scribbling on the tombstone:

To follow you I'll not consent
Until I know which way you went.

Easter says we know which way Jesus went—and where we shall follow because of him. That's what it's all about and why we laugh and shout the joyous "Alleluia!"

. Happy Easter.

16

The Climate of Unbelief

Second Sunday of Easter, Cycle A
John 20:19–31

Theme: countering the culture

The Thomas incident in today's gospel naturally raises questions about belief and disbelief, certainty and doubt. But let me stretch your minds this morning and lead you to consider a wider context within the dynamic of faith. This context proclaims the very plausible theory that people's faith derives not so much from intellectual deduction but rather from their upbringing; that is, the whole complex of emotional overtones and practices of the people that have surrounded them from the beginning, the people who in so many overt and subtle ways affirm their worldview.

In turn, this worldview depends on the social support it receives from the neighborhood, the community, the social institutions like the school, the government, and the dominant means of communication. In short, *faith survives and grows because there is a whole culture that silently conspires and promotes it to keep a religious view of life intact.*

All of which means to say that it is relatively easy, for example, to be a Catholic when the significant people in one's life are Catholic or at least respect Catholicism, when all the institutional forces—like a Catholic neighborhood, a Catholic school, and a Catholic climate—support and confirm this worldview. The same could be said of Jews or Lutherans or Hindus: the social climate can make it seem almost "natural" to be a professed believer.

On the other hand, trouble comes when the climate changes from one of support to one of hostility and ridicule. With the social support system gone, it is far more difficult to believe, to have faith. Or, to put it this way, when the centuries-old Judeo-Christian context comes under assault and is dismantled and is replaced by cynicism, radical doubt, and a pervasive secular spirit, which says that the here and now is all there is; when a world of pluralism drowns individual commitment, then to be a believer, much less a *public* believer, becomes extremely hard.

This challenge becomes enormously compounded if one's primary witness and support group, namely, one's parents, stop practicing the faith, are only nominal Christians, or divorce. Or, in a complaint that ranks as the number one hurt of kids today, if parents are simply absent from their children's lives and so by default leave their children's religious and moral formation to the schools, which must now remain neutral; or to the media, which is hostile to belief; or to celebrities, who have replaced the saints of old as idols to be imitated; or to their peers, who are morally and religiously as much in the dark as they are.

Again, the reality is that faith flourishes within a context of faith-filled people and it languishes in a context of faithless people. That's hardly a revolutionary thought; it's just common sense. It's why some people join communes or do home-schooling. Or, if you want to use the symbolism of the gospel: when Thomas left the faith community, he lost his own faith. When he rejoined the community, he found his faith.

O.K. Let's get to the stories and, for the sake of example, let's stick with Catholics.

Shortly after Ash Wednesday, Brit Hume of Fox News told how Ted Turner, the celebrity mogul, seeing ashes on the foreheads of some workers at CNN, said, "What are you? A bunch of Jesus freaks?" Nothing new. Turner is on record for branding Christianity as a religion "for losers," for labeling pro-life Christians as "Bozo," and for insulting the pope with a cheap joke at a pro-abortion meeting.

Recently, the anti-Catholic play, *Sister Mary Ignatius Explains it All for You*—a play denounced by the Jewish Anti-Defamation League and others as virulently anti-Catholic—was presented at the University Theater of the University of Maryland. The theater brochure actually bragged—and I quote—"In *Sister Mary Ignatius*... [the author] shines a spotlight on the Catholic Church, revealing its blind faith teachings as an extremely dangerous influence on people's lives." A Catholic student attending that play on campus is going to have a hard time defending her faith there.

As we know, it is becoming commonplace for museums to present sacrilegious images of the Blessed Mother. It is not at all unusual to read an article in the magazine *The Nation* calling for laws to force Catholic hospitals to perform abortions and labeling the pope "a homicidal liar who endorses murder."

Television is full of cheap shots at Catholicism, from shows like *Everybody Loves Raymond* and the *Simpsons*. NBC has paid an author named Glenn Kleier one million dollars for rights to produce a miniseries based on his book, *The Last Day*. Rich Horgan, who worked with Kleier on the book, said, "This is a book that's going to be a sort of kidney punch to organized religion and to the Catholic Church specifically." Movies like the delightful *Chocolat* or *All About My Mother* put the church in a bad light. MTV, the darling of the young crowd, endorses beliefs and behavior at odds with Christianity. This scurrilous anti-Catholicism is a staple of many, many plays, movies, and television shows. And it doesn't stop with the media. At some universities, anti-Catholicism and anti-religion are common attitudes among some professors.

What all this is saying is that the national context has changed from support for the Judeo-Christian worldview to indifference, outright disdain, and hostility. The climate has changed and, on the popular front, the steady, unrelenting stream of ridicule and hatred of things Catholic affects the TV-addicted youth of today. The culture has created an undertone of cynicism and embarrassment, and shapes the image of the Catholic Church as an institution no thinking person would admit belonging to. The constant trafficking of anti-Catholic stereotypes, the obligatory sneers on television and in the movies, the intellectual disdain for Catholicism in the universities—all are likely to make it harder for impressionable adolescents or young adults to claim their beliefs or to maintain them. In other words, faith is hard to come by in a culture of disbelief and derision. Doubting Thomases, cut off from a believing community, will multiply.

This points up the urgent necessity for us as a parish, more than ever, to create an image of a caring community, a church that offers liturgies that nourish and a people determined to find ways to encourage parents to go to church, subscribe to Catholic magazines, and consort with people of integrity and faith. Above all, it points up how necessary it is for us, as a group held in contempt, to bear witness in our own lives to the richness of our tradition.

Let me end with a story on how faith is supported by context.

There was a barefooted, big city drifter named George. He had wild hair and he wore tattered pants and an oversized, food-stained T-shirt. One Sunday morning, as he ambled past a big, beautiful church in the heart of the city, he decided to go in. The church was full and the homily was about to begin. George found no seat, and no one moved to try to make room for him. And so, having walked all the way to the front without finding a seat, he squatted down on the floor, in front of the pulpit. The people were incredulous, but did nothing. Then, the priest noticed the church's elderly head usher slowly making his way down the aisle toward George.

There was a certain elegance about the well-dressed usher and, even though he was walking with a cane, he had a confident, authoritative air about him. Everyone was saying to themselves, more or less, "You can't blame that elderly model of correctness for what he is going to do, or say, to that impudent, irreverent young man!"

It took a while for the old usher to reach the young man. The church was silently breathless, other than the click of the old man's cane. Then, with great difficulty he laid down his cane and lowered himself to sit on the floor next to George, guaranteeing that for the rest of the Mass George would not sit alone. Everyone was choked up with emotion. And when the priest finally gained control—and here is the point—he said, "What I am about to preach you may never remember. But what you have just seen, you will never forget."

That's the context of faith.

17

Forgiveness Around the Campfire

Third Sunday of Easter, Cycle C
John 21:1–19

Theme: Forgiveness in time of national tragedy

There once was a little boy who was visiting his grandparents on their farm. And he was given a slingshot to play with out in the woods. He practiced in the woods, but he could never hit the target. Getting a little discouraged, he headed back to dinner.

But as he was walking back, he saw Grandma's pet duck. Just out of impulse, he let fly, hit the duck square in the head, and killed it. He was shocked and grieved. In a panic, he hid the dead duck in the woodpile, only to see his sister watching. Sally had seen it all, but she said nothing. Well, after lunch that day, Grandma said, "Sally, let's wash the dishes." But Sally said, "Grandma, Johnny told me he wanted to help in the kitchen today, didn't you, Johnny?" And then she whispered to him, "Remember, the duck!" So Johnny did the dishes. Later Grandpa asked if the children wanted to go fishing, and Grandma said, "I'm sorry, but I need Sally to help make supper." But Sally smiled and said, "Well, that's all right because Johnny told me he wanted to help." And she whispered again, "Remember, the duck?" So Sally went fishing, and Johnny stayed.

After several days of Johnny doing both his chores and Sally's, he finally couldn't stand it any longer. He came to Grandma and confessed that he had killed the duck. She knelt down, gave him a hug and said, "Sweetheart, I know. You see, I was standing at the window, and I saw the whole thing. But because I love you, I forgave you. But I was just wondering how long you would let Sally make a slave of you...."

Something like that happened in today's gospel and happens in our lives. There was, you recall, a campfire. Around it, Peter, Jesus' hand-picked leader of his group, denied him three times—and with swearing and cursing at that. Then, loaded with guilt, Peter bolted from that fire and fled into the dark streets of Jerusalem. He hid from his friends and ultimately decided to leave the group Jesus had gathered and the way of life he was called to. And still enslaved by his guilt, he returned to his old trade as a fisherman.

That's where we find him in today's gospel. Then, as you heard, he unexpectedly found himself around another campfire. This time he had the chance to affirm his love for Jesus three times and Jesus, who was wondering just how long his guilt would make a slave of him, embraced him and forgave him and set him free. Just as the boy's grandma did. But this should be no surprise. Mercy was Jesus' name and forgiveness was his game, not revenge. That was two thousand years ago. And at that safe distance we can all nod in agreement and gratitude that Jesus will give us a second chance as well, no matter what we do.

Now, a challenge. We enjoyed the Grandma story and got its point. Are you willing to transport its message to a sensitive issue? Let me raise that sensitive issue by introducing you to Bud Welch. Each Wednesday Bud Welch would meet his beautiful twenty-three-year-old daughter, Julie Marie, for lunch across the street from the Murrah Building where she worked as an interpreter. That is, until Wednesday April 19, 1995. On that Wednesday he didn't get to have lunch with her because Julie was a victim of the Oklahoma City bombing. This father lost a lovely daughter. Every day for a year Bud Welch would return to that same spot to grieve her death, and he still goes once a week, after Mass on Sunday.

For the first few months after the bombing, Welch said he was in favor of the death penalty visited upon Timothy McVeigh, the perpetrator. But as time went on, provoked by gospels like today's, he changed his mind and tried to deal with forgiveness. Prior to McVeigh's death, Bob Welch said: "If Timothy McVeigh is executed I won't be able to choose to forgive him. As long as he is alive I have to deal with my feelings and emotions….It's a struggle I need to wage. To me the death penalty is vengeance and vengeance doesn't really help anyone in the healing process." This Catholic man went on to express his belief that the souls of the most "dastardly criminals have a right to be saved—even Timothy McVeigh." Those are his words. And he believes his daughter Julie would agree.

All of this must be hard for Bud Welch—I don't know what we would do or how we would feel if we lost someone in an event like that terrible bombing—but he is, as a matter of fact, only following the gospel. He is dredging up from his Catholic upbringing what Jesus taught: "You have heard it said, an eye for an eye, a tooth for a tooth but I say to you…if anyone strikes you on the right cheek, turn the other also." He remembered that Jesus forbade the accusers to stone to death the woman caught in adultery and, with a rebuke, he made Peter put up his sword in the Garden of Olives. An eye for an eye, a tooth for a tooth, a death for a death is obviously not Jesus' way. He would recall that Jesus taught, "You have heard it said, you shall love your neighbor and hate your enemy, but I say to you, love your enemies and pray for those who persecute you so that you may be children of your Father in heaven."

Then too, like every Catholic, Bud Welch knows that Jesus dealt with murderers in the same way. About those who were murdering him Jesus prayed, "Father, forgive them." And to the criminal on his right who was, as Scripture clearly tells us, a murderer as well as a thief, he says, "Today you will be with me in paradise." In other words, for Jesus, there was always a second campfire for betrayers like Peter and murderers like Paul, whose hands were freshly stained with Stephen's blood. I guess that is why, even though some Catholics disagree—perhaps some of you, especially war veterans and others who have witnessed terrible horrors—the Holy Father and the bishops, heeding Jesus' words, seeing his example and watching his compassion, are opposed to the death penalty.

In any case, the gospel dynamics are provocative and challenging—to Peter, to Paul, to Bud Welch, to us. However you feel, there is one constant: for Jesus Christ there is no need to be enslaved by guilt. For Jesus there always is a second chance. For Jesus, there is always another campfire around which to set things right…for all of us.

No Options

Sixth Sunday of Easter, Cycle B
John 15:9–17

Theme: Christianity costs

It was not you who chose me, but I who chose you and appointed you to go and bear fruit that will remain....

I chose you....

And that's the problem, isn't it? We're backed into a corner. We didn't choose Jesus. He chose us. And, worst of all, he chose us for a mission: to go and bear fruit. I wonder how many of us think: "Thanks a lot! Couldn't he have picked someone else? Chosen someone spiritually classier than I am? Why me?" For some, this "choosing" business is like getting a notice from the IRS saying that they're going to be audited. You don't need this.

Yes, I know there's a sentimental side, a being-flattered side to have Jesus look at me and say, "You have not chosen me. I have chosen you." But after the initial modest blush, there is, I think, a certain anger, or at least an annoyance not too far below the surface, because deep down, we know we've been boxed in. And truth to tell, we don't like it. I mean, the bottom line is this: once I'm chosen, once I'm tagged, once I've been given the baptismal uniform, so to speak, then my options as a Christian are limited. And I, raised in a society of endless choice, in a consumer culture that caters to my infantile fantasy of no parents, no rules, and no limits, resent that.

After all, all day long through massive advertising I am brainwashed by the silly seductions of endless options, and conned by the fantasy of an open-ended lifestyle: "The world has boundaries. Ignore them" is the motto of Isuzu; "No limits" (Foster Grant); "Life without limits" (Prince Matchabelli); "No rules. Just right" (Outback Steakhouse); "No refs. No rules. No mercy" (NFL video game); "Rules? What Rules?" (IBM); "The rules are for breaking" (the Spice Girls); "When I'm in uniform I know no limits" (a recruitment ad for the US Army— pretty scary if you remember Lt. William Calley in Vietnam). But along comes Jesus, and once we put on the uniform of discipleship we *do* know limits, we *must* know limits, and limited options are spelled out. We're stuck. Two examples:

The reporter was interviewing an old man, a grandfather who was obviously still in intense grief over the shooting death of his teenaged grandson. The grandson had been shot during a robbery of the family's little neighborhood grocery store. "Do you want revenge on those who did this?" asked the reporter. "Would you like to shoot the person who shot your grandson?" The old man looked astonished at the question. "No, that's not possible," said the grandfather. "I guess you don't even know for sure who did this," said the reporter. "No," said the grandfather. "It's not that. It's that we are Christians. We are not permitted revenge." There you are. Case closed. Options limited. No getting even, no plotting to kill, none of the beating to a pulp or maiming or murdering so dear to our TV and movie messages. We're stuck. Chosen Christians are not permitted revenge. We're boxed in by mercy and forgiveness and the example of the Master who chose us.

The second example is personal. When I was a pastor and was on my way out of the church late one afternoon, I was chagrined to see a rather forlorn-looking man with a small bag—a wanderer, a vagabond, a drifter, a bum—coming down the road toward the church, seeking a handout. Well, this is what you get for having a church situated near a highway. These drifters come through occasionally, seeking a tank of gas for their trip, a meal, a gift—preferably in cash—for their journey to who knows where. They always have some sad story of woe to tell but the end is always the same: Can you spare about $25.00 in cash?

I sighed as I watched the man approach. It had been a long day. I had to return for a meeting that night, and I was anxious to get home. I decided that I would meet him at the door, head him off, give him the only cash I had—a mere $15.00, as I recall—and then send him, and me, on our way. "What can I do for you?" I asked with some annoyance in my voice. (This was not one my better moments; I'm not proud of this.) "I wondered if you might be able to help a fella on the way South," he said. "I was headed down to…" "Yes, yes," I said, interrupting him. "Well, I'm in a bit of a rush. So here is all I have. A five and a ten. That's all I've got."

The man took the money as I offered it. Looked at it. And without a word, he turned and headed out toward the street. Then he stopped and turned toward me as I locked the church door. "I guess you think I'm supposed to thank you, to be grateful," he said with a surprising tone of defiance. "Well," I said, "now that you mention it, a little gratitude wouldn't hurt." "Well, I'm not going to thank you. You want to know why?" he sneered. "Why?" I asked. "Because you are a Christian. You don't help me because you want to. You have to help me because he (now thrusting his finger up into the air) told you to help me!" And then he left.

I stood there, stunned, angry. The nerve of these people! On my walk back to the rectory it finally hit me. He was right. I was snookered in by the faith. I really had no choice. No options. I was a chosen one.

To be a Christian, you see, chosen by Jesus, means that there are some things for us which are not optional. A person who is a member of the Sierra Club is not a person who sets forest fires. A member of the Boy Scouts cannot be someone who refuses to build a campfire. It goes with the territory. Doing Christlike things and not doing unChristlike things goes with being chosen.

We're caught. Of course, we can bow out—and some have. We can disconnect and say, "No thanks. You may have chosen me, but I do not choose you. I decline the honor." There's a certain honesty to that. Worse, though, is to keep the connection and at the same time keep those options open that make Jesus weep: to keep the label and choose those things that make Jesus ashamed of us. That's traitorous and dishonest. To be a chosen Christian and never say, "I can't do that. I'm a Christian" or "I must do that. I'm a Christian" is to live a lie.

If we are chosen, people should be able to tell.

19
Pentecost

The feast of Pentecost is often called the "birthday of the church." Well, that's a good description—and it isn't. Why not? Because it carries a certain distortion. By that I mean that when we say Pentecost is the birthday of the church we unconsciously think of the church as we know it today.

But look at it this way: when Pentecost happened and the church was born, there *was* no church as we know it today: there was no papacy as we understand it. Oh, there was a leader, a fisherman named Peter, but he often blundered and was sometimes wrong, causing his friend, Paul, to catch him in his error and forcing him to apologize for his mistake.

There was no St. Peter's Square: that would come some sixteen centuries later. There was no Vatican. That would come some eighteen centuries later. There was no pope donning armor like Julius II and going to war against his enemies to defend papal territory. There was no papal territory or armored popes. All of that would come later. There were no encyclicals. The first one was written in 1730. There were no cardinals. That rank was created in the eleventh century. Don't tell Monsignor Murray this but there were no monsignors until the medieval courts, as the word itself testifies: *mon signor*, my lord. There was no canon law until the twelfth century. There was no curia until the eleventh century. There were no church buildings or basilicas or cathedrals until the fourth century and still there was church. There were no brothers, sisters, or monks. Father Dolan's Jesuit order was founded only 400 years ago although Father Andrew's Benedictine order was founded 1500 years ago. But they weren't there at the beginning of the church.

None of them were. All—or some—of the organizational growth of the succeeding centuries may have been necessary, but it had the unfortunate effect of making people identify the church with its developed real estate, bureaucracy, titles, offices, and laws instead of with themselves. But remember, the Holy Spirit fell on *people* that first Pentecost, and the church—composed of those inspirited people— was born.

The Spirit didn't fall on the structure or the externals for, as we have seen, there were none. The Spirit fell on unwashed fisherman, peasant carpenters, ordinary housewives, suspect tax collectors, and seedy marginal folk, and glued them together by three things: baptism into Jesus, the breaking of the bread, and witness by ordinary people. These were the basics of being church. The presumption was that each one upon whom the Spirit fell had gifts to use to spread the gospel.

The author and poet Maya Angelou writes:

In my twenties in San Francisco, I became a sophisticate and an acting agnostic. It wasn't that I stopped believing in God; it's just that God didn't seem to be around the neighborhoods I frequented. One day my voice teacher asked me to read a passage from a book, a section which ended with these words: "God loves me." He said, "Read it again." After about the seventh repetition, I began to sense that there might be truth in the statement, that there was a possibility that God really did love me. Me. Maya Angelou. I suddenly began to cry at the grandness of it all. I knew that if God loved me, then I could do wonderful things. I could try great things, learn anything, achieve anything. For what could stand against me and God?

That is the attitude found in the early church. That is church: a poet joining fishermen and tax collectors; simple people with a variety of gifts. That's why St. Paul could write so forcefully about what it meant to be church:

Now there are varieties of gifts, but the same Spirit; and there are varieties of services, but the same Lord; and there are varieties of activities, but it is the same God who activates all of them in everyone.... For in the one Spirit we were all baptized into one body...and we were all made to drink of one Spirit.... Now you are the body of Christ and individually members of it. (1 Cor 12: 4–6; 13; 27)

That is church. So, you see, when you come right down to it, the miracle of Pentecost was not that people could understand what the disciples said on that first Pentecost. *The miracle was that they could say it in the first place.* The miracle was that ordinary people who recently had been in hiding and full of fear suddenly were church and were making "bold proclamations as the Spirit prompted them."

A church conference was being held by special permission in the city of Leipzig, East Germany back in 1964. It was the custom there to ask a high-ranking city official to bring greetings to the assembled people. But does one invite a communist magistrate to address a church group? Nevertheless, the invitation was extended and accepted. The magistrate, an avowed communist, addressed this conference of Christian people and in the course of his address, he told some of his own experience. Remember, the war and the Hitler were still fresh in people's memories. He told of being imprisoned under the Hitler regime because he was a communist. And he told of another prisoner who had been given some work and limited freedom as a "trustee." For his work that man was given a few bits of extra food or an old shirt or other things which he could well have kept for himself. Nobody would have known.

But that man, whom the magistrate said was a Christian, would share what he got with the other prisoners. He'd toss into their cells, from time to time, a bit of biscuit or tobacco. Whatever he got to make the life of the other prisoners a bit more bearable, he would give them. It was against the rules. It was at great risk to himself that he shared those things. He would have been killed if caught. This communist of Leipzig then concluded his story by saying, "That was the first time I ever thought the church might be worthwhile."

Notice, the magistrate did not say that it was the first time he thought that the Vatican or the titles or the real estate might be worthwhile. No, he said that when he saw the witness of this man, that church might be worthwhile. And that's why people convert: not because of lofty doctrine or loftier buildings, but because they see the church in action in the lives of people who *are* church.

Let me put it this way: if we could time-warp ourselves out of this building and be set down in the middle of the desert, we would still be church. If we would gather in prison cells to celebrate a secret Eucharist, if we would hide in a barn to baptize our babies, if we would bear witness in our office, neighborhood, and schools, we would be church. We have been baptized. We celebrate the Eucharist. And when we witness, that makes us church. Baptism, Eucharist, and witness are still are our defining identities as they were on that first Pentecost when the church was born. Everything else—the Vatican, canon law, this church building—is very helpful, but basically peripheral and incidental to this primal identity of the people as the church of Jesus Christ.

So once more, let me put it this way: if someone should ask you, "Tell me, what is the church of St. Denis like?" you might be tempted to describe this lovely stone building and the beautiful grounds. But, of course, you would be wrong. The building is merely where the church meets to worship, just as the office and school are where the church meets to witness, or the home where the church gathers to grow, or the neighborhood where the church helps its neighbors.

The proper response, therefore, is this: "The church at St. Denis is warm, caring, and gifted." And then, as an afterthought, "Oh, yes, and the buildings are nice, too."

Happy birthday.

Ordinary Time

20

The Holy Shadow

Sixth Sunday in Ordinary Time, Cycle B
1 Corinthians 10:31—11:1

Theme: basic grace

I will pass over today's gospel in order to focus on St. Paul's short epistle, which you just heard. Recall he wrote these opening words:

Brothers and sisters, whether you eat or drink, or whatever you do, do everything for the glory of God.

"Do everything for the glory of God." That sounds nice. But, to be honest, we would like to get some credit. I mean, it's nice to be self-effacing and do things from a high motive, deflecting attention away from oneself and doing deeds out of pure love of God and neighbor without expecting anything in return. As I said, it's nice; but deep down, we know we're not made of such lofty stuff.

Surely one of the great joys in life is to have our good deeds found out and to try to act humble as the spotlight of praise is focused on us, as a secret voice within whispers how good, noble, and powerful we are, and how the world is a better place for our being here. Still, to counteract this bit of self-serving pride, there it is, Paul's words—"do everything for the glory of God." That's a directive found not only in Paul but in all the spiritual masters throughout the ages. Listen, for example, to this ancient tale called *The Holy Shadow*:

As everybody knows, the angelic council meets on Wednesday afternoons from 3:00 to 5:00 to consider earthly candidates for special gifts, rewards, and honors. The list of potential recipients

85

is usually long and a lot of weeding out is necessary. Well, after one particularly tedious meeting, the potential recipient for the week was selected and the name was sent "upstairs." (The angelic council is, of course, purely advisory to the divine source, who has to give the final OK to each nominee.) This time, a memo came down that said, "Approved, but ask her first." And so the angelic council selected a subcommittee. They immediately flew to earth and found their potential recipient. In a formal and solemn presentation, they offered her a gift. "You have been found worthy," they said in unison. (With so much time spent in the angelic choir, angels always speak in unison.) "We are pleased to give you the gift of healing touch. Whomever you lay your hands upon will be healed."

The woman said that she was sure the gift of healing touch was very much needed in the world in which she lived, but she declined the honor. "perhaps someone else would accept it," she said. The angels quickly caucused. Being superior beings, they adjusted their plans to meet the situation and returned with a new offer. "You have been found worthy," they said in unison. "We are pleased to give you the gift of conversion of hearts. Whenever you speak, people will be moved to change their lives for the better." "I am sure that the gift of conversion of hearts is very much needed in the world in which I live," replied the woman, "but someone else must accept that gift. I decline the honor."

Grumbling now, the angels caucused a second time. They returned with a new proposal. "You have been found worthy," they said in unison. "We are pleased to give you the gift of great virtue. People will see your deeds and be encouraged to live lives of high moral values." The woman agreed that the gift of great virtue was very much needed in the world in which she lived, but she insisted that someone else needed to receive it. She declined once again. It was only after the woman's third refusal that the angels remembered what the divine memo had said: "Ask her first." "So, if you don't want the healing touch, the gift of the conversion of hearts or great virtue, what is it you do want?" the angels asked in frustrated unison. The woman answered quickly, for she always knew what she wanted. "I want the gift of doing good," she said, "but not knowing it."

The angels caucused. This was a new and unforeseen request. They were energized and buzzing with the challenge, their wings beating excitedly. After some time, they came upon the way that the "gift of doing good but not knowing it" could be bestowed. They made the woman's shadow a source of goodness. She would go about her life doing what had to be done, but whatever or whomever her shadow fell upon would be graced. As she walked by a withered brook and her shadow fell across it, for example, it would suddenly gurgle with sweet, clear, running water. If her shadow fell upon a sullen child, the child would suddenly smile contentedly. If she passed a world-weary man, he would reawaken to vital purpose and passion.

And so the woman would live, going about doing good and not knowing it. The people in her world respected the humility of the woman. They never told her of the healing effects of her shadow, although many tried to walk behind her. And since her good deeds were never explicitly attributed to her, her name has been forgotten. She is remembered only as the Holy Shadow.

As you can see, this old Sufi story is a variation of Paul's words. It is a reminder to see ourselves as mediums of grace, and not the claimers and doers of good deeds. You see, the mystics like Paul rightly spy a danger in all human gifts and striving. The mystics fear we will not recognize and acknowledge the divine source, that the ego will step forward and pride will claim a place of honor. And we all know how often that can happen and does happen.

But, of course, St. Paul was only repeating what Jesus taught. When Jesus told people they were the light of the world, he urged them to let their good works shine forth. What was the reason he gave? So that people would see them and "give glory to your Father in heaven." In a similar vein, you recall, when a man asks Jesus, "Teacher, what good deed must I do to have eternal life?" Jesus shoots back, "Why do you ask me about what is good? There is only one who is good." The retort is clear: do not take credit for goodness. Humans do not possess goodness; they only reflect the goodness of God. Again Jesus claimed, "I came to do the will of him who sent me," and on his death-cross, "Father, into your hands I commend my spirit." For Jesus, Abba, God, was all: the beginning and the end, the Alpha and the Omega.

We have to ponder this for our spiritual lives. What St. Paul is teaching and what our experience shows is that the ego is forever insistent and pride is our besetting sin, so we must pray and strive and desire that whatever we do, we do it for the glory of God who, after all, is the measure of all things, the One from whom we come and to whom we shall return.

We Catholics, you know, are fond of litanies. We line up saints and plead with them to both influence God on our behalf and be models for our struggling lives.

Holy Mary, pray for us.
St. Joseph, pray for us.
St. Michael, pray for us.
St. Agnes, pray for us.

So we intone. I suggest that perhaps we should add another sentence to our public and private litanies, following St. Paul's injunction, one that is a plea for protection from vainglory and self-idolatry. I suggest that we add, "Holy Shadow, pray for us."

21

The Sick Man's Friends

Seventh Sunday in Ordinary Time, Cycle B
Mark 2:1–12

Theme: faith is communal

Today's dramatic gospel has all the trappings of a good television movie script: a paralyzed man dropped down through the roof top; Jesus talking about forgiving his sins; the scandalized Pharisees who unknowingly were right when they exclaimed, "Who can forgive sins but God only"; the awed crowd. A powerful scene indeed. The center-piece is forgiveness, enough to provoke many well-deserved words on that theme.

But I see another theme here, a deeper theme. Something else is operating that might speak to our hearts. It's the theme of faith. But not our faith; not your children or grandchildren's faith or lack of it, but the faith of friends. In this gospel story, the real miracle, the real focus, is on the faith of the four friends who believed that God willed more for their friend than a lifetime of victimization and incapacity. I'm talking about the faith of the friendship of the four people who carried the paralyzed man to Jesus.

These four friends were not deterred by the difficulty of their task. Not only did they carry the man to meet Jesus, they were willing to brave the crowds and the possible ridicule of others. And when they could not gain admittance to Jesus' presence in the usual way, they took it upon themselves to remove part of the roof and lower the man through the opening. Notice that Jesus attributed their efforts to their faith and that their faith proved to be the catalyst for their friend's spiritual and physical rehabilitation by Jesus. Surprisingly, Mark tells his readers nothing of the paralyzed man's thoughts or motivations, and he makes no comment about his faith. Rather, it was the faith of his friends that proved to be the turning point in the man's life.

At this point, we might be inclined to wonder what would have happened to the paralyzed man had it not been for the lived faith and loving friendship of his companions. Would he have met Jesus? Would he have been healed? Would his sins have been forgiven? Or would he have lived out the remainder of his days crippled and unaware of the tender mercies of God? The whole issue, the whole scene, is reminiscent of the people who make pilgrimages to Lourdes and other such places, who depend utterly on family and friends to take them there and carry them to the healing waters.

In any case, this gospel story demonstrates the responsibility and opportunity we have for one another, both as members of the family of humankind and as brothers and sisters in the faith. At times I will be the one paralyzed by fear, selfishness, pride, greed, and the like. Unaware of the profundity of my own need and unable or unwilling to do anything on my own behalf, I will need you to care for me enough, and to believe in God enough, to carry me where I need to go. I will need your faith to bring me to healing and forgiveness. At other times you will be the one who needs the strength and support of my faith to sustain you and make you whole. Faith is the network that binds each of us to one another and to Christ.

Dr. Boris Kornfeld was a medical doctor in a Siberian prison camp. He was Jewish, but he began to notice one of the prisoners, a Christian a man of quiet faith. The man seemed to find great strength in that horrible place by reciting the Lord's Prayer over and over. We don't know that man's name. We only know that his witness and his friendship began to change Dr. Kornfeld. One day, they brought a guard to Kornfeld for treatment. The guard's artery had been cut in a knifing, and he was bleeding to death. Dr. Kornfeld knew that he could save the man, but he thought about letting him bleed to death. He considered suturing the artery in such a way that it would fail later. Then he caught himself horrified by his own thoughts. He remembered his friend who prayed, "Forgive us our sins as we forgive those who sin against us."

Dr. Kornfeld began to hold himself and others to a higher standard. He turned in an inmate who had stolen food and who had thereby endangered the lives of other prisoners. As a result, he found his own life in danger. He spent more and more time at work where he felt a little safer. One day they brought a prisoner to him, a man who had cancer. The man was seriously ill, but his greatest suffering was spiritual. Kornfeld looked into his eyes, and saw only emptiness and misery. And so Dr. Kornfeld began to tell the man about his Christian friend who had prayed the Lord's Prayer and he began to tell him about his own awakening faith. They became friends.

That night, a prisoner sneaked into Kornfeld's room and took his revenge. He bashed Kornfeld's head with a rock and Kornfeld died. That should have been the end of the story, but it was not. The cancer patient remembered what his new-found friend, Dr. Kornfeld, had said. He recovered from his illness and began his own journey of faith. He became a Christian. He survived that prison camp and he began to write about his experiences there. His name was Aleksandr Solzhenitsyn. Solzhenitsyn's writings turned a spotlight on Soviet cruelty, and they played some small part in the fall of the Soviet Union.

And so we have a progression of unlikely people ordinary people, linked by friendship: a Christian who prayed the Lord's Prayer who became a friend to a Jewish physician who became a friend to a cancer patient who became a friend of freedom. They were trapped in a gulag in the remotest region of the Soviet Union. Their efforts should have come to nothing, but they didn't. These unlikely people started a series of small ripples that grew larger and larger until they helped to destroy the forces of evil that bound them. One believer who became a friend to an unbeliever who befriended another unbeliever—it's like all of them lowering each other down to be touched by Jesus. That is what we are called to do. That is the faith of friendship.

Let's move from that gulag to ours: to friends who are imprisoned even if they don't know it. I won't ask for a show of hands, but I know that most of them would go up if I asked how many here have children or grandchildren, nieces or nephews, or acquaintances who no longer go to church. Some have even joined another religion, usually some evangelical Christian group. Most have just dropped out.

They're good people who endlessly repeat the common mantra, "I believe in God but not in church," or "I'm into spirituality but not religion."

Or there are your relatives or friends who are fighting the demons of illness or addiction or depression or loneliness, many of whom won't go near a church or who have given up. And you would like to bring them to Jesus but they won't have any of that, and besides, you're only one person. But there is friendship. There are friends. Since you can't do it alone, the effective thing to do is join with others in lowering before Christ people who are paralyzed by more than physical illness through the roof of their indifference, anger, or hurt. Their faith, present or absent, weak or strong, doesn't matter, so the gospel teaches. What *does* matter, what is always critical, is the faith of friends. "Where two or three are gathered together in my name, there I am in the midst of them." The message is both simple and clear: it takes more than one person to bring someone to Jesus.

There is, as you know, one good place where faith-friends can meet and, in their collective strength, lower many before Christ. Parish Renew groups start up in Advent and Lent. Joining one of these groups for those liturgical weeks—breaking open the Word of God, sharing reflection and prayer, getting familiar with the workings of faith—is an excellent way to connect with faith friends like those in today's gospel, and with them, help lower the people of your concern to Jesus.

The poet Yeats wrote:

Think where man's glory begins and ends,
And say my glory was I had such friends

That would be more than enough praise from someone you and your friends lowered before Jesus, and who found freedom from their paralysis.

22

The Impossible Imperative

Sixth Sunday in Ordinary Time, Cycle C
Luke 6:17; 20–26

Theme: God's grace is sufficient

Imagine a person who lives in New Jersey and works in New York. He listens intently to the words of Jesus in today's gospel—the gospel you just heard—and decides to try to put them into practice. No longer, he decides, will his life be dominated by resentment, retaliation, and revenge; from now on it will be love of enemies, turning the other cheek, and forgiveness—just as Jesus teaches.

And so on Monday morning, he heads to work intent on being a faithful disciple. He has hardly left the Port Authority bus terminal before being approached by a beggar. "Give to everyone who begs," Jesus said, and so he fishes out some money and places it in the beggar's hand. On the subway, there are other beggars, and more money is provided. At the entrance to his office building a homeless man sits, shivering in the cold. "Do not withhold even your shirt," Jesus said. So our faithful disciple sheds his coat and sweater, and hands them to the man.

Inside the building, office politics, alas, are in full swing as usual. But now, today, with the words of today's gospel in his heart, he has a new attitude. Instead of jockeying for power, the man offers words of affirmation and a spirit of forgiveness. Something new. But, an office rival, sensing a vacuum in power being created by this new way of acting, sensing what he thinks is weakness, moves in skillfully for the power kill. And so, at the end of the day, our disciple may well have lived the gospel command—but he may also be broke, cold, and unemployed.

The man certainly meant well, but his experience shows that Jesus' ideal is almost impossible to put into practice. But Jesus is no dreamer. He knows his program is hard and his teaching difficult. When asked about it, he sympathetically says that what is really impossible for human beings is possible with God. For God, he teaches, really wants us to live this way and God will give us the grace to do so. But meanwhile, while we struggle to achieve the ideal, we must at least be convinced of Jesus' bottom line: *disciples must be different* and live by a different drumbeat. Christians simply must not hold the values and attitudes of everyone else even if we puzzle those who think we're crazy.

Let me give you an example. You may have seen this story on *60 Minutes*. It was about a family consisting of a religiously devout mother in her thirties, a somewhat older and painfully shy father, and their ten year-old daughter, who was bound to a wheelchair by spina bifida. Every year this family made a pilgrimage to Lourdes, where healing is reputed to occur. They were being interviewed by Ed Bradley, a typical sophisticated, urbane, secular man, and he was giving the family a hard time for being so gullible. At one point he turned to the little girl and asked "When you pray, what do you pray for?" She replied, "I pray that my father won't be so shy. It makes him terribly lonely."

That stopped Bradley for a few seconds, but then he pressed ahead, questioning the family's wisdom, saying to the mother that they spend thousands of dollars every year going to Lourdes and that *still* they have no miracle. Looking at her loving daughter, the mother answered, "Oh, Mr. Bradley, you don't get it. We *have* our miracle."

Bradley *didn't* get it. He had his mind set, his expectations, and the only miracle worth noticing, the only miracle that would count, was the one that fit *his* definition: the little girl would get up out of the chair and walk. But he totally missed the miracle of a daughter's growing love, the miracle of a family held together in faith. He missed the miracle of joy growing in soil that should not, by all rights, sustain it. He did not understand that God does not work in the world in the ways we expect, because God's mercy breaks the bounds of our narrow imaginations. That family of disciples had a different value system, had interiorized this gospel which left the secular mind perplexed.

Once a young friend of mine, a seminarian whom I had mentored, told me of his visit home for the Christmas holidays. His father was a deacon at a poor Catholic parish in the inner city in Baltimore. His father lived in the neighborhood and spent every day wrestling with the problems of poverty, unemployment, hunger, and inadequate housing. The seminarian told me that one cold afternoon he and his father went for a walk. As they walked through the sad streets and across the weed-infested local park which lacked the cultivated care and shiny play equipment of parks in the tonier parts of town, they were talking about the mission of the church and the challenge of living out today's gospel in such harsh circumstances.

As they neared the end of their walk they realized that they were hungry. They decided to stop at a pay phone and order a pizza which would be delivered by the time they returned home. But as they headed to the phone a homeless man approached them. "Spare change?" he asked. The boy said his father reached into his pockets and pulled out two handfuls of coins held them out to the street person and said "Here. Take what you need." The astonished man looked at all those coins and replied "Well, I'll take it all." He raked the money from the father's hands into his own.

Father and son resumed their journey to the pay phone, but went only a few steps before the father realized that he had given away all his coins. He had no money for the phone call. So, turning around, he called to the homeless man who was walking away, "Pardon me. I need to make a phone call. Can you spare some change?" The homeless man turned toward the father and held out his hands, now full of coins. "Here," he said, "Take what you need."

A rare moment of mutual sharing. Impossible? But this gospel calls us to live like that. I think that we don't often enough think of ourselves in terms of being disciples. But we should for that's what we are: disciples. Say it to yourself and say it often:

> I am a disciple of Jesus Christ. He is the Master. He teaches and I know that sometimes he teaches hard things but nevertheless I carry his name, Christian, and that says I believe in and want to live by his teachings and example. He has taught in today's gospel. I must try to listen and follow. Lord, I am weak. Make me strong. Make me different. Make me a faithful disciple. Amen.

23

The Mote in the Eye and Other Jokes

Eighth Sunday in Ordinary Time, Cycle C
Luke 6:39–45

Theme: divine humor

We are so accustomed to seeing Jesus on the cross, especially as Lent approaches, and knowing that he fulfilled a messianic prophecy that the messiah would be a suffering servant, that it never occurs to us to ask: did Jesus have a sense of humor?

Did Jesus ever laugh and tell jokes and give out witty sayings? After all, if he were fully human, wouldn't that be part of his makeup, too? Well, not necessarily: all of us probably know someone who is deadly serious. As one person said of his friend, "He has a smile buried inside him that hasn't made it to his face." There is another problem: we may have been taught that laughter has no place in church, which is for serious business. Notice, you do not see statues or paintings or stained glass windows that show a laughing Jesus. A few have been tried, and the result often seems too sentimental.

So, the question again: did Jesus have a sense of humor? Well, the gospel reading for this Sunday before Ash Wednesday—the one we just heard—shows Jesus using illustrations that simply could not have been told with a straight face. It's as if Jesus were saying with a grin, "Hey, did you hear the one about the blind guy who tried to lead another blind guy around? They both fell into a hole. What do you think of that?" Or "How about the one about the man with a huge wooden beam in his eye?" Jesus pokes fun at that man for making a big deal about a mere splinter in his neighbor's eye. Crazy, huh?

Then Jesus talks about farming, slyly reminding his farmer audience that "figs don't come from thorns and grapes don't come from bramble bushes, now do they, friends?" Biblical scholars point out that these must have been funny illustrations, and people must have laughed heartily. Only later, of course, would they realize that a point had been made.

In fact, there is a professor at the Pacific School of Religion in Berkeley, California, named Douglas Adams who claims that the Bible is indeed funny. Very funny. His book on humor in the Bible has the startling title, *The Prostitute in the Family Tree*. It comes from the genealogy connecting the prostitute Rahab to Jesus' family tree. "If Jesus can overcome such a past," Adams argues. "So can we."

Anyway, when he preaches and teaches, Douglas Adams often acts out these humorous biblical stories. While someone in the class is reading today's text about the splinter and the wooden beam in someone's eye, Adams will hold a pillow in front of his eyes as he wanders around, bumping into the students in his classroom. When he does bump into a student he will sometimes say. "I see your difficulty clearly," or "I think my perceptive insight will solve your problem." Adams notes it is clear that he not only fails to see the splinter in the other person's eye, but he doesn't even see the other person!

So in *his* teaching, Jesus does use satire and humor to puncture our pride in thinking that we are better than others, and to remind us that being human means that each of us is at least partially blind. We dare not take ourselves too seriously. There is much to laugh about in life. That is why Jesus, like all of the ancients, told stories—some funny, some serious, and all with a point behind them—because such stories were bearers of truth in a way that all, from the youngest to the oldest, could understand and mull over. Try these variations on Jesus' humor:

When Father Stas first came to St. Denis and rightly began to impress people with his energy and vision, one man was overheard to say, "You know, I have nothing but praise for the new pastor." To which his friend drily replied, "So I noticed when the collection basket comes around." (You can almost hear a little drum roll here.)

Then there's the story about a couple who were walking out of church one Sunday. The wife asked her husband. "Did you see the strange hat Mrs. O'Brien was wearing?" "No," said the husband. "And did you notice those poorly dressed children in the pew ahead of us?" "No, I didn't," replied the husband. "Bill Smith badly needs a haircut, doesn't he?" commented the wife. "Sorry, but I didn't notice," was the husband's response. "Honestly, John," said the wife impatiently, "sometimes I wonder if you ever get anything out of going to church." (But there's a point here somewhere, isn't there?)

In the more serious department—and Jesus would tell a story like this—a holy man heard that his apprentice was able to walk on water. "How did you do this?" he asked the apprentice. "At every step I simply repeated your saintly name, " said the apprentice, "and that is what held me up." So the holy man ran to the river bank and stepped onto the water. "Me, me, me," he said, and sank to the bottom.

Funny, but deeply serious. Like some of Jesus' sayings in today's gospel. OK, here's a final story to think about, the kind Jesus would tell.

A voyaging ship that was wrecked during a storm at sea and only two of the men on it were able to swim to a small, desert-like island. The two survivors, not knowing what else to do agreed that they had no other recourse but to pray to God. However, to find out whose prayer was more powerful, they agreed to divide the territory between them and stay on opposite sides of the island.

The first thing the first man prayed for was food. The next morning, the first man saw a fruit-bearing tree on his side of the island, and he was able to eat its fruit. The other man's parcel of land remained barren. After some days, the first man was lonely and he decided to pray for a wife. The next day another ship was wrecked, and the only survivor was a woman who swam to his side of the island. On the other side of the island, the second man had nothing. Soon the first man prayed for a house full of clothes, and more food. The next day, like magic, all of these were given to him. However, the second man still had nothing.

Finally, the first man prayed for a ship, so that he and his wife could leave the island. In the morning, he found a ship docked at his side of the island. The first man boarded the ship with his wife and decided to leave the second man on the island. He considered the other man unworthy to receive God's blessings, since none of his prayers had been answered. But as the ship was about to leave, the first man heard a voice from heaven booming: "Why are you leaving your companion on the island?"

"My blessings are mine alone, since I was the one who prayed for them," the first man replied. "His prayers were all unanswered and so he does not deserve anything."

"You are mistaken," the voice rebuked him. "He had only one prayer, which I answered." "Tell me," the first man asked the voice, "what did he pray for that I should owe him anything?"

"He prayed," said the voice from above, "that all your prayers be answered."

I think Jesus would tell a story like this, smile, and then walk away and let his audience think about it. A good idea....

24

Why I Am a Christian

Thirteenth Sunday in Ordinary Time, Cycle B
Mark 5:21–43

Theme: the woman with the hemorrhage provides grounds for identity

Does it strike you that we just heard a two thousand-year-old story? Two thousand years it's been around and two thousand years it's been told and retold. And here we are today, sophisticated, wired, savvy, well-off Western Americans still hearing and resonating with that old story from the Mid-East. Why? What's its attraction? The answer is, basically, when you come right down to it, this story tells us why we are Christians. Christians believe in Christ and bear his name. This story reveals why Jesus captured the people who first heard him, and why he captures us today. It's the kind of story that began it all—the "it" being Christianity.

The outline of this familiar story is simple. Jairus, the leader of the synagogue, beseeches Jesus to come and heal his daughter. Jesus agrees to come to this important man's house—but on the way, he is interrupted by an unimportant woman who, unlike Jairus, doesn't even have a name. And here's where we begin to get captivated.

Now I don't know what Jesus thought, but this women was an intrusion. She was pushy. He was on an important mission—couldn't she see that? —and here she was irritatingly interrupting, grabbing at the hem of his garment. I mean, she could accidentally trip him. Can't she see he's preoccupied, has things to do? In a hurry? He doesn't have time for her. But I'm reading myself into Jesus for, as usual, this unusual man does the unexpected and from his actions, from this story, I learn the five things that tell me why I am a Christian.

First of all, this Jesus not only has *time* for the unimportant but a *preference* for them. Remember, Jesus was with the synagogue leader, a high-powered man—and yet he stops to encounter a marginalized woman. That in itself is remarkable. In that time and place in history, when women had no standing, much less a contaminated woman, much less a poor woman—"she spent all her money on doctors"— this was revolutionary. As the saying would go in modern times, Jesus showed a preferential option for the poor. Jairus, the important man, can wait while Jesus deals with the unimportant woman. And right away, this attitude raises the hope that he will pause for me as well.

Second, Jesus has time for losers. He who has the habit of seeing people on the margins senses that here is a woman with losses. She has lost a lot of blood, a lot of life. Down and out, having given up *on* her doctors and maybe *by* her doctors, she is a loser easily relegated to life's sidelines. But not for Jesus. Precisely because she *is* sidelined she catches his attention. That raises the hope that he will notice me as well; that he, in fact, has.

Third, Jesus has time for affirmation. So far, this woman has been identified only by her bleeding and her pain. But Jesus pauses; he wants to see a face and hear a name. He takes time to see her, not as an intrusion, a nonentity, but as a human being in need. So he speaks to her not as his patient, not as a recipient of the health care delivery system, but as an equal. He calls her "daughter." That is, she is more than someone in pain. And furthermore he affirms her by giving her credit. "Your faith has made you well." This raises the hope that he will see me not as a face in the crowd but as who I am, and call *me* by name. I, like millions of others, find that compelling.

Fourth, Jesus ignores the naysayers. I can hear the complaints of exasperation at his demand to know who touched him, "No, Jesus, we cannot dawdle here. We have a job to do. Let's go." "How can you ask in this crowd who touched you? Let's move on." And when he reaches Jairus' house, more negative voices. "You're too late. She's dead. Why bother?" And when he *did* bother, they laughed. This raises the hope that the people who put me down, who are always negative toward me, who laugh at me, are wrong and that Jesus is right to deal with me and see me alive and not dead as they think.

Fifth, the story, when it's all said and done, reminds us of a deep truth. Too often we feel that in order to be a good Christian we have to try hard and believe this or that, whether we, in fact, actually do believe it or not; that we first have to straighten out our life and get it together, and feel this or that in our hearts, in order to be pious and worthy.

But listen again to this story. In the stories of Jairus and the hemorrhaging woman, nobody does anything except cry out in the face of death and sickness. No one, as far as I can tell, believes, or feels, or thinks. As writer Robert F. Capon put it: "Jesus came to raise the dead. The only qualification for the gift of the gospel is to be dead. You don't have to be smart. You don't have to be good. You don't have to be wise. You don't have to be wonderful. You don't have to be anything. You just have to be dead. That's it." And this raises the hope that I don't have to be virtuous or "worthy" or even spiritually alive for Jesus to raise me up. In fact, it seems the more "dead" I am, the more he cares.

So what do I learn from this story? I learn why I am a Christian and believe in Jesus, and why I am here. I have never met anyone so open and accepting, so ready to have mercy on my nothingness and my bleeding. I learn that if I am unimportant to the world or even to those whose love I crave, I know, deep down, that I am important to Jesus. No matter how small, how minor a figure in society, how overlooked or unpopular, how sidelined, how much of an outcast—no matter how "different" I am, there is always one who notices me with love and compassion.

I learn that if I am the chronic loser, the nerd whose every project turns to dust, whose every attempt to be liked and wanted is met with ridicule and rejection, whose brain is slow and body uncoordinated and talent nonexistent and whose life is leaking away, I know that, deep down, I am a winner with Jesus. To him I am not, "Hey you!" but he calls me son, daughter. He knows me by name. I learn that if no one ever praises me, never notices my strivings, rewards my efforts, pats me on the back, makes me feel that I count, Jesus affirms me and says, "Your faith in me will make you well."

I learn that if everyone in my life is a naysayer, telling me that I am too far gone, too much of a sinner, too obviously a hypocrite; if everyone is negative, I know someone who is positive, who will ignore them all and pay attention to me anyway.

I learn that even if I'm dead, spiritually or physically, I qualify even more as a candidate for his concern. So I, like so many others through-out the ages, ultimately ask, what kind of a person is this? Is it any wonder I would rally around his love and join with others that also do so and call ourselves a church?

You know, it's funny how the mind works. I thought of this gospel and Jesus one day when I was watching an interview on TV. The per-son being interviewed was a heroic mother who had singlehandedly raised a large family. In spite of all the frustrations, disappointments, and obstacles, she had persevered, and every one of her children had made remarkable achievements, not only in their schooling but also in their vocation. It was an inspiring story worth celebrating, for it revealed the heights and depths of human greatness. But during the interview, the mother was asked her secret by the reporter who said, "I suppose you loved all your children equally, making sure that all got the same treatment."

The mother's answer was stunning and brought me back to this gospel. She replied, "I loved them. I loved them all, each one of them, but not equally. I loved the one the most that was down until he was up. I loved the one the most that was weak until she was strong. I loved the one the most that was hurt until he was healed. I loved the one the most that was lost until she was found."

Amen to her. Amen to Jesus. That's why I'm a Christian.

25

The Seventy-Two

Fourteenth Sunday in Ordinary Time, Cycle C
Luke 10:1–12, 17–20

Theme: we, today's seventy-two, are sent

At that time the Lord appointed seventy-two others whom he sent ahead of him.

Some of us here may be old enough to remember when there were no automatic dishwashers in our homes. Some of us can remember when there were three or more children in almost every home. *And* most of us can recall what happened after each meal. "No, it's *your* turn to wash, *her* turn to dry, and *my* turn to put the dishes away!" Always the bickering about whose job it was to do what.

Well, it's the same way in the church. We keep on saying, "It's the priest, the nuns, the brothers, the lay ministers—the professional inner circle—it's their job to witness to the good news. I'm not trained for that." But training isn't the answer. By our baptism and confirmation each and every one of us, no matter how high or how low on the holiness scale, is called to witness, to discipleship, to spread the good news. The Vatican II document on the laity forcefully reminds us:

> There are innumerable opportunities open to the laity for the exercise of their apostolate of making the gospel known and people holy. The very testimony of their Christian life and good works done in a supernatural spirit, have the power to draw people to belief and to God.

But what can I say? These are just words, aren't they? We've heard them before. So what can I do to make them sink in, to put flesh and blood on them? My answer is that I will replay them, wrap them up, so to speak, in a true story. All that I ask you is to quiet your hearts, don't count the minutes, and enter into it. The story, a very personal one, I should tell you, comes from a man I know, a former priest and now recovering alcoholic, Brennan Manning. Listen as he tells it.

A few years ago, I lay desperately sick on a motel floor in a southern city. I learned later that within a few hours, if left unattended, I would have gone into alcoholic convulsions and might have died. At that point in time I did not know I was an alcoholic. I crawled to the telephone but was shaking and quivering so badly that I could not dial. Finally, I managed one digit and got the operator. "Please help me," I pleaded. "Call Alcoholics Anonymous."

She took my name and address. Within ten minutes a man walked in the door. I had never seen him before and he had no idea who I was. But he had the breath of the Father on his face and an immense reverence for my life. He scooped me up in his arms and raced me to a detox center. There began the agony of withdrawal. Anyone who has been down both sides of the street will tell you that withdrawal from alcohol can be no less severe than withdrawal from heroin. Anyway, to avoid bursting into tears, I will spare the reader that odyssey of shame and pain, unbearable guilt, remorse and humiliation. But the stranger brought me back to life. His words might sound corny to you, like tired old clichés. But they were words of life to me.

This fallen-away Catholic, who had not been to Mass in years, told me that the Father loved me, that he had not abandoned me, that he would draw good from what had happened. He told me that right now the name of the game isn't guilt and fear and shame but survival. He told me to forget about what I had lost and focus on what I had left. Above all else, he affirmed me in my emptiness and loved me in my loneliness. Again and again he told me of the Father's love; how when his children stumble and fall, he does not scold them but scoops them up and comforts them.

Later I learned that my benefactor was an itinerant laborer

who shaped up daily at Manpower, a local employment agency. He put cardboard in his work shoes to cover the holes. Yet, when I was able to eat, he bought me my first dinner at McDonald's. For seven days and seven nights, he breathed life into me physically and spiritually and asked nothing in return. Still later I learned that he had lost his family and fortune through drinking. In his loneliness he turned on his little TV at midnight and talked to John Wayne, hoping he would talk back. Every night before bed he spent fifteen minutes reading a meditation book, praised God for his mercy, thanked him for what he had left, prayed for all alcoholics, then went to his window, raised the shade and blessed the world.

Two years later I returned to the same southern city. My friend still lived there but I had no address or telephone number. So I called AA. In one of life's tragic ironies, I learned that he was on Skid Row. As I drove through Skid Row looking for him, I spotted a man in a doorway whom I thought was my friend. He wasn't. Just another drunk wino who was neither sober nor drunk. Just dry. He hadn't had a drink in twenty-four hours and his hands trembled violently. He reached out and asked, "Hey man, can you gimme a dollar to get some wine?" I knelt down before him and took his hands in mind. I looked into his eyes. They filled with tears. I leaned over and kissed his hands. He began to cry. He didn't want a dollar. He wanted what I wanted two years earlier lying on the motel floor: to be accepted in his brokenness, to be affirmed in his worthlessness, to be loved in his loneliness. He wanted to be relieved of what Mother Teresa of Calcutta, with her vast personal experience of human misery, says is the worst suffering of all: the feeling of not being accepted or wanted. I never located my friend.

Several days later I was celebrating Eucharist for a group of recovering alcoholics. Midway through the homily, my friend walked in the door. My heart skipped. But he disappeared during the distribution of communion and did not return.

Two days later, I received a letter from him which read in part: "Two nights ago in my own clumsy way I prayed for the right to belong, just to belong among you at the holy Mass of Jesus. You will never know what you did for me last week on Skid Row. You didn't see me, but I saw you. I was standing just a few feet away in a storefront window. When I saw you kneel down and kiss that wino's hands, you wiped away from my eyes the blank stare of the breathing dead. When I saw *you really cared*, my heart began to grow wings, small wings, feeble wings, but wings. I threw my bottle of wine down the sewer. Your tenderness and understanding breathed life into me and I want you to know that."

Friends, have you noticed, have you noticed? You've got a couple of drunks here, a bunch of winos, fallen-aways, a pack of losers, flawed and addicted to their toenails. And yet—and yet—see how they ministered to one another. See how they breathed the breath of life and love into strangers.

I like to think of them as among the seventy-two "non-professional" disciples, flawed people like you and me, sent out in their brokenness to minister where they are even if that means the back alleys and twisted ways of sin and shame. I tell you this standing here in church: after that story, after listening to this gospel, I can't think of one single reason why you and I, child, teen, or adult, can leave being Christ to someone else. There *is* no "someone else." We are the seventy-two.

We have been sent.

26

Come Apart and Rest

Sixteenth Sunday in Ordinary Time, Cycle B
Mark 6:30–34

Theme: need for solitude

Come away to a deserted place all by yourselves and rest a while.

In a world that equates busyness with success and constant activity with importance, that brings its laptops and cell phones on vacation, that works more hours than thirty years ago, that continually escorts its children away from home, and forever sing-songs, like a mantra, the national motto that "there is never enough time"—the words of Jesus seem more critical and more compelling than ever: *Come away and rest a while.*

This rest is not only necessary for our physical and mental health, but also for our spiritual health. Of course, we know this intellectually, but emotionally we're caught in an addiction—indeed, busyness and hurriedness and the feelings they produce are addictions. For example, a recent survey shows that seventy-nine percent of people feel rage towards others, especially when they have to wait. Psychiatrists offer two reasons for this feeling of rage. One is a new kind of self-centeredness that says everyone should make room for me and the other—the one we're interested in today—is caused by trying to cram too much into too little time. That's us. But all living things, from plants to children, need space and solitude in order to grow and form a center that rises above all that. As Christian de la Huerta writes in *Coming Out Spirituality*:

All human beings are spiritual simply by virtue of being human, even if not all of us are equally in touch with that part of our nature. So how can we develop or deepen an awareness of our spiritual nature? Probably the best—and maybe even the only—way to really discover this is in solitude and silence. In these days of multimedia, hi-tech sensory overload, it has become increasingly important that we consciously seek out time and space to spend alone. Otherwise we risk feeling disconnected and alienated, trapped in the superficial challenges and dramas which life will inevitably present.

That's why so many people *do* feel disconnected, find themselves off-center, have a hard time with relationships, have difficulty finding the real "me" beneath all the veneers that society imposes.

We are seeing this disconnection more and more in children. The old cliché, which, like all clichés, is true, is that we must give children "roots and wings"—roots that ground them in a core identity and values that will sustain them in the shifting fortunes of life, and wings that will help them soar to challenges. But today, it seems, all we give them is wings—wings that take them to each and every activity, entertainment, happening, or sports event. They must miss nothing. They are, proudly, like their parents, "kids on the go." Hopefully it will turn out otherwise but, if the trend continues, there is the possibility that they may grow up as adults wonderfully able to negotiate the Internet, know the names and histories of the people on *Survivor* and *Big Brother*, be masters of trivia, get good jobs—and then, in mid-life, find that they cannot jump the hurdle to the marvelously deeper life that beckons. They might one day suddenly discover that they are missing the core resources for a coherent philosophy of life, a guide for the spiritual path.

And they may not know how to handle the crisis. Maybe, they might think, as was done in the past, a new "ism," a new religion, a New Age gimmick, a new car, a new drug, a new spouse, will help. So they try them all. But nothing seems to work. The trouble is that they basically will have become alienated from themselves. They are, they may discover, hollow, devoid of inner spiritual resources to fall back on or moral roots to tap, roots that could only have grown in solitude. As Stephen Covey wrote, "It's incredibly easy to get caught up in an activity trap, in the busyness of life, to work harder and harder climbing the ladder of success only to discover it's leaning against the wrong wall." So many grow up only to find themselves one day leaning against the wrong wall, and they don't know how to get down. But what if they—and we—learned early on the secret of solitude?

That secret is revealed to us in this story from Sister José Hobday, a Franciscan nun and a Seneca Indian. She tells of the time when she was young, and she was being so obnoxious at home that her father lost patience. She says,

Finally, my father said to me, "Get a book, a blanket, and an apple, and get into the car!" I wanted to know why, but he only repeated the order. So I obeyed. My father drove me about eight miles from home to a canyon area, and said, "Now get out. We cannot stand you any longer at home! You aren't fit to live with. Just stay out here by yourself today until you understand better how to act. I'll come back for you this evening."

I got out, angry, frustrated, and defiant. The nerve of him! I thought immediately of walking home; eight miles was no distance at all for me. Then the thought of meeting my father when I got there took hold, and I changed my mind. I cried and threw the book, apple, and blanket over the canyon ledge. I had been dumped and I was furious. But it is hard to keep up a good, rebellious cry with no audience, so finally there was nothing to do but face up to the day alone.

I sat on the rim, kicking the dirt and trying to get control of myself. After a couple of hours, as noon approached, I began to get hungry. I located the apple and climbed down to retrieve it— as well as the book and the blanket. I climbed back up, and as I came over the top I noticed the piñon tree. It was lovely and full. I spread the blanket in the shade, put the book under my head, and began to eat the apple. I was aware of a change of attitude.

As I looked through the branches into the sky, a great sense of peace and beauty came to me. The clouds sat in still puffs, the blue was endless, and I began to take in their spaciousness. I thought about the way I had acted and why Daddy had treated me so harshly. Understanding began to come, and I became more objective about my behavior. I found myself getting in touch with my feelings, with the world around me. Nature was my mother, holding me for comfort and healing. I became aware of being part of it all, and I found myself thinking of God. I wanted harmony. I wanted to hold the feeling of mystery.

I wanted to be a better person. It was a prayerful time, a time of deep silence. I felt in communion with much that I could not know, but to which I was drawn. I had a great sense of discovering myself as great, of seeing the world as great, of touching the holy. This sense lasted a long time, perhaps a couple of hours. I found I liked being alone, enjoyed the rich emptiness, held the stillness. It was as if I had met another person—me—who was not so bad after all.

By the time my father came to get me, I was restored. Daddy did not press me about the day. He asked no questions and I gave him no answers. But I was different and we both knew it. My father had dumped me into solitude and had challenged me to grow. Before I got out of the car, I thanked him. And from that day on, especially during the summers, I would take a day to go out alone. I loved those times of solitude, of contemplation, of prayer. I loved the person, the world, the God I had met that day.

That's what solitude has to offer. Will we ever offer ourselves, our children, that most needful experience? As Brennan Manning puts it:

Silence is not simply the absence of noise or the shut down of communication with the outside world, but rather a process of coming to stillness. Silent solitude forgets true speech. I'm not speaking of physical isolation; solitude here means being alone with the Alone, experiencing the transcendent Other and growing in awareness of one's identity as the beloved.

The fact is that soul work requires that we give ourselves solitude, time to replenish the spirit. Thomas Merton was right when he wrote,

"It is in deep solitude and silence that I find the gentleness with which I can love my brothers and sisters." And Jesus was right, "Come, tread the road less travelled; come apart a while and rest."

I have two suggestions here. The first is to do some spiritual reading. Summer is a good time for escapist reading but come the Fall, determine to read a good spiritual book. Ask your pastor for advice. Second, plan a day or overnight retreat away. There are lots of places around that offer them. Don't have time? If you can take a day off for the bus ride to Atlantic City, you can find time for a day of solitude and prayer.

Now I leave you with a question: What comes directly after the orchestra conductor raises his baton for the initial upbeat? Dead silence. To appreciate music, you must also appreciate silence. To appreciate the music of life, you must also appreciate solitude. *Come apart and rest.*

27
When the Miracles Stop

Seventeenth Sunday in Ordinary Time, Cycle B
John 6:1–15

Theme: faith in hard times

Jesus went across the sea of Galilee. A large crowd followed him because they saw the miracles he was performing.

It's vacation time, it's summer time, when the livin' is easy. Should I try to tease your minds and hearts in such a context? Should I offer the challenging homily this gospel provokes? Well, why not? You can always complain to the pastor.

It's the opening words of the gospel I just cited that raise the issue: *"A large crowd followed him because they saw the miracles...."* Well, I ask, who wouldn't follow? You'd be dense not to. My challenging question is this: what happens when the miracles cease? When they dry up? Will we follow Jesus when there are no more miracles?

Will I follow when my child is born genetically defective and all the prayers in world aren't pulling in the miracle that would make her any different than a prospect for lifelong care? When my spouse is killed in an automobile accident and there is no miracle of resurrection, when I am diagnosed with a terminal illness and no miraculous cure appears? When bad things happen to good people and there are no miracles to right the equation? When, in a word, there are no miracles and no more God, at least none that I can detect, when faith is shaken if not evaporated altogether? Will we follow then? So again, my question: will we follow Jesus when we no longer see miracles?

A woman who lost her child at birth and almost her faith writes:

All my multi-layered, carefully constructed faith was stripped away as I focused on one thing: the injustice that our little girl didn't have a chance to take even a single breath….Prayer seemed so futile, even unnecessary, like throwing a glass of water on a burning house. I had prayed my entire pregnancy for the baby to be healthy—and she was. Carly was perfect but she wasn't alive, cooing in my arms. How could I not feel betrayed?…

In the weeks following Carly's death, well-meaning friends and relatives called and sent hundreds of cards and letters offering helpless words of condolence. Most of their efforts said the same thing: "It was God's will. We cannot understand God's will." Those words kept me up at night for months, spinning through my frantic mind, tying me in philosophical knots. I know they were trying to help, but every time the issue of God's will sprang up, I was miserable. It got to the point where I couldn't even numbly smile or nod any more when the phrase inevitably popped up. I just clenched my teeth to keep from saying something I'd regret.

Finally, exhausted, this woman who lost her child and almost her faith, punctuates her long sorrow with these plaintive words:

Some may wonder why, after our experience, I still want to make the painful effort to believe. I can only respond that, despite my doubts, having seen the breathtaking perfection of my daughter's peaceful face, it is impossible to think God was not there.

Somehow, beyond the miracle that never came, she sensed Someone.

Let's hold that in mind while I move to a short story I once read about a doubt-ridden Jesuit priest. Since the age of ten, he had been plagued by doubts. Finally, however, he develops a doubt that will not pass; he begins to doubt the love of God. In the face of his doubt, he prays for faith, but none comes. So, he prays for hope, but when that is not given either, he simply goes on with his duties—teaching, preaching, saying Mass. Then, one bright, clear day, after saying Mass, he is driving home to the rectory when he comes across a terrible automobile accident. A young man lies dying, trapped in an over-turned car. The priest is able to force open the crumpled car door and manages to cradle the nearly dead man in his arms.

Taking a vial of holy oil from his pocket, the priest anoints the dying man, pronouncing, "I absolve you from all your sins. In the name of the Father and of the Son and of the Holy Ghost. Amen." But, then, nothing happens. There is no shift in the world, no change in the dire situation, no word from heaven, not even any human rescuers come. Only the silent world and the dying young man's harsh, half-choked breathing. The priest begins to pray recited prayers, rote prayers, prayers about Mary, prayers to the Father in heaven. He feels foolish, but what else can he do, what else can he say? He wants that miracle.

He wonders, what would God do at such a moment, if there were a God? "Well, do it!" he says aloud, and hears the fury in his voice. "Say something!" But there was silence from heaven....What could anyone say to this crushed, dying thing, he wonders. What would God say if he cared as much as I?....The young man suddenly turns in some dying reflex, and his head tilts in the priest's arms, trusting, like a lover. The priest could see death beginning across his face. At once the priest, faithless, unrepentant, gives up altogether, bends over him, and whispers, fierce and burning, "*I* love you." He continues until there is no breath: "*I* love you, *I* love you, *I* love you," a cry which means that even if God didn't come through with a miracle, *he* loves the dying young man. What now?

This is hard, but I suggest in this story that the priest is fundamen-tally a converted man even though he doesn't know it. He is a man who has quite painfully moved from a childish faith to a mature and hopeful one.

What happened is that the priest, when you come right down to it, was forced to give up his immature idea of a God who comes with miracle in hand when we whistle to make everything all right, in favor of a God who summons the faithful to be present when a need arises, to be his incarnate divine mercy at this time and place. In other words, the priest, lacking a miracle, himself becomes the miracle. God was there and held that dying boy through the arms of the priest.

So today's gospel in its own way poses the question: will we follow

Jesus when the miracles stop? When our daughter dies, when our son is killed? Will we, like the woman who lost her child, see the absent miracles as an invitation to seek the miracle worker himself? Will we consider the possibility that, when all is said and done, after the shock is over and the tears are dried, *we* ourselves might be the miracle?

I don't know. It's tough to stand in someone else's shoes. I just know that, of course, the folks in the gospel story were sensible and savvy enough to follow Jesus *because* of the miracles he was performing. But I also know that folks are even more sensible and spiritually savvy enough to realize that magic tricks are just that: tricks to get you to the magician and to be discarded once you have found him. And so we are challenged to love Jesus for who he is rather than for the free bread he can give us. Dried-up miracles can help us focus on the real miracle: that we are called to be the compassion and presence of God. It is, as I said, a tough call, but a call nevertheless.

Anyway, it's something to think about on a summer day. As you heard, the gospel story had a happy ending. Lots of people saw miracles and were fed with a new one. But it's also time to think about those who saw none and were left excruciatingly hungry...hungry for some answers, some sign, some way, ultimately, to live without miracles and still live with Jesus.

28

Hunger

Twentieth Sunday in Ordinary Time, Cycle B
John 6:51–58

In the gospel of John, one never knows. Water is not really water but baptism. Wind is more than wind; it is the spirit that blows where it wills. Bread is not only bread; it is life. It is hunger—hunger *for* God, and hunger *by* God.

Many people, sadly, know physical hunger. So much of the world doesn't have enough to eat. But all people know spiritual hunger. Maybe that's why you came to church today: because you are hungry and will be disappointed if not fed.

I've heard people say that: "We're really not being fed at this or that church." They didn't mean that the church didn't have enough potluck suppers. They meant their souls weren't being nourished. There wasn't enough nourishment in the preaching or the music or the worship to sustain them through the week and the daily demands of being a good Christian. When I ask people why they are here in church that's one of the main reasons they give me: "I'm here to get nourished to make it through the week."

I wonder if we do that. I wonder if we preachers *do* nourish or are we so out of touch that we fail to fill the hunger? Maybe we don't listen enough to you or maybe we don't remind you enough of what *is* nourishing here, what are some of the "nourishments" before you right now that you ought to notice. If that's the case, allow me to take the opportunity to recall them to you.

The first nourishment is the others here. Some people you know, some you don't. Some are natives, some are vacationers. But all have felt, for one reason or another, the compulsion to come to church today. All share the same beliefs, though with different motivations, commitments, and degrees of fidelity. There are among us sinners and saints, the shameful and the shameless, true believers and hypocrites, rich and poor, famous and unknown, hot shots and nerds, the successful and the failures, the proud and the humble—but all are equal here right now. We've left all distinctions outside and here we are, all of us, simply and profoundly, a vulnerable and needy people of God each seeking something in his or her own way.

This motley crew, this odd mix, is your faith family, your fellowship in the Lord. These others here pray with you, are present with you. And there are millions and millions of them right now all over the world doing the same thing. You should remember then that one of the nourishments here is that, every time you come to church, you are a part of something larger: a branch in the vine, a stone in the building, a member of the mystical body of Christ. You belong no matter where you stand, no matter how out of sync you are, physically, sexually, spiritually, or emotionally. You belong. This congregation, even the strangers, are your brothers and sisters in the Lord. You should be nourished by that fact. Your hunger for family and meaning should be met here.

Second, you are nourished by a blast of honesty. Honesty, because outside of your homes, this is the one place where you can be openly religious and declare yourself as such. You can be seen going to and coming from church. You can respond to the prayers and sing the songs and openly proclaim, without apology or embarrassment, that Jesus Christ is Lord. Think about it. There are not too many places you can do that. Maybe, for all I know, not too many people even know you're Catholic. But here, all is revealed. Here, once you came in that church door, you're forced out of the closet.

Here the label for us all is clearly "disciple." Every weekend you are reminded of your truest identity. In a world where we all, at one time or another, try on other people's faces and clothes and values, it's good to know that, deep down, beneath the makeup and toys, we can know who we really are: one beloved by God and a disciple of Jesus Christ. And that truth, above all the other veneers that the culture imposes, is the real nourishment of our lives.

Third, you are nourished by a 2000- to 5000-year-old Scripture. You are inheritors of an ancient wisdom that has nourished David, Mary, Joseph, Peter, Martha and Mary, Augustine, Ignatius, Catherine, and Mother Teresa. The Word of God—the very gospel story we heard today, for example—has been heard by billions before us in every time and place and people have been comforted by its message of hunger satisfied. By the ancient Scriptures we have been enfolded into the larger stories of Abraham, Moses, Solomon, Rachel, Priscilla, and St. Paul.

Finally, you are nourished here by the Eucharist. Two thousand years ago Jesus broke the same bread and shared the same cup as we do and told us to do this in his memory. And we do. Through this Eucharist we are connected to him and to one another and that makes us an ancient people wired to an ancient tradition. We are still fed with the Great Presence as countless believers have been and are today.

These are the nourishments that feed our gnawing spiritual hungers, and I just wanted to recall them for you. But I am forced to go on. There is one more powerful hunger to note, one that is highly dangerous, one that you are exposed to and reminded of every time you come here. *You and I are exposed to the hunger of God.* And that terrifies us. God is, in the imageries of many stories, the Hound of Heaven, the Stalker, the Shepherd, the Seeker, who for some reason which escapes us, is madly in love with us and is hungry for our companionship.

In his marvelous Narnia Chronicles series, the great Christian writer C.S.Lewis has a scene in which a little girl, Jill, comes face to face with the great lion. In the story, Jill has been whisked away from her boarding school in England by magic. She is very thirsty, and begins to search for water. Hearing a stream, she starts to approach but sees an enormous lion blocking her path—it's Aslan, the Christ figure—directly between herself and the stream. Listen:

> It lay with its head raised and its two fore-paws out in front of it. She knew at once that it had seen her, for its eyes looked straight into hers for a moment and then turned away—as if it knew her quite well and didn't think much of her.
>
> "If I run away, it'll be after me in a moment," thought Jill. "And if I go on, I shall run straight into its mouth."
>
> Anyway, she couldn't have moved if she had tried, and she

couldn't take her eyes off it. How long this lasted, she could not be sure; it seemed like hours. And the thirst became so bad that she almost felt she would not mind being eaten by the lion if only she could be sure of getting a mouthful of water first.

"If you are thirsty, you may drink."…For a second she stared here and there, wondering who had spoken. Then the voice said again, "If you are thirsty, come and drink," and…[she] realized that it was the lion speaking.

Anyway, she had seen its lips move this time, and the voice was not like a man's. It was deeper, wilder, and stronger; a sort of heavy, golden voice. It did not make her any less frightened than she had been before, but it made her frightened in rather a different way.

"Are you not thirsty?" said the lion.

"I'm dying of thirst," said Jill.

"Then drink," said the lion.

"May I—could I—would you mind going away while I do?" said Jill.

The lion answered this only by a look and a very low growl. And as Jill gazed at its motionless bulk, she realized that she might as well have asked the whole mountain to move aside for her convenience.

The delicious rippling noise of the stream was driving her nearly frantic. "Will you promise not to—do anything to me, if I do come?" said Jill. "I make no promise," said the lion.

Jill was so thirsty now that, without noticing it, she had come a step closer. "Do you eat girls?" she said.

"I have swallowed up girls and boys, women and men, kings and emperors, cities and realms," said the lion. It didn't say it as if it were boasting, nor as if it were sorry, nor as if it were angry. It just said it.

"I daren't come and drink," said Jill. "Then you will die of thirst," said the lion.

"Oh dear!" said Jill, coming another step nearer. "I suppose I must go and look for another stream then." "There is no other stream," said the lion.

It never occurred to Jill to disbelieve the lion—no one who had seen his stern face could do that—and her mind suddenly made itself up. It was the worst thing she had ever had to do, but she went forward to the stream, knelt down, and began scooping up water in her hand. It was the coldest, most refreshing water she had ever tasted.

A nice parable. It tells us that, sooner or later, we must give in. We must take the risk of drinking from the way, the truth, and the life. There is no other way, no other stream. But we fear God, the Lion of Judah. We fear his love and, like Jill, ask him to go away. We fear his hunger for our hearts and souls—that hunger which has swallowed up so many people from Francis of Assisi to Dorothy Day—because we would like to divide them among so many others.

Like Jill, we are both fascinated by and frightened of God's love. And yet, by coming here, we flirt with it and are exposed to it. And maybe someday, just maybe, we'll become like that ancient desert father, Abbot Macarius, who when he announced his decision to go to the desert to wrestle with God, his incredulous disciples asked, "And you hope to win?" he answered, "No, I hope to lose."

So, here we are on a Sunday that talks about hunger. And I thought it might be worthwhile to review the nourishments we find here. The nourishments of each other, true identity, Scripture, the Eucharist, and the threatening presence of a lion God hungering for our love. And I suppose it's to our credit that we still come, knowing that each time we do, we move closer to the danger.

29

Subtracting Evil

Twentieth Sunday in Ordinary Time, Cycle B
Ephesians 5:15–20

Theme: what we can do in the face of so much evil

"Brothers and sisters," wrote St. Paul in today's second reading, "watch carefully how you live, not as foolish persons but as wise, making the most of the opportunity because the days are evil."

Ah, "the days are evil." So what else is new? Our daily diet of television news confirms that. Yet, what does Paul advise? "Make most of the opportunity." What opportunity? To do good among so much evil, to be a light in the darkness, to make acts of kindness so that people, awash in so much deceit and dishonesty and the existence of prosperous sinners, won't lose heart. These good acts are more important than you think. They don't eradicate evil, of course. We know that. They simply and profoundly, like a light in the night, are signs that evil will not ultimately triumph.

An example: as you may know, there's a group of Mother Teresa's sisters living in Asbury Park. They are not relieving all the hurt and all of the drug abuse and all of the hunger in Asbury Park. They know that. But by their presence and their charity they are a font of kindness amid so much harshness, a sign of hope for people who desperately need it.

They cannot feed everyone in Asbury Park. They cannot attend to every sick person there. But the few they reach and touch with love give the others hope. They are only following Mother Teresa who, when asked how she expected to make even a small dent in the human misery of Calcutta, for the task seemed so overwhelming, so hopeless, she replied, "I do not think the way you think. I do not add up. I only subtract from the total dying." That's our job: to subtract from the total evil.

Novelist and former New York *Times* columnist Anna Quindlen, someone not always in tune with church, nevertheless gave a fine commencement address at Villanova University last year that underscores this point. She admonished the young graduates:

> People don't talk about the soul very much anymore. It's so much easier to write a résumé than to craft a spirit. But a résumé is a cold comfort on a winter night or when you're sad, or broke, or lonely, or when you've gotten back test results and they're not so good.
>
> Here's my résumé. I am a good mother to three children. I have tried never to let my profession stand in the way of being a good parent. I no longer consider myself the center of the universe. I show up. I listen. I try to laugh. I am a good friend to my husband. I have tried to make my marriage vows mean what they say. I show up. I listen. I try to laugh. I am a good friend to my friends, and they to me. Without them, there would be nothing to say to you today because I would be a cardboard cutout. But I call them on the phone and I meet them for lunch. I show up. I listen. I try to laugh.
>
> I would be rotten or at best mediocre at my job if those other things were not true. You cannot really be first rate at your work if your work is all you are. So here's what I wanted to tell you today: get a life. A real life, not a manic pursuit of the next promotion, the big paycheck, the large house. Get a life in which you are generous....Care so deeply about life's goodness that you want to spread it around....Work in a soup kitchen. Be a big brother or sister. All of you want to do well. But if you do not do good, too, then doing well will never be enough.

Doing good. Doing good, one on one, one at a time, consistently, is what we're talking about. And so even though we can truthfully ask, "Oh my God, there is so much crime and violence and terribleness in the world, what can I do?" the answer is that we can make the most of the opportunity to subtract evil.

There's an old Indian story that provides us with a good image of our task. It's about a twelve-year-old boy who died of snake bite. The poison took away his life and his grieving parents carried his body to the holy man and laid it before him. And the three of them sat around the body sadly for a long, long time. Then the father finally arose from his grieving, went over to his child, stretched out his hands over the feet of the child, and said, "In all my life I have not worked for my family as I should have." And the poison left the feet of the child.

Then the mother rose and she stretched her hands over the heart of the child, and she said, "In all my life I have not loved my family as I should." And the poison left the heart of the child. And the holy man stretched out his hands over the head of the dead boy and he said, "In all my life I have not believed the words I have spoken." And the poison left the head of the child. The child rose up, and the parents and the holy man rose up, and the village rejoiced that day.

That's the way it goes. A little poison subtracted here, a little there— they all add up to bring back life. And that's our calling, our vocation, what we're here for: to make a difference, to make, again in St. Paul's words, "the most of the opportunity [to be a disciple of Jesus] because these days are evil."

All of us have some measure of power to do so as did Sam Plimsoll. Sam Plimsoll started his work life as a lowly government clerk in Sheffield, England, in the last century. He later went on to become a member of Parliament. Anyway, he was disturbed by how many sailors were lost at sea because greedy ship owners overloaded their vessels—that's the evil. And so he looked for some opportunity to subtract from this evil and eventually he devised a simple way of knowing if a ship was overloaded. A line was painted on every ship permitted to enter a British port. That line had to stay above the waterline, otherwise the ship was considered unacceptably overloaded. After a while, the "Plimsoll line" became a standard feature on all ships plying international trade, and remains so today.

Our point? St. Paul's point? Who knows how many lives have been saved because one obscure man cared enough to persist with an idea he knew to be very good? And who knows how much evil will be subtracted because someone like you makes the most of the opportunity to be like Jesus Christ?

30

A Cloud of Witnesses

Twentieth Sunday in Ordinary Time, Cycle C
Luke 12:49–53

Theme: awareness

The wise old Mother Superior was dying. The nuns gathered around
her bed, trying to make her comfortable. They gave her some warm
milk to drink, but she refused it. Then one nun took the glass back to
the kitchen. Remembering a bottle of whiskey received as a gift the previous Christmas, she opened it and poured a generous amount into the
warm milk. Back at Mother Superior's bed, she held the glass to her
lips. Mother drank a little, then a little more, then before they knew it,
she had drunk the whole glass, down to the last drop. "Mother,
Mother," the nuns cried, "give us some wisdom before you die!" She
raised herself up in bed with a pious look on her face, and pointing out
the window, she said, "Don't sell that cow!"

There. I'm glad I made you laugh because the readings today— about
harassed prophets, Jesus bringing fire and division, and a cloud of martyred witnesses—have forced me to share thoughts that are not guaran-
teed to make you smile. But it's like these lines from T.S. Eliot's poem,
"The Rock":

Why should men love the church?
Why should they love her laws?
She tells them of life and death
And all they would forget.
She is tender where they would be hard
And hard where they would be soft.

She tells them of evil and sin
And other unpleasant facts.

And so it is my unenviable task, in the light of today's Scripture readings, to speak to you, to remind you, of two unpleasant or disturbing facts, one which I shall give in the form of a report and the other in the form of a fable.

First, the report. Here it concerns those "clouds of witnesses," the divisions they caused and their consignment, Jeremiah-like, to the cisterns of prison and death. And to summon up those clouds of witnesses, I tapped into the Internet where there is a site called The Voice of Martyrs, www.persecution.com, a nonprofit organization dedicated to assisting and listing the persecuted Christians around the world. The material there is staggeringly enormous, page after page. Here's but a tiny scattering of the material I found. I discovered, of course, the familiar names of Cardinal Jozsef Mindszenty of Hungary, Cardinal Aloysius Stephanic of Croatia, and the Lutheran minister Dietrich Bonhoeffer, who died in a Nazi concentration camp; the Catholic Archbishop Oscar Romero gunned down in his church in San Salvador, the slaughtered Jesuits and their housekeepers in El Salvador, Maximilian Kolbe whose feast we just celebrated who took the place of a condemned prisoner at Auschwitz, and so on.

But I learned more. I learned that under the Taliban regime in Afghanistan, untold numbers died for openly professing their faith in Christ; that Christians in Algeria have been suffering for more than thirty years under the death-dealing regime of a hostile government. I discovered that to this very day public witness by Christians continues to be illegal in China, which has destroyed more than 15,000 religious sites and routinely sentences believers, including two Catholic bishops, to its religious gulags. Christian public witness is forbidden as well in the Comoro Islands, equatorial Guinea, Iran, Laos, Mauritania, Morocco, North Korea, the Sudan, where more than one million non-Muslims are reported to have been killed, and Saudi Arabia, which outright forbids freedom of religion.

I learned that after the Persian Gulf war, tens of thousands, including Christians, were gassed, shot or forced to leave their homes in Iraq.

In Kuwait, where Sunni Islam is the state religion, Christians cannot become citizens. Christians in Egypt are forbidden to build, repair, or repaint churches. In 1995, fifteen Christians there were murdered as they prayed. In 1998, 1,200 Christians were detained and tortured by Egyptian army security officers. In the mid-1960s Fidel Castro denounced Christians as "social scum" and sent many of them to forced labor camps. Only in 1992 did the Cuban government grant religious freedom; but then, in 1996 the Ministry of Justice ordered all house churches closed.

The list and the horror stories are simply endless; they go on and on. It's so hard for us who are sitting here to fathom that right now, as I speak to you, hundreds of thousands of Christians are being persecuted, imprisoned, and killed precisely because they are Christians. Protected as we are, it is difficult for us to grasp the truism that, statistically, more Christians have been persecuted, imprisoned, and put to death in this past century than in all the previous nineteen centuries put together. This is something we never refer to, something that never surfaces in our consciousness, in our distracted lives, something we never, ever hear about, as worldwide and horrific as it is, something that never officially becomes public because some of those persecuting governments are supplying us with oil.

Anyway, the unpleasant fact that I call to your attention is these people are today's Jeremiahs being tossed into the cisterns of countless prisons for living the faith. These numberless people are the cloud of witnesses of whom Paul writes. And that's why I thought, in light of such Scripture, that I should bring this report to your attention in hope that you and I, for a moment at least, will think of our brothers and sisters suffering and dying for what we take so casually for granted, and to remind ourselves to pray for them. So much for the disturbing report. Now, if you're ready, the equally disturbing fable. It goes like this:

> In heaven, each morning at sunrise is an Easter. The bodies of those who die on earth arrive in the night and are placed in giant morgues outside the pearly gates to await the sunrise. Accompanied by Archangel Michael who carries files and personal data on each of the dead, God visits the morgues one by one.

Opening the door to the first large morgue one early morning, Michael said, "These are the bodies of those who died as small infants. The number stays steady at about 40,000 a day, fifteen million a year." "And the cause of death?" asked God. "For ninety-six percent of them it's a lack of food and medical care," answered Michael. God picked up a dead child and rocked it like a sorrowful mother. "I don't understand," wept God. "Oh, there's an abundance of both food and medicine on earth, but there's a problem of distribution," said Michael.

God gently placed the child back on the slab. Heaving a great sigh, God moved the divine hands over the dead infants. "Let there be light!" God exclaimed. And suddenly the large building exploded with laughter and vitality .

God and Michael then moved to the next large morgue. It was filled with thousands upon thousands of skinny, deformed, diseased bodies. "And these?" asked God. "These, Divine One, are victims of starvation, contaminated water, or lack of medical care." "How is that possible?" asked God. "I gave the people of earth all they need to provide food and care for all my children." "Again, the problem is one of distribution," answered Michael, flipping open his file. "These dead are from Burundi in Africa where they have only one doctor for every 45,000 people. And these are from Somalia, Guinea, and Angola, where the life expectancy is only about thirty-eight to forty years." "And what is it in America?" asked God. "The life expectancy is...let's see...about seventy-six years. But, of course, America has one doctor for every 520 persons. It's the same problem: distribution!"

Like a father viewing the dead body of his only son, God sobbed in agony. Then, drying the tears, God made a sign over the dead, saying, "Let there be light!" And the morgue instantly transformed into a great festival hall of joy and dancing.

As they walked to the next large morgue, Michael pointed down to earth. "Look, O God, your children are praising you!" God and Michael looked down upon a group of thousands with upraised hands, singing the praises of God. They were led by a preacher wearing a three-piece suit and a gold Rolex watch who had just completed a hell-fire sermon condemning X-rated films, dancing, and the sins of the flesh. In another place they saw a white frame church in which people were clutching their Bibles and singing of how pure and prayerful are the friends of Jesus. And then there was an ornate cathedral with giant golden candlesticks, silk vestments, and clouds of incense rising above gem-encrusted vessels and a massive organ thundering out the music of Bach. God watched for a moment and then said, "It's a mirage, Michael, only a mirage. Pay no attention to it. I don't!"

They then entered the final large morgue. It was filled with bodies of the well-dressed and well-fed dead. They hardly looked dead, but only seemed to be asleep. "And these?" asked God. "These, O God, are the dead who arrived last night from America and Western Europe."

God stood stone still, expressionless; then turned and went to the door. Michael asked, "Divine One, your blessing?" But God only turned and stared into the sunrise and then began to walk away. "But God, you are love without end. You are mercy itself." "Yes, I know," said God. "While my love is endless, I have a problem—what did you call it? Ah, yes, I have a problem of distribution! No, Michael, leave them dead. Store them away in the warehouse with the others."

A report and a fable to challenge our minds and hearts. To make us aware. To incite us to pray. Perhaps even to urge us to enter into the cloud of witnesses.

31

Will You Also Go Away?

Twenty-first Sunday in Ordinary Time, Cycle B
John 6:60–69

Theme: why I stay while others have left the Church. This homily was first
preached following World Youth Day held in Rome in 1999.

---

*As a result of this, many of his disciples returned to their former way
of life and no longer accompanied him. Jesus then said to the twelve,
"Do you also want to leave?"*

I won't ask for a show of hands, but if I did I am fairly certain that
hardly anyone here hasn't had someone who said "yes" to that question. Many of Jesus' disciples—your children, your grandchildren,
your friends, your neighbors—no longer accompany Jesus. Some have
left angrily, some have left because of the "hard sayings" on divorce,
chastity, and fidelity. Most, I suspect, have just slowly drifted away,
their faith eroded by a steady, alluring, attractive materialism and secular way of life where the good times roll, the living is easy, and the
money is fabulous. That many have walked away is evidenced by the
small percentage of those who come here every Sunday. Indeed, the
university pundits, seeing all this, confidently, gleefully, and routinely
predict the demise of religion altogether.

So the pundits weren't prepared for the nearly two million young people from all over the world who rallied in Rome last week to see the pope.
They and the Baby Boomers from the sixties, who are now in charge of
the nation as teachers, journalists, TV producers and trendsetters, are
simply at a loss to explain an old man and his followers. Outside of official sneering or sour-grapes snide remarks, they're frankly baffled.

Figure it out. If you take all of the rock concerts of the past thirty years and think of the biggest events you possibly can, their combined total audience comes nowhere near the showing in Rome. It's the largest youth gathering Europe or America has ever seen since the world began. And still it is only half of the four million youth who gathered for the pope when he went to the Philippines. There has never been anything like it.

Those aging Baby Boomers for whom Woodstock, as the acid-head guru Timothy Leary said, was about "turning on, tuning in, and dropping out," about instant gratification, drugs and "everything goes," are utterly confused. They simply don't know what to make of it. To think that their grandchildren are rushing to see a frail, eighty-year-old man in Rome's unbearable heat blows their minds.

They themselves have long ago found Jesus' sayings about divorce and fidelity and loving one's neighbor more than oneself hard sayings to follow, and when asked "Do you also want to leave?" they fell all over themselves fleeing. And their children followed; they felt liberated. But, now, here are their grandchildren falling all over themselves to return, going to confession at the Circus Maximus and making the Stations of the Cross at the Colosseum—500,000 young people at this event alone!—showing the world that not all of today's youth live in a secular, morality-free world. The Boomers must be thinking, "Where did we go wrong?"

My guess is that their grandchildren, like the rest of us, have seen that the sixties didn't work. They are sick and tired over their parents' divorces, over being abandoned by them as they pursue their careers, over empty casual sexual encounters, over dog-eat-dog economics, over television's siren call to hedonism, over the constant "this-is-all-there-is" philosophy they are taught in college. Watching the emptiness of their parents' lives, a society with no moral moorings, awash in "I am the center of the universe" lifestyles, they are simply yearning for better guideposts on how to live. One young woman from Dallas said it openly, "It's about spirituality." Another, an eighteen-year-old from Paris, said, "One of the main principles of this whole thing is to prove to people that the new generation still believes."

So, it seems that when asked, "Do you also want to leave?", more and more of our youth are answering with Peter, "Master, to whom shall we go? You have the words of eternal life." Perhaps it's time to recall once more one college student's words. In his small book, *Life After God*, Doug Coupland writes:

> Now here is my secret: I tell it to you with an openness of heart that I doubt I shall ever achieve again, so I pray that you are in a quiet room as you read these words. My secret is that I need God—that I am sick and can no longer make it alone. I need God to help me give, because I no longer seem capable of giving; to help me be kind as I no longer seem capable of kindness; to help me love as I seem beyond being able to love.

He speaks for so many youth and maybe that's why they are attracted to an old man with Parkinson's disease. They know they need God and they sense somehow that the old man in white can reveal that God. They know that he leads a church that still distributes the Bread of Life and passes on the traditional eternal truths such as that the one who would hug his life to himself will lose it while the one who loses it for Christ's sake will find it; to be chaste in thought and action, to set aside the road and air and all the other rages and instead be compassionate and forgiving, that, in spite of the secular gospel of unremitting advertising, we do not live by bread alone, that Jesus really is the way, the truth, and the life.

When someone is a symbol of such straight talk, a purveyor of such wisdom, and a rock in shifting sands, no wonder the youth, drowning in a million alternate "lifestyles," are attracted. Two million youth in the west, four million youth in the east—there's never been anything like it before in human history. Though it baffles the sophisticates we know that this is simply and profoundly a huge and enduring sign of the hunger for God.

And know this and attend to my words: you who have remained, who did not leave because of the hard sayings or troubled times in and out of the church, you are playing a significant and critical part. Like the Holy Father, you are a steady witness to Jesus, and—don't be fooled—out of the corner of their eyes, the youth are noticing and the affluent young adults of so many toys are being slowly subverted as they begin to wonder, among the growing emptiness of their lives, if maybe *you* are on to something.

The message? The phenomenon in Rome last week and the witness in Manasquan this week are interconnected.

Thank you for that.

32

Humility

Twenty-second Sunday in Ordinary Time, Cycle C
Luke 14:1, 7–14

Today's gospel lends itself to the topic of humility, not always a well-understood subject. So let us try to get a practical insight into this virtue and offer three contrasts of what it is and what it isn't.

First, humility is appreciation, not abasement. That is, it deals with truth not insincerity. For example, to have Tiger Woods stand up here with downcast eyes and say, "Ah, shucks, folks. I'm not that good a golfer. I just putter around a bit, that's all," would strike us not as being humble but as being insincere. Humility is truth. We do have certain talents. We have achieved certain things. We are gifted in certain areas. We possess certain objects of which we're rightly fond and proud. To appreciate such gifts, to rejoice in them and not deprecate or lie about them, is the first step toward true humility. Denying, abasing, belittling one's gifts is a form of reverse pride. Humility, as we indicated, is truth. It isn't abasement.

Second—and this balances the first point—humility is stewardship, not ownership. Things not ours have been entrusted to us for a time to be used for the good of, and in service of, others. We are humble when we remember and practice that. We are proud when we don't. It's as simple as that. We are humble when we think of ourselves as stewards: temporary gift-holders from God. We are proud when we think of ourselves as owners: permanent possessors in our own right.

We become proud when our God-given gifts slip into a sense of self-possessed and self-deserved ownership, and when that happens, then status with a capital "S" is not far behind. Then slowly we find we are acquiring possessions for their own sake in order to show people how rich we are; then we begin to consume much more than we need—all designer brands, of course; then we find that we are setting ourselves above the rest of humankind. Then we begin to think we are the origin of our gifts and we are deserving of our talents and we were set by God above the rest of ordinary folk who, sooner or later, become invisible to us, especially the poor and needy, and we no longer have a sense of simple stewardship. Insensitivity, blindness, isolation, and greed enter in behind our gated communities. We get an inflated sense of self, begin to think of ourselves as the center of the universe, and don't even see those who are on the other side of the gate. Status and ego have taken hold. We are proud.

Finally, humility is openness, not closedness. Which is to say, humility is always open to the Spirit and sensitive to where God wants one to serve, where, forgetful of self, one ought to share one's gifts and be alert to the needs of others. I guess that's because the truly humble know they are stewards; they know they rely on God for everything, for life itself. They know ultimately that they are dependent—something quite intolerable for the proud person. Pride is not open to the Spirit. So full of oneself, one doesn't even know the Spirit is there calling for them to pay attention to others.

Sometimes, however, if prideful people are lucky, there is an unexpected breakthrough into their self-contained world. Let me share one such story, about a yuppie hotshot, a young and successful executive, who was traveling down a neighborhood street going a bit too fast in his spiffy new Jaguar. He was watching for kids darting out from between parked cars and slowed down when he thought he saw something. As his car passed, no children appeared. Instead, suddenly out of nowhere, a brick smashed into the Jag's side door! Furious, he slammed on the brakes and spun the Jag back to the spot where the brick had been thrown.

He jumped out of the car, grabbed some kid, and pushed him up against a parked car shouting, "What was that all about, and who are you? Just what the hell are you doing?" Building up a head of steam, he went on. "That's a brand new car, kid, and that brick you threw is going to cost you a lots of bucks. Why did you do it?" "Please, mister, please. I'm sorry! Please! I didn't know what else to do," pleaded the youngster. "I threw the brick because no one else would stop." Tears were dripping down the boy's chin as he pointed around the parked car. "It's my brother," he said. "He rolled off the curb and fell out of his wheelchair, and I can't lift him up." Sobbing, the boy asked the executive, "Would you please help me get him back into his wheelchair? He's hurt, and he's too heavy for me."

Wham! Right in the yuppie gut. Moved beyond words, he lifted the young man back into the wheelchair, and took out his handkerchief and wiped the scrapes and cuts, checking to see that everything was going to be okay. "Thanks, mister," the grateful child said to him. The man got back into his car and watched the little boy push his brother down the sidewalk toward his home. To his credit, the young man never did repair the car's side door. He kept the dent to remind him not to go through life so self-centered, so fast, that someone—God?— had to throw a brick at him to get his attention.

Anyway, this homily is intended to be a mild form of brick-throwing in its reminder of what humility is and isn't. To repeat: humility is grateful appreciation, not insincere abasement. Humility is possessing a sense of stewardship not ownership. Humility is openness to the Spirit, not closedness.

The line at the airport was long, the crowd pressing. The man at the head of the line was furious. "I want to be seated now! I can't wait in this line. I've got first-class tickets," he screamed. He went on and on. The attendant behind the counter was patiently trying to explain to him the problems but he would have none of it. Finally he shouted, "Do you know who I am?" Immediately, the sharp-witted attendant picked up the microphone and announced. "Attention, we have a gentleman here who doesn't know who he is. If anyone can identify this man, please come to the front desk."

We laugh at this because it's funny and we laugh because we are glad the man had his comeuppance. We laugh because a proud person has been rightly toppled. But, more to the point, beneath the laughter, we have been reminded of the advice of St. Thérèse of Jesus, the Little Flower, who wrote: "Never mention anything concerning yourself which people account praiseworthy, such as learning, goodness, birth, unless with the hope of doing good thereby, and then let it be done with humility, remembering that these are gifts of God."

33

Healing

Twenty-third Sunday in Ordinary Time, Cycle B
Mark 7:31–37

Theme: healing on the everyday level

Jesus healed many people during his ministry. Some were healed instantly, some with a word; some with a little ritual, like the laying on of hands or the spit and clay of today's healing. Some were healed in stages, like the blind man who saw only gradually as people first looked like trees and then real; some only after a little sparring, like the Phoenician woman with the quick tongue who wouldn't take an initial refusal; and some only after many, many years, like the man at the pool of Siloam.

Some were healed because they were lucky enough to have good friends to help them, like the crippled man's friends who lowered him through the roof top or the friends in this morning's gospel who brought the deaf man to Jesus. Some were healed at a distance, like the Roman centurion's servant. Some were healed not in body but in spirit, like the tax collector Zacchaeus or the Samaritan woman at the well. Some weren't healed at all because, as Mark says bluntly in his gospel, they did not believe. Others for whatever reason just weren't healed, period. But enough were healed so that people knew the compassion and mercy of God was among them.

Healing. In one sense, every one of us in this church right now has the power to continue the healing ministry of Jesus. I mean that we all have power to lighten a burden, share a sorrow, speak a word of hope and comfort, and therefore help heal a heart. And healing can happen quietly, almost unconsciously, and often takes place where we don't expect it. I have three stories of ordinary healing to share—not spectacular ones—but tiny, soft healings caused by an unlikely trio: a husband, a baseball manager, and a rock star.

The first story was told to me by a surgeon a few years ago and it deals with the power of words. It's the case of John, who, he said, was one of those strong, self-reliant men who rarely expressed their emotions outwardly. One night John had to rush his wife to the hospital for emergency surgery. The ensuing operation was successful, but the woman's condition deteriorated. Despite blood transfusions and intensive care, she continued to lose strength. The doctor was puzzled because by all medical standards, she should have been recovering. Finally, he became convinced of the reason for her steady deterioration: she was not *trying* to get well.

The surgeon, an old family friend, went to her bedside and said, "I would think you would want to get well for John." She replied, weakly, "John is so strong, he doesn't need anybody." The doctor called John to his office and told him what his wife had said. John went immediately went into his wife's room, took her hand in his and said, "You've got to get well." Without opening her eyes, she asked, "Why?" He replied, "Because I need you!" At this point, the nurse who was monitoring the blood transfusion said she noticed an immediate change in the woman's pulse rate. Then the patient opened her eyes and said, "John, that's the first time you ever said that to me." Two weeks later she was home, fast recovering.

Commenting on the case, the doctor said it wasn't merely the blood transfusion but her husband's word, his declaration of his need for her and therefore, her importance to someone she loved that made the difference between life and death for that woman. The husband didn't say, "Arise and walk," but his words were every bit as effective in healing her.

Here's the second story. On a stifling afternoon in Philadelphia, relates New York Yankees manager Joe Torre, he was about to walk through the players' entrance at Veterans' Stadium when a middle-aged man called his name. Torre is not one of those celebrities who walk past people head down as if they didn't hear a thing. So he stopped, assuming he would be asked for an autograph. He was wrong. "I met you almost thirty years ago," the man said, "I was in high school and I wanted to drop out. My parents asked you to talk to me one day because they thought I might listen to a ballplayer. They were right. I'm a lawyer now. I just wanted to tell you thanks." Torre was pleased by the story, albeit a bit stunned. "I had a little, tiny, vague memory when he brought it up," he said, "but that was it."

Before he could take the last few steps to the players' entrance, Torre was stopped again by a younger man. "Twenty years ago I had cancer," he said. "They thought I was terminal. You were with the Mets. You came to see me an gave me a pep talk. I never forgot it. When you were sick, I realized I never said thank you." Again, Torre was rendered almost speechless. Later he said, "It makes you realize what all of us...can do....A word here, a pat on the back there, a phone call...we all have tremendous effect on people." Joe Torre didn't put his finger in anyone's ears or touch anyone's tongue, but he was every bit as effective in healing people.

The final story comes from a former rock star, British musician Cliff Richard. I don't expect you to remember his name. Anyway, Richard, who was once a bad boy of rock, became a Christian. In the 1970s, he visited missionary camps in Sudan and Bangladesh, where he saw people with open sores and all kinds of health problems living in very primitive conditions. But, like us, he tried not to touch anything or anyone. If he found it necessary to shake hands with someone, he went quickly to a faucet where he could wash.

Then he tells about one of those transforming moments when God broke through the hardness of his heart: "I was bending down to one little mite," he says, "mainly for the photographer's benefit, and trying hard not to have too close contact, when someone accidentally stood on the child's fingers. The child screamed out, and as a reflex, I grabbed hold of him, forgetting all about his dirt and his sores. I remember now that warm little body clinging to me, and the crying instantly stopped. In that moment, I learned of the enormous power I had to heal." Cliff Richard wasn't the Messiah, but he could heal every bit as much as if he were.

I share these stories because when we talk about healing we always tend to think of the great dramatic ones, the miraculous cures that make the news. And they are rare. Far more common and far more within our reach is our own power of healing: the words "I need you, I love you, I'm here for you," or the gesture: the pat on the back, the phone call, the presence, or the heroic act such as an impulsive embrace of the needy. These aren't the dramatic stories of Scripture, but they are real healings nevertheless.

My fellow Christians, we have all received the Spirit in baptism and confirmation. The healing ministry of Jesus is in our hands. We are, all of us, miracle workers. It's a matter of knowing our power and using it.

34

Vocation

Twenty-third Sunday in Ordinary Time, Cycle C
Luke 14:25–33

Theme: we are all called

The other day, I was reading an article on the shortage of priests, and
the writer was saying that that shortage must be seen in the larger context of vocations in general. That is, he says, certain secular vocations
are also struggling, areas like nursing, medicine, social work, youth
work. The vocational crisis, in other words, is part of a wider social
picture that reveals the heart of our modern society. This heart lies in
the fact that an external marketplace mentality has replaced a sense of
internal calling. He quotes a report about nursing, for example, which
says, "Nursing's collapse is a cultural and spiritual one, a failure of the
notion of charity and compassion, not the result of failed pay bar-
gaining rounds."

In others words, a consumerist culture places its emphasis primarily on attending the right school and making the right connections in
order to get the right job, the big money, and prestige. A vocational
culture, on the other hand, is one in which people have a sense of
being called to make life better, a sense of possessing a gift to offer, a
sense of a mission to be accepted and completed, a sense that they
have to live a worthwhile life and do things that count on the human
level, whether or not it brings them money and fame. If they are religious, they have a sense of God calling them regardless of the difficulty, danger, or lack of worldly rewards.

This sense of vocation is at the opposite pole of society's meaning
of success which is displayed only in terms of image, prestige, letters

behind one's name, what we buy and consume or, if we're really successful, celebrity. In the secular society, it doesn't get any better than that. And the dominance of that mentality is why we face a shortage in many critical areas and why society can so easily, without blushing, offer a baseball player 250 million dollars to play ball and a caretaker of the elderly only nine dollars an hour.

And yet—people are dissatisfied. It is commonplace for some to reach the top and say, "Is that all there is, my friend?" There's an emptiness for people who have it all when that "all" does not include the "four Cs": care, compassion, charity, and a cause larger than our own egos. Shrewd people, however, sense the deeper longing behind the materialism, feel the void that consumerism is trying to fill, and learn to appeal to a latent sense of a vocation, a calling.

For example, a recruiter from the Teach America Program came to a nearby university a couple of years ago. This organization recruits the nation's best college and university students to go work in the most impossible teaching situations in the country. This recruiter from Teach America knew his audience of hot shot, ladder-climbing yuppies. So he looked out on the crowd of students and began by saying:

> I don't really know why I am here tonight. I can tell just by looking at you that you are probably uninterested in what I have to say. This is one of the best universities in America. You are all successful. That is why you're here, to become an even greater success on Madison Avenue, or Wall Street, or in law school.
>
> And here I stand, trying to recruit some people for the most difficult job you will ever have in your life. I'm out looking for people who want to go into a burned-out classroom in Watts and teach biology. I'm looking for somebody to go into a little one-room schoolhouse in West Virginia and teach kids from six to thirteen years old how to read. We had three teachers killed last year in their classrooms. And I can tell, just by looking at you, that none of you wants to throw away your lives on anything like that. On the other hand, if by chance there is somebody here who may be interested, I've got these brochures and I am going to leave them here and will be glad to speak to anybody who is interested. The meeting is over.

With that, all of the students jumped up, rushed into the aisles, rushed down to the front, and started fighting over her pamphlets, just dying to apply for Teach America.

People are good and instinctively look to something larger than themselves. They are hungry to give their lives to something more important than themselves. They want a vocation, not a résumé. It is a fact of life, not only that everything costs us something, but that, in our better moments, we are even eager to pay the price.

Chiune Sugihara was born on a day of new beginnings—January 1, 1900. As a boy, he cherished the dream of becoming the Japanese ambassador to Russia. By the 1930s, he was the ambassador to Lithuania, just a step away from ambassadorship to Russia. He was on his way to a successful career, a big name on the international scene with money and prestige galore.

Then a vocation, not a job, came unexpectedly calling. What happened was that, one morning, a huge throng of people gathered outside his home. They turned out to be Jews who had made their way across treacherous terrain from Poland, desperately seeking his help. They wanted Japanese visas, which would enable them to flee Eastern Europe and the Gestapo. Three times Sugihara wired Tokyo for permission to provide the visas; three times he was rejected. Now came his moment of truth—his calling, so to speak, versus his job. He had to choose between the fulfillment of his dream as an ambassador and people's lives, and he chose the latter. He dared to disobey orders.

For twenty-eight days he wrote visas by hand barely sleeping or eating. Recalled to Berlin, he was still writing visas and shoving them through the train windows into the hands of the refugees who ran alongside. Ultimately he saved six thousand lives. He lost his job, his fame, his money, his career, and he wound up humbly selling light bulbs, of all things. But he had found his calling.

Let me lay this one on you. Parents, we know, are fanatical about getting their children into the right schools, and kids kill themselves with overactivity in order to parlay an overstuffed résumé into acceptance. Parents give their kids every possible leg-up advantage that money can buy. But my question, the gospel question, is this: where is the equally passionate concern that their children be moral and visionary and follow a calling rather than a career?

William Willimon, the well-known chaplain at Duke University, has a wry remark. He writes:

> I have been a campus minister for over a decade. In that time I have received only one or maybe two phone calls from an anxious parent saying, "Help, my daughter is addicted to alcohol," or "Help, my son is sexually promiscuous." However, in that period of time, I have probably received a dozen phone calls from anxious parents saying, "Help, I sent my child to Duke to become a lawyer and she has become a religious fanatic." "Religious fanatic" is usually defined as someone who wants to go and work in the Catholic nutritional program in Haiti rather than go to Duke law school.

Look. All that I have said so far is but a variation on today's gospel, which is a call to vocation of discipleship. "Whoever does not carry his cross and come after me cannot be my disciple." "Hate" your parents and children, which is the Semitic way of saying, put all things in perspective.

We are a faith community with a sense of being tapped by God. Each of us has been given a vocation. We have been recruited by Jesus Christ who offers us the cross. There is something we have to do before we die, no matter how small, that lifts us above ourselves. There is an urgency, no matter how deeply we have buried it, to answer a call.

The gospel simply asks, "Do you hear it? Have you answered yet?"

35

Spiritual Blindness

Twenty-sixth Sunday in Ordinary Time, Cycle C
Luke 16:19–31

Theme: learning to be spiritually sensitive

There is nothing in this familiar gospel story to indicate that the rich man was bad any more than there is any indication that Lazarus was good. There is no hint that the rich man had gotten his wealth by evil means. He was, simply put, a rich man enjoying his hard-earned wealth; he was entitled to a little luxury.

According to the way Jesus tells the story, the rich man's problem was spiritual blindness; that is, he saw Lazarus but passed him right by. He saw him and yet he didn't see him, any more than he noticed the tree in his yard or the color of the sky. He simply lived his own unreflective, self-conscious, self-contained life. The point of the gospel? Spiritual people—people who belong to Jesus—should do more, see more, than that.

One who did is another rich man whose feast we celebrate this week, or rather, the son of a very rich man who would inherit his father's wealth. He was also blind—at least he started out that way. Confronted with his Lazarus, a poor man begging on the wayside, he passed him by, spurring his horse on. But, as he rode on, he had second thoughts. He turned around and came back to the beggar who was a leper, saw him this time for what he was, a child of God, kissed his hand, and gave him all the money he had. And thus history was made. John Bernardone became Francis of Assisi. Two rich people. One had sensitivity to see. One did not. The one who did not is the sorry object lesson of our gospel.

But let's be honest. It isn't easy to be spiritually sensitive. Most people are born with sensitivity but it soon gets dulled.

One morning Janice Anthony and her husband were on their way to work when they unexpectedly came upon a cow in the road. Janice swerved to miss the cow and ended up crashing into a telephone pole. Both she and her husband were injured. The next day, Janice returned to work at a day care center, but she was quite self-conscious about the bruises on her face, and worried that her appearance would upset the children. The first child at the day care center that day was a bubbly four-year-old named Elizabeth. Little Elizabeth ran to give Janice a hug, but stopped short when she saw Janice's face. Then, Elizabeth announced with wonder, "Ms. Jan, you have a rainbow on your face!"

Where Janice had seen the ugliness of bruises, little Elizabeth had seen the beauty of a rainbow.

I think we all start out like Elizabeth but soon lose such innocence. For one thing, our society is not conducive to sensitivity, is it? There's too much noise, too much hurrying, too fast a lane in which to travel, too much to be done. We work and work more than any other industrialized nation. "There's never enough time" is the unofficial motto of the United States. We don't mean to, but in full speed we pass by our Lazaruses, who are often times members of our own families. Until, of course, something like the World Trade Center disaster happens. Then suddenly, in the shattering recognition of how frail life is, we realize who we've been missing, who we've not been seeing. We're hit with the realization that there are many people outside the gates of our lives whom we have been looking right past: those near and dear to us whom we forget to hug and those in want whom we forget to feed.

Unfortunately, this kind of insensitivity can happen to whole countries too. Let me relate a true story about the citizens on the island called Nauru, a tiny paradise of an island in the Western Pacific Ocean. With abundant natural resources and rich fishing waters, Nauru provided its citizens with a very comfortable, caring, peaceful life. But one day that all changed. A chemist studying a piece of wood from the island discovered it to be very rich in phosphates, which are used extensively in fertilizers. Quickly, the government of Nauru set about mining the phosphates, and soon became exceedingly rich from its export. And because the government subsidizes the lifestyles of its inhabitants, the people of Nauru also became quite rich in the process.

As a result, the newly rich folk slowly began to lose their spiritual balance, their spiritual sight. For one thing, they became very conspicuous consumers, stocking their houses with every kind of high-tech household gadget. And even though—and this is ridiculous— their little island had only one road, they became so spiritually blind that most native families bought two or more cars. Finally, the government began importing large amounts of food from other countries, and made it available to the people at very low prices.

Gradually, irresponsible mining practices devastated the island's habitat and natural beauty, and the phosphate stores began to run out. The final result? Today, ninety percent of the once healthy and trim inhabitants are obese, and diabetes and heart disease rates have skyrocketed. Their island, once a place of exquisite beauty and comfortable living, has been ravaged by greed. Worse, a once caring people have become a callous reflection of the rich man of the gospel. Spiritual blindness took over as they no longer saw and blessed the water and the sky—or each other.

On a spiritual level, their sad story becomes a symbol, a parable, of creeping blindness. Like them, little by little, we lose sight of what really counts. Gradually we take on the characteristics of the rich man in today's gospel: a good man, distracted by the rat race and wealth, who over time grew morally obese and spiritually insensitive to the needs of others.

Once there was an encounter between a jailed rabbi and the chief jailer. The deep piety of the rabbi touched the jailer deeply. A thoughtful person himself, the jailer began talking with his prisoner and questioning him on various points of Scripture. Finally, one day the guard asked the rabbi: "Rabbi, how are we to understand that God, the all-knowing, had to say to Adam in the garden, 'Where are you?'" The rabbi countered, "Tell me, do you believe that the Scriptures are eternal and that every era, every generation, and everyone is included in them?" "Yes, I believe this," said the jailer. "Well then," said the rabbi, "in every era, God calls to everyone 'Where are you? Where are you in your world?' So many years and days of those allotted to you have passed, and how far have you gotten in your world? God, for example, says something like this: 'You have lived forty-six years. How far along are you?'" When the chief jailer heard his age mentioned, his heart trembled.

You see, the point is that God did not ask of Adam, "Where are you?" expecting to learn something new. Rather, God used the question to confront Adam with the state of his life just as today's gospel story is basically confronting us. Where are you? Where are you on the spiritual path? Have you too started out like sweet-seeing Elizabeth and become the blind rich man? Do you need the hell-fire of the rich man to finally see? Do you need a terrible disaster to finally see? "Friends," Jesus is saying with this parable, "Lazarus is at the gate."

Have you noticed?

The whole point is that parables like the one found in today's gospel, no matter how well-known, familiar, and often-repeated, are meant to challenge our spiritual standing and convert our hearts so that someday we will be able to sing, with meaning and truth, our favorite religious song:

Amazing grace, how sweet the sound,
That saved a wretch like me!
I once was lost but now am found;
Was blind, but now I see.

36

A Week of Super Saints

Twenty-seventh Sunday in Ordinary Time, Cycle B
Mark 10:2–16 (October 8, 2000)

In Catholic circles, this past week has offered an unusual array of
some popular and fascinating saints parading across the church's liturgical calendar. On September 29, we had a trio of archangels: St.
Michael, who, in the book of Daniel, defends Israel against its enemies and, in the Book of Revelation, leads God's army to victory over
Satan; St. Gabriel, also appearing in the book of Daniel then later, to
a frightened little girl in Nazareth to announce startling news; and St.
Raphael, who was little Tobias' disguised traveling companion
through a series of adventures, which included the healing of his
father's blindness and, at the very end of the story, as in an exciting
novel, one who reveals his true identity.

On September 30, we celebrated the feast of St. Jerome. Irascible,
cantankerous, ill-tempered, he was noted for his sharp tongue and
sharper pen. He skewered more than one well-known personage. He
fought with everyone from Pope Damascus to his friend, St.
Augustine. Yet, he was captivated by the word of God and, after years
of study and five years in the desert, finally wound up in a cave outside Bethlehem where he died. He translated the Bible into Latin from
the Greek, giving us what is known as the Vulgate. It was from the
Vulgate that the first English translation of Scripture, the Douay-
Rheims edition, was written in the late 1500s.

The next day, October 1st, was the feast of St. Thérèse, the Little
Flower, as unknown in her lifetime as Jerome was famous in his and
as gentle as he was harsh. She was young, in poor health, cloistered in
an obscure Carmelite convent in Lisieux, France, doing nothing but

routine chores, while infusing that routine with the love of God. "I prefer the monotony of obscure sacrifice to all ecstasies. To pick up a pin for love can convert a soul," she was to write later in her famous autobiography. That is why she became a co-patron of the missions. Before her untimely death she wrote, "I want to spend my heaven doing good on earth"—and that "good" is symbolized by the shower of roses with which she is usually pictured.

The feast of Thérèse was followed the next day by the feast of the Guardian Angels. Though honoring these angels was first promoted back in the sixth century by St. Benedict, and in the twelfth century by St. Bernard, their actual feast day was not established until the seventeenth century. The Guardian Angels are our invisible guides on our spiritual path.

The feast of the exalted angels was followed on October 4 by the feast day of a rather unexalted John Bernardone, a foppish young man with a rich merchant father, who regaled his companions in the taverns of Assisi, who so liked French finery that his friends called him Frenchy and eventually Francis. This Francis, after a bout with illness and imprisonment revealed to him the emptiness of his life, became a hero, a wandering beggar, who at first was an embarrassment to his old friends and held as a religious nut by his neighbors, but then won them all over for he had discovered Jesus and it showed. Although he died early—at the age of forty-four, half-blind and seriously ill—Francis became the troubadour of God and the modern world's favorite saint, and he left to us not only the tradition of the Christmas crèche but a profound teaching of respect and love for the environment.

October 6 saw the feast of a saint less known to us, St. Bruno, a hermit who lived in the thirteenth century and who has the distinction of founding the Carthusian order of priests—which he established so well that it's the one order in the church that has never had need of reform. Quite a feat.

October 7 was the feast of Our Lady of the Rosary, established in 1573 to thank God for the victory of the Christians over the Turks at Lepanto. The rosary was originally prayed by uneducated Christians, who said 150 Our Fathers instead of the 150 psalms in the Divine Office prayed by monks. Later, it became the practice to say 150 Hail

Marys while reflecting on fifteen mysteries in the life of Jesus and Mary. Starting in the early thirteenth century, St. Dominic and his followers promoted this form of prayer throughout Europe.

Finally, tomorrow is a minor feast to most of the world, but not to this parish. It's the feast of St. Denis, martyred in the third century and held to be the first bishop of France. More likely, he was a holy man sent to Gaul or France from Rome and beheaded in the persecution under the Roman emperor Valerius in 258 AD. One of the more exotic legends about St. Denis says that, after he was martyred on Montmartre in Paris, he carried his head to a village northeast of the city where, in the sixth century, St. Genevieve built a basilica to honor the site. This is why we see pictures of him carrying his head.

So, there we are: a remarkable week graced by some remarkable people: Michael, Gabriel, and Raphael, the mighty archangels; Jerome, the scold; Thérèse, the consumptive; Francis, the playboy; Bruno, the hermit; Denis, the martyr. A motley crew from different centuries and walks of life, no different from anyone else in their time—except for one thing, which is why I am telling you about them. The one thing these flawed people had in common was that at some point in their careers, they let go of their titles and toys, their securities and images, and surrendered to Jesus. One thinks, for example, of Francis literally taking off his fine, rich clothes in the public square to walk into a new life with Lady Poverty.

Well, I have a fable that fits these saints—and every saint—and I'd like to end with it. Remember, the fable is not entertainment or a distraction. It must be heard as a challenge. It is their story and maybe someday, we must pray, it will be ours as well. Listen.

Once long ago in a distant land, a prince was riding through a deep forest far from his home with his company of soldiers, looking for new lands to conquer. Quite suddenly he came upon a clearing in the trees. There before him stretched a meadow leading to a glorious hill. The meadow and hill were covered with blossoming trees, bushes, and wildflowers. At the top of the hill was a castle that seemed made of pure gold. It sparkled so in the sunlight that the prince was nearly blinded.

Fascinated, the prince signaled to his regiment, and together they rode closer and closer, and up the hill toward the castle. The birds sang sweetly, the perfume of flowers was lovely. As they drew near the castle, he saw that a window opened for a moment in the wall and a face appeared, a face that shone more brilliantly than the sun and yet more gently than any flower. Then it was gone. Instantly he fell in love.

He knocked upon the castle door. "Who is there?" came a voice softer than the bluest sky. "It is I, Prince Rindleheart. I am known throughout the land for my bravery. My armies are the strongest. My castle is but two days' ride from here. May I please come and be with you?"

"There is only room for one of us here," was the reply.

He left downcast and in his desperation he sought the wisdom of a wise woman. "Perhaps your armies intimidate her," she suggested.

"Of course," he thought. He returned to the castle alone and knocked upon the door. "Who is there?" came the sweet voice.

"It is I, the prince, alone," he replied humbly.

"There is only room for one of us here," said the sweet voice.

He went away again, dejected and confused. He roamed the wilderness for some years until he met a famous wizard. "Perhaps she cannot know you with all of your armor and weaponry," he suggested.

"Of course," said the prince.

So he returned and laid down his armor, his shield, and his sword. He walked humbly to the castle door and knocked. "Who is there?" asked the voice. "It is I, your humble servant. No soldier, just a man."

"There is only room for one of us here," came the reply.

For seven more years the prince wandered alone in the wilderness, forsaking his kingdom, thinking only of his beloved. He sought wisdom only from the stars in the sky and the wildness inside him.

Finally one day the prince returned to the castle on the hill. He had no armies, no armor, no horse. He walked up the hill, past the bushes heavily laden with fruit , and knocked upon the door.

"Who is there?" came the sweet voice.

The prince took a breath, and said, "It is *thou*."

And the door was opened to him.

37

The Rich Young Man

Twenty-eighth Sunday in Ordinary Time, Cycle B
Mark 10:17–30

Theme: letting go for the sake of the kingdom

InterVarsity Press, a Protestant publishing house, published a book several years ago titled *101 Things to Do With a Dull Church*. In it they printed a tongue-in-cheek liturgy for congregations to use on the occasion of a stock-market crash.

> Minister: Oh, Lord, you did not promise us an easy life, and surely now our enemies afflict us sorely on all sides. Our share prices tumble, our creditors rave and our cell phones grant us no rest. Oh, Lord, in this our hour of our need, hear our prayer.
> And the congregation responds: *And answer it quickly.*
> Minister: When we are reduced to our final Mercedes,
> *Sustain us, Lord.*
> Minister: When our loved ones are deprived of their designer footwear,
> *Preserve us, Lord.*
> Minister: Grant unto us, out of your manifold grace and abundance, those cars,
> *Those large cars.*
> Minister: And houses,
> *Very large houses.*
> Minister: That declare your greatness to all that behold them, and make life quite pleasant for us,
> *Amen.*

Well, that's clever, but there's no use in taking that litany or this morning's gospel and using it as platform to denounce rich people. Having wealth of itself is no sin. Many rich people and corporations use their wealth well, give to good causes and charitable organizations, and make possible our way of life. The gospel is simply pointing out common human wisdom, that wealth, as the lawyers would put it, is an attractive hazard. It's attractive because of all the things we can buy and the power it gives us, but it's a hazard because, like sex which is good, money carries a built-in compulsion, a strong, seductive tendency to become an end in itself rather than a means, an idolatrous and demanding master rather than a servant.

Very few, it seems, without a deeper philosophy, can handle well the potential and power of money. Which is why Jesus could make the common observation, "How hard it will be for those who have wealth to enter the kingdom of God," and follow up with his exaggerated figure of speech that it is "easier for a camel to go through the eye of a needle than for someone rich to enter the kingdom." These are not castigations against wealth but simply tributes to the temptations and pitfalls inherent in it.

In this gospel, what Jesus offers as an antidote is a balancing principle on the use of money and wealth. It is this: it is not what you have but *what you can let go of, must let go of,* for the sake of the kingdom that matters. That's the gospel measurement: what can you let go of for the sake of the kingdom—the kingdom being any higher moral good?

Those of you old enough to remember Jack Benny, whose radio persona was that of a tightwad, might recall the classic scene where Jack is held up by a thug who barks, "Your money or your life!" There is a long pause. The hold-up man demands, "Well?" and Benny replies, "I'm thinking, I'm thinking!" We always laughed at his dilemma because it was so obviously disproportionate. But "your money or your life" has become a more urgent issue because some people are seriously in a dilemma, unwilling to let go of their wealth at the expense of their human life, their compassionate life, their moral life—life lived as human beings who have their priorities and values straight.

In *Dilbert*, the comic strip about corporate life, the head of the company confronts an employee and says, "Alice, it has come to my attention that you are spending time with your family at night. That's time that could be used productively to do extra work for no extra pay." Alice asks him, "Do you have a family?" To this he replies, "Hmmm... that would explain the people in my house."

Now *that's* the rich young man who can't let go for the sake of the kingdom. But some do.

Before co-founding Habitat for Humanity, Millard Fuller was a successful businessman who followed his estranged wife Linda to New York to try to convince her to come back to him. She was not easily convinced that he could turn back from his headlong rush for material wealth. Millard recalls:

> We were in a taxi right after Linda and I had a very tearful session. We'd gone to Radio City Music Hall and they showed the movie *Never Too Late*. It was about a woman getting pregnant after she thought it was too late. The message was that it's never too late to change anything.
>
> I had a sensation of light in that taxi. It was not anything spooky. All I can say is it just came into my head: give your money away, make yourself poor again, and throw yourself on God's mercy. I turned to Linda and said, "I believe that God just gave me the idea to give all our money away; give everything away." She said, "I agree. Let's do it."
>
> Friends, family, even pastors tried to talk us out of it. I told them no, if I think about it I won't do it, because it's not logical. But I believe that God is calling us to do this.

For Fuller it was wealth or life with his wife. He chose to let go of his wealth, which was good for the sake of the kingdom, the higher good, in this case, his wife. Others, we know, have chosen to let go of their spouses.

"I am the great-grandson of Oscar Meyer" wrote this man of the famous name. He continued:

> In 1961, I inherited a little less than half a million dollars, which I immediately gave away to various charities. If I had kept that money and invested it in an index fund that tracked the S & P

500, I'm told that it might now be worth $6 million. Why did I give it away? Because I didn't want my life to be governed by things that happened four generations ago. For me the money was like a spiritual barrier to finding my own path in life. I don't regret the decision. Once in a while I think it would be nice to have more economic security, but now I'm in the same boat as most people I know. If we go down we'll all go down together. I don't want to live in a different America than everybody else.

Oscar Meyer let go of his position and wealth for the sake of the kingdom, for the higher good of being more human, and of finding his path in life.

A few years ago Tom Bloch resigned as chief executive officer of H&R Block, the $1.7 billion tax-preparation and financial-services firm. Tom left behind his prestigious job to become a teacher at St. Francis Xavier middle school in Kansas City, Missouri. His annual salary suddenly dropped to less than $15,000 a year, about three percent of his old salary. But Bloch knew his hectic schedule as CEO had been interfering with his top priority: his wife and their two sons. "The hardest part was telling my father," Bloch says, referring to H&R Block chairman Henry Bloch, who founded the company. Bloch continues, "But I didn't want to look back on my life and say, 'Gee, you had an opportunity to play a bigger role in your children's lives and didn't take it.'" For the sake of the kingdom—in this case, a wife and two sons whom he wanted to parent and be with—he let go of position and money to teach in a Catholic school.

All these stories carry the meaning of this gospel: what can we—ought we—let go for the sake of the kingdom? Two days ago, the Asbury Park Press had a bold headline, "Fifty million children live in poverty," and the article went on to describe the plight of children in this country and abroad. We, who are wealthy by the standards of a world in which most people are desperately poor, are challenged to let go, to share, to give to the poor for the sake of the kingdom.

People of God: we live in a time when we offer ourselves as candidates for *Who Wants to Be a Millionaire?* perhaps even for *Who Wants to Marry a Multi-Millionaire?* Such shows are simply modern signs of an old conceit: to measure people, to measure life, by a standard of wealth. How about the better standard? Jesus would ask: "Who wants to be human? Who wants to love their spouse and children? Who wants to rejoin the human race? Who wants to be compassionate to the poor of the world and share what they have?"

If you and I, each of us like the rich young man of the gospel, raise our hands and cry out, "Me!" Then Jesus, who looks at us with love as he looked at that young man, will ask his last question: "Then, what can you let go for the sake of the higher good, for the sake of that kingdom?"

That is the urgent question behind today's gospel.

38

First Place

Twenty-ninth Sunday in Ordinary Time, Cycle B
Mark 10:35–45

Theme: pride and humility

"Teacher, grant that in your glory we may sit one at your right and the other at your left."…Rather, Jesus replied, "Whoever wishes to be great among you will be your servant."

The motivational speaker Zig Zigler tells a story of two men in the hot summer of the South working in a rail yard, driving spikes into railroad ties with eight-pound sledgehammers. As they worked in the heat, a private railcar and engine came upon them and slowed to a stop. A man stuck his head out of a window and yelled at one of the two workers, "Charlie, is that you, my friend?" One of the workers put down his sledgehammer and replied, "Joe, I haven't seen you in years." The man in the window asked for Charlie to come aboard.

A little while later, Charlie and Joe shook hands and Charlie left the car. His coworker, still with the sledgehammer in hand, said, "Charlie, do you know who that is? That's the president of the railroad. How do you know him?" Charlie replied that the two of them began working for the railroad together twenty-five years earlier. The friend had to ask, "If you and the president started out swinging sledgehammers together, then how is it he's the president of the railroad and you're still here?" Charlie replied, "Twenty-five years ago I came to work for $1.25 an hour. But he came here to work for the railroad."

James and John came to work for self-interest, and Jesus wanted them to work for the kingdom.

On Clement Street in San Francisco there is a pipe organ at the Pacific Ocean Studios called the Chamberlain Music Master. What's different about this pipe organ is that is has a special button, and when you push it, you get an immediate round of applause—and not just tepid applause, but large concert hall-size applause. So you can play anything, any way, press the button, and get a virtual standing ovation.

James and John wanted applause but not the cross.

We have to understand this gospel. It doesn't say that self-interest is bad, that we should not desire praise or want to feel wanted, appreciated, and rewarded. These are good, natural, human desires—which is why the first lesson salespeople learn is "make the client feel important." Few of us are completely altruistic, and without a pat on the back and an acknowledgment of all we do and are, we shrivel up or seek harmful ways to get some self-esteem. Sometimes unfaithful wives and husbands, or risk-taking teens, are looking for what they don't get at home.

All the gospel is saying is that it ought not *stop* there, that self-measurement alone can't be the way to live. There has to be a higher goal outside of and beyond oneself if we are to be both happy and fulfilled human beings and disciples of Jesus. This means drinking the cup of self-denial and being baptized into the cross, that symbol of dying to self in order to rise to another. It means embracing the paradox that whoever wishes to be master must be servant, whoever wishes to be first must be last. It's like Joe, the president of the railroad, who saw beyond his own paycheck to the larger picture. It's like the organist who has to work hard to move beyond the canned, self-induced applause to the applause that genuinely comes from pleasing other people.

Jesus teaches a philosophy of leader-as-servant. That's a hard lesson to take in these days of self-promotion, fed by a huge billion-dollar image industry and the idolatry of celebrities—whom someone has described as people who fight half their lives for recognition and then have to wear dark glasses to avoid being recognized!

In contrast to the gospel, the self is the goal and object of life in the new thinking. David Brooks' scintillating, bestselling book, *Bobos in Paradise*, does a great job in dissecting the Bobos, those fabulously rich, counterculture folk, the privileged and free folk who revolve their world around the self, promoting higher consciousness and greater and greater self-esteem. He cites, for example, an ad for a computer company that asks, "What do you want?" And the answer is given in a young woman's voice:

> I want to write my own ticket. High tech is a wide-open field. I'm helping to create public relations programs for companies that are on the leading edge of software development. What I'm learning is making one fabulous career. I want to hit the beach. I grew up on the West Coast. The ocean has always been my second home. Whenever I need to think things through, this is where I come. I want to keep climbing. Each year, my role gets bigger. My managers support my growth with professional development and mentoring programs. It's like being back in college. I want to go to Africa. Next year, I hope...I want to be my best. If there's a limit to what I'm capable of achieving, I'm not sure where it is or when I'll reach it. Never, I hope.

There it is, Brooks writes, in a nutshell:

> ...college, learning, growth, travel, climbing, self-discovery. It's all there. And it's all punctuated with the little word "I," which appears in that short paragraph fifteen times....The current ethos puts "me" first.

No hint here of of giving to or serving others. This is the James and John syndrome. They wanted privilege, position, and power without service. And Jesus simply reminded them that, paradoxically, you gain these things by renouncing them.

Another one of Jesus' followers, Mother Teresa, had it right. Following a two-day workshop for her and some of her sisters, the workshop leader and the good mother were having a cup of tea together. Referring to her famous ministry to society's rejects, the workshop leader asked, "What is your biggest problem, Mother?" She quickly replied, "Professionalism." Her strange, one-word answer left the leader momentarily speechless. In his words,

My jaw dropped. I had expected her to say something about the difficulties involved in trying to hold her community of nuns together. Or the difficulty of determining who would be her ultimate successor as the authority figure among the sisters. Instead, I got "professionalism."

Seeing that I was dumbfounded, Mother Teresa then spelled out her answer, saying, "I have five sisters getting M.D. degrees and far greater numbers getting R.N., L.P.N., and M.S.W. degrees. But a funny thing happens. When they come back from their education, they are concerned about titles and offices and parking privileges. So I take all of that away from them and I send them to the hospice of the dying. There they hold people's hands, and pray with them and feed them. After six months of that, they typically get things straight again and remember their vocation to be a spiritual presence first, and a professional presence second."

And *that* sums up the gospel.

39

Justice and Charity

Twenty-ninth Sunday in Ordinary Time, Cycle C
Luke 18:1–8

Theme: justice first, charity second.

There was a judge who feared neither neighbor, God, nor anyone, for
that matter. And there was a widow who used to come all the time and
demand from him simple justice. Not charity, notice, just basic, fundamental justice. Well, as you heard, the judge ultimately does give
the justice he should have given anyway if he weren't so corrupt,
because he's being worn down. And the woman finally—finally—has
her rights honored. Unfortunately, in our haste to focus on persistent
prayer, the first lesson of today's gospel, we tend to slide over the
major motif of justice, which is the other lesson. And we shouldn't let
it slide. No, this gospel is definitely about justice as well as prayer.
Even Jesus, you recall, speaks of God securing the rights of his chosen
ones. And so it is justice that we shall explore today—even if it makes
us slightly uncomfortable.

Let me explore this theme by turning to a modern, updated version
of it, one that comes from a really fine Catholic novelist, John Hassler.
In his book, *The Green Journey*, we are introduced to Agatha McGee.
What is striking for us is that Agatha McGee bears more than a passing
resemblance to the widow in the parable of today's gospel. For one
thing, you should know that Miss McGee, as she was still called by gen-
erations of students who had passed through her sixth-grade classroom
at St. Isidore's School in Staggerford, Minnesota, was not one who, like
our gospel widow, would allow an injustice to go unchallenged, particularly when it was inflicted by the powerful against the powerless.

163

Here's the storyline. At the beginning of the novel, we find the far from conventional Miss McGee taking the very pregnant and very much unmarried teenager, Janet Raft, one of her most promising former students, into her home on Christmas Eve. Janet's family lived out in the country, too far away from the hospital should she go into labor after the expected winter storm had arrived. Not surprisingly, Janet is more than a little apprehensive and ill at ease as she arrives at the door of her former teacher, whom she knows would not approve of the behavior that got her into this condition. She mutters "Hello, Miss McGee," while staring at the doorstep.

Agatha, with a spirit showed by our lady in the gospel, responds, "Please look me in the eye and say that, Janet," and when Janet does so Agatha provides her own characteristic brand of unsentimental and common sense encouragement: "Oh, that's ever so much better. You see, this is no time for hangdog expressions. This is a time for strength. You're about to give birth in a blizzard, and the poor baby's father is a thousand miles away and God knows if he'll come home and marry you. And furthermore, if you insist on keeping the baby you've got years of great responsibility ahead of you. So promise you'll refrain from self-pity. Promise you'll be strong." With a small bright smile Janet does so and soon heads off to midnight Mass with her baby's future godmother.

Well, as it happens, neither the blizzard nor the baby arrive right away, and Janet goes into labor just before midnight on New Year's Eve. Stephen Raft is born early on the morning of January 1, three hours ahead of Daniel Buckingham III, son of the owner of the local furniture store. So far, so good, but now the plot thickens, as they say. And our gospel theme subtly intrudes when it is Daniel rather than Stephen who is named in the newspaper as the winner of the supply of gifts presented by the local Chamber of Commerce to the first New Year's baby.

Janet, caught up in the initial bliss of new motherhood, is content to let the injustice pass. But of course, not Miss McGee. Agatha is outraged. Like the woman in the gospel, she drags a reluctant Janet and her even more reluctant father, also a former student whom Agatha still calls Francis though to everyone else in town he is Frank, over to the furniture store where she confronts Daniel Buckingham Jr. about the "mistake."

By a combination of cajolery, threats, and promises she manages to have the various merchants provide a duplicate set of gifts for the genuine New Year's baby—and then, as an afterthought, demands that they provide a cash equivalent for a couple of previous illegitimate babies, now in their teens, who had been likewise cheated.

To read about this small, white-haired woman in her late sixties with an unbending, persistent sense of right and wrong, making a grown man squirm as though he were still a sixth-grader is to be brought right back into the gospel where the widow made the unjust judge squirm—and us as well. Why us? Because the gospel raises an issue we don't often think of—and we should if we are serious about the spiritual life. The gospel today does not ask if we are charitable, but before we even get to charity, are we just? The gospel reminds us that, yes, we are all anxious about charity—and quite good at being charitable, in fact—but our charity is sterile unless we first do justice. That's the biblical bottom line.

It's nice, for example, to give a turkey to your employees at Thanksgiving—that's charity—but if you're underpaying them all year long, that's injustice. Before the turkey can count, the wage must be adjusted. Before your charity can count, you must first be just. So say the prophets. So says Jesus. So says this gospel. In a word, you can have justice without charity but you can't have real charity without justice.

This reminds me of the lawyer, a very involved Catholic, who gave witness talks to Cursillo groups, was a eucharistic minister, and coordinated the food baskets for the poor. At a retreat weekend, the priest moderator, commending this man for his involvement and his charity, asked, "By the way, what about your professional life? Do you pay a just wage to your secretaries? Do you take pro bono cases? Do you practice ethics in a sometimes win-at-any-cost atmosphere?" The lawyer responded, "Hey, I don't even want to get into that." He had a segregated life. His charity, wide as it was, was morally suspect because he didn't first do justice.

Let me end with a brief but telling story I read about a good man who did charity but was brought up short on justice. The man's name is Clyde Best, Jr., of Redwood City, California. He is a maintenance instructor for United Airlines. Often on his way to work Clyde will stop at a doughnut shop and get doughnuts for his students. There is usually a "street person" hanging around asking for change. Sometimes, out of charity, Clyde gives him some, but usually he ignores him.

One day, when Clyde didn't have a class, he saw this man and felt compelled to stop. They ended up sharing some coffee, apple fritters, and conversation on a bus stop bench. But when Clyde offered charity by asking the street person if he could pray for him, the man caught him off guard by quietly demanding justice. He said, "I don't need anybody to pray for me, I just need somebody to talk to that will treat me like a human being."

This gospel catches us off guard too. It suggests that before we ever start considering charity as a measurement of our spiritual health, we must take the measurement of justice in our lives. So, in its own way, it leaves us with a question hanging in the air: are we just?

40

Bartimaeus

Thirtieth Sunday in Ordinary Time, Cycle B
Mark 10:46–52

Theme: sight and insight

By way of introduction, the story about a blind man of the past con-
jures up a story about a blind man of the present. At a celebrity party,
singer Stevie Wonder met golf champ Tiger Woods. Wonder mentioned that he, too, is an excellent golfer. Tiger was a bit skeptical that
the blind musician could play golf well, but he was too polite to say
anything. "When I tee off," the singer explained, "I have a guy call to
me from the green. My sharp sense of hearing lets me aim." Tiger was
impressed, and Stevie suggested that they play a round. When Tiger
agreed, Stevie asks, "How about if we play for $100,000?" Tiger insist-
ed he wouldn't play for money, but Stevie argued until Tiger finally
relented and said, "So, when do you want to play?" Stevie laughed and
replied, "I'll play on any night you choose."

It is significant that today's gospel comes right after last Sunday's
gospel about James and John seeking to sit at the right and left hand
of Jesus, not realizing, not seeing what this would involve. The side-
by-side position of these two episodes says that Jesus' intimates had it
all wrong and today's stranger had it all right. In short, the apostles,
physically able to see, were morally blind. This man in today's gospel
is physically blind, but morally full of sight and insight. We know this
by the way he answers Jesus' question, "What do you want me to do
for you?"

Pause for a minute. What would be your answer? What would you
want Jesus to do for you? To win the lottery? To get the raise? To regain

167

health? To reclaim a lost child? To be rich and famous? To be happy? "What do you want me to do for you?"

All the other healings in the gospel are done to anonymous people. We never are told their names. The exception is this gospel. We have a name for the man cured, Bartimaeus. Why did they remember his name and not the others? Perhaps it was because he was the only one who gave the right answer to Jesus' question when he answered, "That I might see."

Whether he was cured or not, he wanted to see; that is, to see the meaning behind it all, to see what life was about, to see how to really live, to see some sense in life's confusion and unfairness, to see the hand of God somewhere present, to see beyond his physical blindness. He was, in a word, asking for faith, for goodness, for moral insight. Would that be our prayer?

> Some of us are blind to our own faults.....Lord, we want to see.
>
> Some of us always focus on the weaknesses of others....Lord, we want to see.
>
> Some never acknowledge many of life's blessings....Lord, we want to see.
>
> Some are blinded by unbridled desires for pleasure, money, and self-promotion and fail to notice the needs of others, the presence of the poor....Lord, we want to see.
>
> Some have eyes darkened by prejudice and hatred....Lord we want to see.
>
> Some are blinded by ambition and step all over others' feelings....Lord, we want to see.
>
> Some are blinded by pride which makes them think that they are the center of the universe....Lord, we want to see.
>
> Some wallow in their own self-pity and are turned in on their own sins and never notice God's mercy....Lord, we want to see.
>
> Some don't have their prayers answered and need to sense something deeper happening in the crosses they bear....Lord, we want to see.

We want to see, like John Newton, who had a conversion experience and became a priest in the Church of England, and devoted his life to serving others. In St. Mary's Woolnoth Church in the City of London there is a large memorial tablet with Newton's own words on it. It reads:

John Newton, Clerk, once an infidel and libertine, a servant of slaves in Africa, was, by the rich mercy of our Lord and Saviour Jesus Christ, persevered, restored, pardoned, and appointed to preach the faith he had long labored to destroy. Near sixteen years at Olney and twenty-eight years in this church.

It was he, who knew what he was talking about, who gave us our one unofficial national religious hymn:

Amazing grace, how sweet the sound,
That saved a wretch like me!
I once was lost and now am found;
Was blind, but now I see.

That's the kind of sight Bartimaeus was asking for: to see as Jesus sees, to see what's important. Which is why the gospel adds that he immediately followed Jesus. That is, once he saw what was really real, what really counts, he left all, like John Newton, to give his life to Jesus.

According to the gospel, you recall, many rebuked Bartimaeus, telling him to keep silent. We have the same today. Many—meaning the media that keeps us endlessly distracted with trivia and a culture that offers us bread and circuses as the means of salvation—many rebuke us, telling us to keep silent, not to bring up all that "spiritual" stuff and the real issues of the spirit. But, like Bartimaeus, we must cry out all the louder our deepest and most heartfelt needs when Jesus stops before us and asks,

"What is it that you really want me to do for you?"

Your answer?

41

Everyday Saints

Thirty-first Sunday in Ordinary Time, Cycle B
Mark 12:28b–34

Hear O, Israel. You shall love the Lord your God with all your heart,
soul, mind and strength and you shall love your neighbor as yourself.

So proclaims the ancient teaching before Jesus and reaffirmed once
more by Jesus. How does such love begin?

Writer Kathleen Norris tells the story of a friend named Willie who
had fallen in with a drug dealer in Wyoming and dreamed up a
scheme to make some truly big bucks. Willie thought that things were
working out just fine—making good contracts, setting up a network—
but one day he and his drug dealer colleague were cruising down the
road when the drug dealer saw a man traveling in the opposite direction. "I need to kill him," said the dealer quite matter-of-factly, reaching for a gun that was stashed under the front seat.

"It was right then I decided to get out," said Willie, badly shaken.
"This was over my head."

And *that*, concluded Kathleen Norris, is where the path to love and
salvation begins—in the sudden awareness that a particular path is
leading to death, in the naming of something that is wrong and taking steps to get away from it. The saints are people who, having flirted with sin—like Paul of Tarsus or Francis of Assisi—come to such an
awareness. The saints are those who heard today's gospel as if for the
first time and embraced that truth that love of God and neighbor are
the real directives of life and humbly realize that they have far to go.

When the poet Maya Angelou appeared on *The Today Show* a few
years ago, she was asked about her lifetime goals. She answered, "I

want to become a Christian." This surprised the show's host, who asked, "But aren't you already a Christian?" To which the poet replied, "When people come up to me and say they are Christians, I think, 'Oh my, already?'"

To become a saint, a Christian, is an ongoing process. And it happens in the way Rabbi Harold Kushner points out: "When people ask me 'Where is God?' I tell them I would rather rephrase the question to '*When* is God?' God is there when we love him and our neighbor."

As in this story: a woman was in great distress because she had lost the sense of God in her life. "Why doesn't God make me feel that he is there? If only I could feel him, know that he touched me." And the old woman to whom she was complaining said to her, "Pray to God. Ask God to touch you. He will put his hand on you." The woman closed her eyes and began to pray earnestly—and suddenly she felt the hand of God touching her! She cried out, "He touched me!" and went into an ecstasy of joy. But then she paused and said, "But you know, it felt just like your hand."

And the old woman replied. "Of course it did. It *was* my hand." "It was?" "Sure, what did you think God would be doing? Did you think he would extend a long arm out of heaven to touch you? He just took the hand that was nearest and used that."

Like the story of the woman who, during the course of earning her master's degree, found it necessary to commute several times a week from the town of Victory in Vermont to the state university in Burlington, a good hundred miles away. Coming home late at night, she would see an old man sitting by the side of her road. He was always there, in subzero temperatures, in stormy weather, no matter how late she returned. He made no acknowledgment of her passing. The snow settled on his cap and shoulders as if he were merely another gnarled old tree. She often wondered what brought him to that same spot every evening—what stubborn habit, private grief, or mental disorder.

Finally, she asked a neighbor of hers, "Have you ever seen an old man who sits by the road late at night?" "Oh, yes," said her neighbor. "Many times."

"Is he...a little touched upstairs? Does he ever go home?" "He's no more touched than you or me," her neighbor laughed. "And he goes home right after you do. You see, he doesn't like the idea of you driving by yourself out late all alone on these back roads, so every night he walks out to wait for you. When he sees your tail lights disappear around the bend and he knows you're okay, he goes home to bed."

Like the story of the woman, both divorced and an unwed mother, who, in the 1920s, worked for a series of leftist publications and lived a bohemian lifestyle in New York's Greenwich Village. Then one day she realized that she was in over her head, and so in 1927 she, of all people, became a Catholic and then led a quiet rebellion within the church to reach out to the poor, the needy, and the desperate. She was a pacifist, an anarchist, and a crusader for social justice—not your standard-issue saint. And yet right now her name is in fact being processed for canonization, even though in her lifetime she perceptively said she didn't want to become a saint because, in her words, she didn't want "to be dismissed that easily." Which is to say, once you put the label "saint" to a person's name, we say, "Oh, well, he or she could do those things because, after all, they were saints. But that's not for me."

She didn't want people to think that what she did was extraordinary because what she did—loving God and neighbor—was in fact to be the ordinary way any Christian should live. She protested that loving God and neighbor wasn't meant to be unusual or artificially elevated to the stuff of sainthood, out of the reach of ordinary people. It was simply what everyday Christians were meant to do. This woman is Dorothy Day, whom the archbishop of New York recently called, "a model for all in the third millennium."

The law and the prophets, Jesus says, are summed up in loving God and neighbor. This is not something over and above daily life, but the very kernel and heart of daily life, the springboard for our actions, the basis for our decisions, the grounding of our prayer life, the motivation of our careers, the purpose of our being here to begin with.

I suspect that if people today have trouble discovering where God is, it is because they have not experienced *when* God is. The gospel invites us to show them.

42

The Zacchaeus Moment

Thirty-first Sunday in Ordinary Time, Cycle C
Luke 19:1–10

Theme: the time to say yes is now

We have it in the Bible. We have it in the movies. We have it in life.

The Bible. We heard just a few Sundays ago, for instance, the story of the great general Naaman, the Syrian general who had leprosy and was directed to go to the prophet in Israel. Once there Naaman became angry because he was told to go and wash in what was essentially a mudhole. As he said he had two wonderful sparkling rivers back in his homeland, why should he bathe in a little squeedunk, backwater pool? So he sat on his high horse while his servants pleaded with him. "No!" he said, "this is stupid. I'd be a fool to get down and go into that water if that's what it's called." But his servants wore him down and finally, with reluctance, he got down from his high horse, paused at the water muttering, "I feel like an idiot," and finally stepped in. And, says the Scripture, he was cured.

Then there was King David, so overjoyed that the Ark was being brought to Jerusalem, his new capital, that he himself went before the ark gyrating and dancing his head off in his short tunic so people could see his underwear only to be scolded by his mortified wife who scornfully reminded him that, after all, he was king and it was unseemly and disgraceful for him to be dancing in front of all those people and exposing himself like some kid at a rave dance. Good God, had he no sense of dignity? And the only explanation David could give was, "But this is the Ark! God among us!"

Then there was the father in the story of the prodigal son who did the same thing. When he saw his wayward, hangdog son at a distance, he should have waited imperiously with his foot tapping till the lad reached him. But, contrary to all norms, flinging away all social decorum that forbade a father to run to his son and not the other way around, he unceremoniously tucked up his robe like a flapper from the 1920s and, with his bare legs showing, ran like a banshee, out of breath, to embrace his son. Utterly foolish. Utterly redemptive.

Then there's today's gospel. A less than honorable cheat, called "runt" behind his back, nevertheless Zacchaeus, because he was a man of wealth no matter how he had gotten it, had a certain social position, a certain standing among the people. Kind of like a mob boss whom everyone knows gets his wealth from murder and corruption but they invite him to their homes because he is a celebrity and rich.

And this man, this cheat, this pillar of society suddenly gets infected with the same impulse that grabbed Naaman, David, and the prodigal's father, and he steps out of character. He hitches up his robe and, in front of everybody, shimmies up a sycamore tree like a monkey searching for a coconut. In fact, he probably *looked* like a monkey. And the people stand there with open mouths watching this surprising and embarrassing episode. But Zacchaeus didn't care; Jesus was passing by.

All these illustrations are examples of what I call "the Zacchaeus moment": the moment we must all earnestly and ceaselessly pray for; the moment that says that sometime in our lives, at some point, we too have to act like fools. At some time in our lives we have to let down our defenses, throw caution to the wind, scandalize our family and friends, play the fool for Christ, and say "yes" to the saint we were called to be.

The movies. Remember that delightful romantic comedy, *Overboard*, where Goldie Hawn leaves behind her stuffy husband, her socialite mother, and her multimillion-dollar yacht to jump overboard and go live with Kurt Russell and his four sons in a shack? Of course, any woman might want to leave anything for Kurt Russell, but the point is that she utterly shocked her friends, her high-class circle, by basically seizing "the Zacchaeus moment," becoming an utter fool for her heart's fulfillment.

In a recent Hollywood film, *Family Man,* Jack, the character played by Nicolas Cage, is initially shown at an airport preparing to catch a flight. He is going to London for a year to intern at an important bank. We see him saying goodbye to his college girl friend Kate, who is remaining stateside to begin law school. He tells her that their love is strong enough to reunite them after their year apart. Then we are abruptly shifted to his life fourteen years later.

Jack is now a highly successful Wall Street investment banker. He has never married, since he and Kate did not in fact reconnect after their separation years ago. But one Christmas Eve he is miraculously transported away from his glamorous life in Manhattan to a glimpse of the life he would have had if he had returned from London and married Kate years earlier. He finds that they have two wonderful children but their lives are quite ordinary; he is a retail tire salesman in New Jersey, she is a non-profit lawyer.

Jack initially cannot accept that many of the dreams he had as a young man fresh out of college were never realized in the sacrifices and difficulties of this married life he would have had. But slowly, painfully, he begins to adapt to his life as a family man. He is slowly converted in his heart to see the value of living for others; he casts his dreams of wealth and independence aside.

So at the end of the film, when he is returned to his hitherto life of wealth and independence, he shocks his friends by embracing "the Zacchaeus moment." He turns his back on all the glitz and glamour, and immediately begins to seek out Kate, the one he really loves and needs, to try and make this would-have-been scenario come true.

Real life. Many years ago, former Secretary General of the United Nations, Dag Hammarskjöld, wrote in his book titled *Markings*:

> I don't know who—or what—put the question. I don't know when it was put. I don't even remember answering it. But at some moment I did answer yes to Someone—or Something—and from that hour I was certain that existence is meaningful and that, therefore, my life, in self-surrender, had a goal.

These incidents from the Bible, the movies, and life are all variations of today's gospel. Yes, Zacchaeus hesitated, shifted from foot to foot, looked around at the admiring crowd, thought of his position and all that he had to lose. But, at some point—at some point—he decided to play the fool. He simply had to see Jesus and open himself to the invitation of grace and repentance. When he did, he was never the same again.

Most of us are probably still in the early foot-shifting stage. Still, time is running out. The gospel is asking, when we ever get down from our high horse? When will we ever dance in public before the Lord? When will we ever forget our dignity and position and run and embrace another? When will we ever leave everything and jump overboard for Christ? When will we let go of our comfortable life and reconnect with Jesus, our first love?

In short, when will we ever grab hold of our "Zacchaeus moment"? Hopefully, in time. At least right now it's worth praying over because deep down, we know the gospel is right. It's the only way—the only way—Jesus can declare that, for us, "today salvation has come to this house."

43

Money

Thirty-second Sunday in Ordinary Time, Cycle B
Mark 12:38–44

Theme: money as spiritual measurement

Because the gospel prompts me so, I want to talk to you about money. And even though I am not going to ask for it, I can feel the tension. Money is the one subject, I have found, that immediately provokes defensiveness either from the wealthy—because they sense they're going to be publicly denounced—or from the ordinary person, who bristles with resentment that anyone would dare intrude—because "my money, my income, what I make and what I do with it, is my business and nobody else's."

Now that we have that hostile truth out in the open, let me make one statement that we will explore together. When people seek to take measure of their spiritual lives, they examine themselves on such things as their prayer life, their honesty, their truthfulness, the fact that they have been faithful to their spouses, have been chaste, have not cheated or lied to any great extent, been violent or maligned another's reputation. The laundry list could go on. But the fact is, the one single, most reliable, most accurate practical measure of our spiritual lives, how we stand with God, is our use of money. Let me repeat that: the one single, most reliable, most accurate practical measure of our spiritual lives, how we stand with God, is our use of money.

Money is necessary to live. We work for it, spend it, save it. Think of it: making it, saving it, and spending it takes a large portion of our lives. We need it, want it, and spend most of our human energy, most of our time, acquiring it. And yet, with money being such a hugely proportionate part of our lives, we still claim that it is neutral, private, and totally irrelevant to who we are as Christians. That doesn't make sense. Money, being a dominant force in our lives, has to significantly figure in the equation of whether we are good people and whether we will get to heaven or not.

At least Jesus saw it that way for it was much on the mind of Jesus. Sixteen of his thirty-eight parables were concerned with how to handle money and possessions. In the gospels, an amazing one out of ten verses deals directly with the subject of money. The whole Bible offers 500 verses on prayer, fewer than 500 verses on faith, but more than 2000 verses on money and possessions. Think about that.

So what can we, should we, say about money? There are several things to ponder. First, money, like sex, is an attractive hazard—attractive because, like sex, it is powerful, sustaining, joyous. It is a hazard because, like sex, it has built-in passions we cannot always control. There's something about the very nature of money that not only pushes us to excess but, worst of all, to pride and idolatry. Very few people can handle lots of it well—and many people *have* lots of it. Merrill Lynch tells us that the number of millionaires in the United States and Canada has risen almost forty percent since just three years ago, which means that two and one-half million millionaires and 216 new billionaires are now living among us. In terms of percentage of wealth relative to the average American, this means that if Bill Gates wanted to buy a $250,000 Lamborghini, the purchase would set him back sixty-three cents.

This doesn't mean that the super-wealthy are all obsessed with money. Some really don't want to be wealthy; it just happens in this high-tech Wall Street economy. Some, in fact, fear that sudden wealth might make them greedy or insensitive. Some are quite generous. But others, of course, revel in their wealth and live extravagantly and wastefully, totally insensitive to the poor of the world—who are the majority. They build their multimillion-dollar enclaves, monuments to their ego and status, plunder the environment, compete for financial status among their peers, and shelter their children from life's harshness. In short, money has a tendency to blind people to the needs of others, while inflating egos with more and more rare and expensive possessions and what are called "lifestyles." The blindness and pride inherent in money figure in our spiritual lives.

Second, sooner or later money tends to get seen as a earned right for private use when in fact it is an unearned gift for public use. In short, we are not owners of money, but stewards. And, in that word, we are at the heart of the matter and Jesus' concerns. Sooner or later Christians must see money solely and only in terms of stewardship. We've got to wholeheartedly embrace that biblical concept. Money is, so to speak, on loan to us. We are its servants, not its masters. How we use this temporary gift—remember the old sayings that no hearse carries a U-Haul or no shroud has pockets—is the critical factor in our spiritual odyssey and development and growth.

The point is, once again, that if we are looking for a real litmus test as to our spirituality, we must ask ourselves how we and our family are stewards of our money. How do we master it, or how it has mastered us? We must ask ourselves, do we tithe? Give ten percent of our income to the poor? Let me point out that, according to a Gallup poll, when you compare Catholics to Protestants and Jews, we do not come up smelling like roses. In a recent year, American Catholics gave 1.3 percent of their income to their parish and charities. In that same time span, however, Protestants gave 2.4 percent and Jews 3.8 percent. And the scribes and the Pharisees best us all. It was normal for them to give ten percent right off the top.

It is helpful to remember that money used for others—for feeding the hungry, giving drink to the thirsty, clothing the cold and naked—are precisely those works of mercy that, according to Jesus, form the basis—the *only* basis—of our judgment when we die.

I am an ordinary man. I make enough money to sustain my life. I have a car, a house, food, and clothing. But I know that I am enormously and fabulously wealthy in comparison to the rest of the world. I remember reading about a woman from a poor village in Bangladesh who was visiting a family in Boston, and the morning after she arrived she looked out of the window of the people's home. "Who lives in that house?" she asked the woman from Boston. "Which house?" "That one right there." "Oh, that. No one lives there. That's a 'house' for the car." The woman from Bangladesh was nonplused. "A house for the car," she kept saying. "A house for the car." I picture that woman looking out my kitchen window and seeing my garden shed, puzzled, saying again and again, "A house for shovels. A house for the lawn mower."

Let me share something personal. When I first went to the seminary in Baltimore a long, long time ago, for the first time I met boys from other parts of the country. We all soon sensed that a lad named Gary, from Georgia, was not as well off as the rest of us. Later we were to find that "not well off" was not even close. It was a gentle term we used for outright poor, something we had never experienced. After a year or so, when we had gotten to know one another, we asked him about being poor. He couldn't tell us face to face because it was too painful, so he wrote a little note and left it with us. (I still have it, as I suspect the others have kept it too.) This is what he wrote, quite unselfconsciously:

Being poor is witnessing the agony on your mother's face as she places hot cloths on your belly to quiet the hunger pains.

It's watching your illiterate father succumb to alcohol because he is not equipped mentally or physically to raise seven children.

It is stealing potatoes from the school cafeteria so that the family can eat supper that night.

It is being put to bed early on Christmas eve because there are no toys and no food.

It is having your childhood's only birthday cake made without sugar or shortening.

It is being called to the school cafeteria where your younger brother has falsely sworn that he brought vegetables from home in exchange for a hot lunch, and both you and he being brought to tears by a lecture on why children shouldn't ever lie and being sent back to your classroom without food.

It is selling a dozen eggs needed by the family because you cannot have the shame of not bringing your share of soft drinks for the school picnic.

It is eating flour and meal mixed and cooked with hot pepper so that you won't eat too much.

It's having your brother and sister drop out of school in the third grade because she doesn't have a dress and he is being laughed at for wearing a shortened version of your mother's tattered old coat.

In my wildest dreams I could never even imagine this kind of poverty, then or even now. But it made an impact on us all and on the necessity of sharing our "enormous" wealth. It might be revealing for us to examine the last three months of our lives and see what we spent for necessities, enjoyment, and luxuries, and what we spent on the poor.

Anyway, I just wanted to make three points about money. One is that the subject is not really as "none-of-your-business" as we like to think. Money is *everyone's* daily business, and being such a big business it *has* to come under the scrutiny of the gospel.

Two, money is a necessary and wonderful commodity—look at all the good you can do with it—but as insightful and experienced Christians we know that it is a two-edged sword and we must acknowledge its seductive power, abetted by a massive advertising industry: the power to pull us into blindness (not seeing the poor), selfishness (not sharing what we have), and pride (defining who we are by what we have).

Three, our use of money, no matter what you say, is still the best barometer of our spiritual status. Our petty virtues and vices pale beside this mathematically dominant part our lives; and it is this part, over and over again, with which Jesus is concerned. In fact, he seems obsessed with it.

The real question is, why doesn't it bother us?

44

Heaven Can Wait

Thirty-second Sunday in Ordinary Time, Cycle C
Luke 20:27–38

Theme: skip the questions; focus on Jesus

We all want to go to heaven. But not just yet.

A prosperous doctor one day encountered his rabbi, a charismatic character, in the marketplace. The teacher grasped the doctor's arm and cried ecstatically. "Just think, Chaim, the Messiah is coming soon!"

The younger man paled and shrank back at these words. "God forbid!" he cried. "I have finally built up a good medical practice; my wife and I have just moved into a new house, our children are in excellent schools…and we have tickets to *The Producers*! When the Messiah comes we shall have to give up all of this and move to Jerusalem." The rabbi wagged his finger in gentle rebuke. "Ah, you must not upset yourself, Chaim," he replied. "Calm down. Surely the God who freed us from Pharaoh, who gave us victory over the Philistines and protected us against Haman, surely he will save us from the Messiah!"

We're like the doctor. Yes, we want to go to heaven but not just yet. Save us from it. Besides, to be honest, in spite of all those holy pictures, we're not so sure what it's all about. We more readily mouth Shakespeare's King Claudius' quandary when he speaks of "the dread of something after death" and goes on to ponder,

> The undiscover'd country from whose bourn
> No traveller returns—puzzles the will,
> And makes us bear the ills we have
> Than to fly to others we know not of. (*Hamlet*, act III, scene 1)

Well, the Sadducees went King Claudius one better. They held there
was no undiscovered country to worry about to begin with, no here-
after, no heaven. And, if in fact there was one, they posed a crafty rid-
dle to Jesus to show that it would be an absurd concept anyway. What
they didn't realize was that in bringing up that silly case about the
woman with the seven husbands and how all those connections would
work out in heaven, they were unknowingly asking our questions
about heaven—if not about matrimonial status, about other matters.

We wonder, for example, whether babies who died as babies will
still be babies in heaven, and whether those who die at great age will
be of great age, and if not, what age will they be? And for that matter,
what age will we or anyone else be? In the fourth century St. Augustine
worked on this question and came up with an answer that satisfied
him. He decided that everyone would be thirty-three—which was generally thought to be Jesus' age at his resurrection.

We wonder whether we will recognize one another, and—at least in
some cases, whether we will *want* to recognize one another, at least
whether we want to be recognized by everyone. There are people we
don't like on earth and we surely don't want to pal around with them
in heaven. Will our pets be in heaven? (Dogs certainly!) Will we be
surprised at who's there, not the least of whom ourselves? Will our
scars be gone? Our receding hairline? Our embarrassments? Will we
get bored after a while? What will we do all day? Will it be air conditioned? In short, what is heaven like?

Through the ages, as you know, we have had no lack of people pur-
porting to give us answers. Crystal balls, mediums, books about near-
death experiences, the psychic channel, the new age junk, and a good-
ly number of offbeat versions of the Christian faith have all promised
to give us that information. So it is important to pay careful attention
to what Jesus has to say to the Sadducees when they ask him what will
happen to the woman with seven husbands when they all die. He says
that the woman in the story is not going to be anybody's wife. He said,
in effect, that their whole question was irrelevant. Why? Because things
will be different, people will be different, heaven will be different. All
will be radically different. In a word, forget about your questions
because all will be beyond our questions, beyond our imaginations.

Just as five hundred years ago, our ancestors could not imagine an artificial heart or a computer or television, so we cannot imagine heaven. I would think, in that same vein, that the crawling, homely caterpillar in its wildest dreams could never imagine it would fly and fly as a gorgeously colored butterfly. Jesus is saying: forget all your categories, all your paradigms, all your preconceptions. Heaven is beyond time, beyond experience. Heaven, eternal life with God, is so entirely different, so completely beyond our present thinking, so spectacularly full and rich, that no questions fit, no answers would be understood.

So, only one thing really counts, only one thing remains: faith. A faith that does not come from knowing whose wife the woman will be or from knowing any details, not even from knowing answers to the best and most reasonable of questions. It's a faith that comes from believing Jesus, and trusting that when he says heaven will be different, it will be different. Our faith comes from trust that Jesus died for our sins, that he loves us beyond measure and desires that all be saved.

We are given no specifics, no answers, no solutions, no picture postcards. Instead we are called simply to surrender our questions and our difficulties and our logical puzzles, and to trust that God will handle things better than we could ever imagine; and that God's love and care for us will surpass all that we can ask or imagine. In short, we are to remember that when we die, and when those we love die, that God does not die. God's love for us—a love that has already carried us through so much, a love that has already been so gracious to us—does not die. That love will continue and that love will grow; *that* is all we need to know about heaven. And that's enough.

OK, now it's all right that we try and visualize heaven, and it is surely right and proper that our prophets, artists, and poets try as best they can to convey what heaven is like. After all, we're creatures of imagination. Isaiah's version of heaven, for example, is a banquet—a good metaphor for a people always living on the edge:

> On this mountain of the Lord of hosts will make for all people a feast of rich food...he will swallow up death forever. The Lord will wipe way tears from all faces and the disgrace of his people he will take away from all the earth. (Is 25:6–9)

And the poets and songwriters can chime in. For example, during the time of slavery in this country, shoes were reserved only for the privileged "white gentry." So in this Negro spiritual, heaven meant:

I got shoes.
You got shoes.
All God's children got shoes.
When I get to heaven, gonna put on my shoes
And gonna walk all over God's heaven.

And the artists come along and paint heavenly scenes with harps because they know that music is the nearest thing we have to ecstasy on earth, and gold crowns because gold is the one metal that doesn't rust, indicating the eternity of heaven.

But, still, the artists and the musicians and the poets are all straining. When all is said and done, when we think about heaven, we still have to come back to St. Paul's words, which echo Jesus': "No eye has seen nor ear heard nor has it even entered into the heart of man what God has prepared for those who love him" (1 Cor 2:9).

That's what Jesus is really saying about heaven. Case closed. It's the final word. Not very satisfying, I grant you, and not an answer to our off-the-mark nosiness. But on the issue of heaven, it really does come down to this: believe deeply that Jesus loves you and that that love endures through time and eternity, and the curiosities about heaven will take care of themselves. Just be prepared to be surprised at answers you never had questions for.

45

Christ the King

Feast of Christ the King, Cycle B
John 18:33–37

It is helpful to remember that John, the author of this gospel, is fond of irony. It's shot all through his work. For example, in his gospel the blind man sees while the sighted Pharisees and scribes do not. That's ironic. Nicodemus is a teacher and yet he comes by night to learn from Jesus. The Samaritan woman at the well has buckets to draw water, yet she is thirsty; while Jesus has no bucket to draw water, yet he is the water that springs up to eternal life. The soldiers come armed to arrest Jesus and they fall down before the unarmed Jesus. And so it goes.

Today, in another striking episode from John's pen, we get that same irony. The powerless prisoner is the king while the powerful ruler is the subject. How is this so? John gives the answer in the following dialogue: "Then you are a king?" asks Pilate. Jesus replies, "You say I am king." And then he explains it. "For this was I born and for this I came into the world, to testify to the truth."

And there it is. "To testify to the truth." That is what it means to be king, to be royal. What this episode is saying and what this feast is all about is *integrity*. Wherever truth reigns, one is king no matter how lowly, imprisoned, tortured, or rejected. In other words, we are in the realm of moral witness with this feast. We are always king when we testify to the truth.

I must return to one of my favorite scenes from Robert Bolt's play, *A Man for All Seasons*. King Henry VIII is trying to coax his subject, Sir Thomas More, to agree to his divorce of Catherine. They are in the garden as Henry is speaking: "You must consider, Thomas, that I stand in peril of my soul. It was no marriage; she was my brother's widow.

186

'Thou shalt not uncover the nakedness of thy brother's wife'; Leviticus, chapter eighteen, verse sixteen."

More replies: "Yes, Your Grace. But Deuteronomy…"

Henry interrupts angrily: "Deuteronomy's ambiguous!"

More replies quietly: "Your Grace, I'm not fit to meddle in these matters—to me it seems a matter for the Holy See.…"

Once more Henry interrupts: "Thomas, Thomas, does a man need a pope to tell him when he's sinned? It was a sin, Thomas: I admit it; I repent. And God has punished me; I have no son.…Son after son she has borne me, Thomas, all dead at birth or dead within the month. I never saw the hand of God so clear in anything.…I have a daughter, she's a good child, a well-set child. But I have no son. It is my bounden duty to put away the Queen and all the popes back to St. Peter shall not come between me and my duty! How is it that you cannot see? Everyone else does."

More answers: "Then why does Your Grace need my poor support?"

And Henry comes back with those powerful words that everyone one of us would like to hear: "Because you are honest. What's more to the purpose, you're known to be honest.…There are those like Norfolk who follow me because I wear the crown, and there are those like Master Cromwell who follow me because they are jackals with sharp teeth and I am their lion, and there is a mass that follows me because it follows anything that moves—*and there is you.*"

Henry, in the presence of More's integrity, knew who was really king and who was really the subject.

One day, as Mahatma Gandhi stepped aboard a train, one of his shoes slipped off and landed on the track. He was unable to retrieve it as the train was moving. To the amazement—and the mockery—of his companions, Gandhi calmly took off his other shoe and threw it back along the track to land close to the first. Asked by a fellow passenger why he did so, Gandhi smiled. "The poor man who finds the shoe lying on the track will now have a pair he can use." And everyone with two shoes on his feet knew in his heart that the shoeless man had testified to the truth. They were subject to their pride; he was king in his compassion.

Finally, let me tell you about a special priest who was ordained in

1946, in the same year as Pope John Paul II. His name is Father Anton Luli, SJ, of Albania, and he died in March 1998 at the age of eighty-eight. But he was able to get to Rome in November 1996 to celebrate his golden anniversary of ordination with the Pope and with many other priests ordained in 1946. While in Rome, Father Luli shared some of his experiences and testified to the presence of God in his life. Here is a true account of his experiences, in his exact words:

> On Dec. 19, 1947, they arrested me and charged me with provoking unrest and with propaganda against the government. I lived in solitary confinement for seventeen years and for many more in forced labor. On Christmas night that year (how could I forget?) they dragged me from that place and put me in another lavatory on the second floor of the prison. They forced me to strip and hung me up with a rope passed under my arms. I was naked and could barely touch the ground with the tips of my toes. I felt my body slowly and inexorably failing me. The cold gradually crept up on my limbs and when it reached my breast and my heart was about to give in, I gave a desperate cry. My torturers arrived; they pulled me down and kicked me all over. That night, in that place and in the solitude of that first torture, I experienced the real meaning of the Incarnation and the cross.
>
> But in this suffering, I had beside me and within me the comforting presence of the Lord Jesus, the eternal high priest. At times, his support was something I can only call "extraordinary," so great was the joy and comfort he communicated to me. But I have never felt resentment for those who, humanly speaking, robbed me of my life. After my release, I happened to meet one of my torturers in the street: I took pity on him; I went toward him and embraced him. They released me in the 1989 amnesty. I was seventy-nine years old.
>
> This was my experience as a priest throughout these years. It is a very unusual experience compared to that of many priests, but certainly not unique. There are thousands of priests who have been persecuted in their lives because of the priesthood of Christ. Their experiences differ, but they are united by love. The priest is

first and foremost someone who lives in order to love; to love Christ and to love everyone in him, in all life's circumstances, to the point of giving up his life. Everything can be taken from us, but no one can wrench from our hearts our love for Jesus or our love for our brothers and sisters.

Who was the king here? The priest who embraced his torturer or the torturer who thought he had all the power? These stories all have one thing in common: they tell us what was going on at the trial of Jesus before Pilate. They tell us that although powerful Pilate would have captive Jesus tortured and killed, he still remained the prisoner because he lived a lie, and the prisoner still remained king because he kept his integrity and testified to the truth to the last.

"Then you are a king?" Jesus answered, "You say I am a king. For this was I born…to testify to the truth." This gospel, the feast of Christ the King, remind us that each of us was born for the same reason.

Holidays

46
Mother's Day

Beyond the sentimentality and especially the commercialism of Mother's Day there lies a deeper religious reality, an example of which we find in today's gospel; namely, "I give you a new commandment. As I have loved you, so you also should love one another." The operative word is, of course, "as" and if you want to know the content of "as," you look at Jesus washing his disciples' feet or the crucifixion. That explains "as." Jesus, in short, was wise enough to know that he couldn't just say something abstract about love. He had to make it concrete. Love has to have a content, a pattern, a demonstration for it to mean anything, to catch on. So he used his own life and death as an example of love.

This, of course, is a common truism: we learn how to love from being loved, from seeing love in action. It's as simple and profound as that. And that's why I said that behind the Mother's Day hype lies a deeper religious reality: we honor our mother because, in almost all cases—there are some exceptions—her love gets to us first and is the first concrete lesson we have in love. So to this extent, Mother's Day is a celebration of all those, parents or not, who nourish or cherish others and teach them the meaning of love. It's just that mothers are the most evident, most visible, most endearing teachers and that's why we honor them, remember them and their concrete examples of love. A daughter writes:

A few years ago, when my mother was visiting, she asked me to go shopping with her because she needed a new dress. I don't normally like to go shopping with other people, and I'm not a patient person, but we set off for the mall together nonetheless. We visited nearly every store that carried ladies' dresses, and my mother tried on dress after dress, rejecting them all. As the day wore on, I grew weary and my mother grew frustrated. Finally, at our last stop, my mother tried on a lovely blue three-piece dress. The blouse had a bow at the neckline, and as I stood in the dressing room with her, I watched as she tried, with much difficulty, to tie the bow. Her hands were so badly crippled from arthritis that she couldn't do it.

Suddenly, as I watched her fumbling with her arthritic hands, it hit me. Suddenly my impatience gave way to an overwhelming wave of compassion for this woman, my mother. I went over to tie the bow for her. The dress was beautiful, and she bought it. Our shopping trip was over, but the event was etched indelibly in my memory. For the rest of the day, my mind kept returning to that moment in the dressing room and to the vision of my mother's hands trying to tie that bow. They are old and stiff now, but I couldn't get it out of my mind that these were the loving hands that had fed me, bathed me, dressed me, tied my shoelaces and bows, caressed and comforted me, and, most of all, prayed for me.

Later in the evening, I went to my mother's room, took her hands in mine, kissed them and, much to her surprise, told her that to me they were the most beautiful hands in the world. I'm so grateful that God let me see with new eyes what a precious, priceless gift a loving, self-sacrificing mother is. I can only pray that some day my hands, and my heart, will have earned such a beauty of their own.

This daughter was learning to love others as her mother loved her.
Alicia Sferrino was just twenty years old when she was diagnosed with severe kidney failure. Although dialysis would help for a while, doctors made it clear to Alicia's family that she would die without a kidney transplant. Like any loving parents, Deanne and Vincent Sferrino would have gladly given a vital organ to save their precious daughter. But they couldn't. You see, Alicia was adopted, and they had no idea who her real parents were.

So began an arduous search to connect with Alicia's birth mother. All they had was her name, Ruth Chiasson, and the state in which she gave birth. After making extensive telephone calls to this town, they learned that Ruth had married and now her last name was Foisy. But they couldn't find a Foisy anywhere. Finally, Deanne and Vincent tracked down the priest who had married Ruth and her husband. He agreed to send her a letter from the Sferrinos.

When Ruth Foisy first opened the Sferrinos' letter, she was stunned. At seventeen, she had become pregnant and given birth to a baby girl. Her parents pressured her to give the baby away. Ruth had never gotten over the heartbreak and guilt of that act, and for twenty years she had burned a candle on the date of Alicia's birth. Now, the child she had given life to needed her to give that gift a second time. Ruth the mother knew what she must do for her child of long ago. It wasn't easy to gather her present children around and tell them that they had a half-sister they never knew. It wasn't easy to relive the story of giving away her baby for adoption. But when she was finished, Ruth's children rallied around her. They would support her all the way.

Ruth went through with the donation, and today both women are doing well. Alicia Sferrino is healthy, her new kidney functioning fine. She is married now, and the mother of a baby daughter herself. In a time of physical and emotional crisis, these two women gave each other a special gift. Ruth gave Alicia life a second time; Alicia gave Ruth the forgiveness she sought for so long.

Love is like that and that's how we learn it. It's today's gospel in another guise.

Finally, on a lighter note, in these days when motherhood is devalued in some quarters, let me end with this account from a woman who writes:

A friend of mine went to the County Clerk's office to renew her driver's license. "Do you have a job, or are you just a…?" the recorder asked her. My friend, fuming, snapped: "Of course I have a job. I'm a mother." The recorder replied, "We don't list 'mother' as an occupation. 'Housewife' covers it."

Well, I found myself in the same situation one day when I was at our own town hall. The clerk was obviously a career woman, poised, efficient, and possessed of a high-sounding title, like

"Official Interrogator" or "Town Registrar." She asked, "And what is your occupation?"

I don't where they came from, but all of a sudden the words popped out of my mouth: "I'm a Research Associate in the field of Child Development and Human Relations," I said.

The clerk paused, pen frozen in midair. I repeated the title slowly: "I'm a Research Associate in the field of Child Development and Human Relations." The clerk wrote my pompous title in bold, black ink on the official questionnaire.

The clerk said, "Might I ask just what you do in your field?" I replied, "I have a continuing program of research in the laboratory and in the field. I'm working for my Masters (the whole family) and already have four credits (all daughters). Of course, the job is one of the most demanding in the humanities, and I often work fourteen hours a day. But the job is more challenging than most run-of-the-mill careers and the rewards are in satisfaction rather than just money."

There was an increasing note of respect in the clerk's voice. She completed the form, stood up, and personally ushered me to the door. As I drove into our driveway buoyed by my glamorous new career, I was greeted by three of my lab assistants—ages thirteen, seven, and three. And upstairs, I could hear our next experimental model (six months old) in the child development program, testing out a new vocal pattern.

I felt triumphant. I had scored a beat on bureaucracy. And I had gone down on the official records as someone more distinguished and indispensable to society than anyone else.

I was a mother.

47
Memorial Day

The famous ship, the Queen Mary, now sits at a dock in Long Beach, California and is enjoying life as an exclusive restaurant attraction after sailing for over a half a century on the high seas

The Queen Mary has a fabled history. Let me recall it. The ship was built in Scotland and launched in 1934. After Her Majesty Queen Mary presented her personal standard, it embarked on its maiden voyage on May 27, 1936, departing Southampton, England. It took only a record five days to reach New York. The Queen Mary has four propellers weighing thirty-five tons each, a 140-ton rudder and overall weighs 81,234 tons. In its glory days it carried nearly two thousand passengers serviced by a crew of over a thousand. It was *the* premier luxury liner of the time.

Something was to change all that, however. World War II broke out, and so the Queen Mary underwent a transformation. The ship became known as the "Grey Ghost" when it was camouflage-painted and its portholes blacked out. Because its four, 40,000-horsepower turbine steam engines could outrun German U-boats, it became a military transport. Servicing the war effort, it traveled more than 600,000 miles and carried over 800,000 troops. One historic journey to New York in May 1943 included passenger Winston Churchill and 5,000 German prisoners of war. Quite a history.

Is there something here for us to contemplate? Yes. When given the choice between becoming a museum for gawking curiosity seekers and being a ship on the high seas outrunning the enemy, bringing glory to the British crown, the Queen Mary opted for glory. And now once again, when the Queen Mary's use as both luxury liner and transport carrier is clearly no longer possible, she is creatively surviving as a floating restaurant attracting thousands of tourists every year and exposing them to her past, present, and future glory. She's no museum; she's earning her way in yet another way.

Why do I tell you this story? Because, for our purposes today, the story of the Queen Mary functions on three deep spiritual levels. First, on this Memorial Day weekend, it reminds us of all those men and women whose lives, like the Queen Mary, were changed when war broke out. Their placid everyday routines were dramatically impacted and turned upside down. Thousands of men and women were called to be, as it were, camouflage-painted into a hundred different jobs, campaigns, and service here and abroad.

With unified purpose, these men and women sailed the seas in high adventure and constant danger. They all knew that, like the mighty ship, they had their choice of selfishness or service. They chose service and many of them paid with their lives. And now, just as the Queen Mary sits at the dock as a reminder of its former glory, so we build our monuments, celebrate our holidays, and call up our memories to remind us of the dreadful glory earned on the battlefields of the world and of those who paid the price for it.

But, as I said, the story of the Queen Mary functions on a second level as well, a different, more personal one. It's a paradigm of what happens to us. Like that ship, we too start out great, so to speak. Then, as life goes on, we find that the unexpected comes along and we must keep on making adaptations. For example, we simply didn't bargain for our personal wars—sickness, depression, a divorce, a child on drugs, financial setback, loss, widowhood, the relentless ravages of time and aging—any more than the Queen Mary bargained for a global war, but there they are.

Suddenly, we have our choice: to forever keep looking back like a perennial Baby Jane, keep propping up our old persona like an aging movie star loading the makeup on a face that won't lie anymore. Or, like the Queen Mary, we learn to adapt to new circumstances, new challenges, to new stages in our lives. And to adapt creatively; that is, in a way that both serves others and makes us grow. Like, for example, Audrey Hepburn who, after her marketable looks wore out, became an advocate for poor children. So, again the story of the Queen Mary forces us to ask in life's changing circumstances, how can I grow now?

How can I serve now? How can I love now? What is God calling me to now? Not then, but now?

Finally, realize it or not, the Queen Mary story functions as a challenge. We are making our future now. While we must rightfully strive for immediate success in our chosen field, we must always, at the same time—it can't be recovered—be building for the future. Which is to say: as I work and live now, what kind of person am I turning into? If I am successful and am gaining fame and fortune—which I must let go of sooner or later—what enduring values have I embraced and nourished along the way?

Here's a true story that catches what I'm trying to say.

While at the park one day, a woman sat down next to a man on a bench near a playground. "That's my son over there," she said, pointing to a little boy in a red sweater who was gliding down the slide.

"He's a fine looking boy," the man said. "That's my son on the swing in the blue sweater." Then, looking at his watch, he called to his son. "What do you say we go, Todd?"

Todd pleaded, "Just five more minutes, Dad. Please? Just five more minutes." The man nodded and Todd continued to swing to his heart's content.

Minutes passed and the father stood and called again to his son. "Time to go now." Again Todd pleaded, "Five more minutes, Dad. Just five more minutes." The man smiled and said, "O.K."

"My, you certainly are a patient father," the woman responded.

The man smiled and then said, "My older son Tommy was killed by a drunk driver last year while he was riding his bike near here. I never spent much time with Tommy and now I'd give anything for just five more minutes with him. I've vowed not to make the same mistake with Todd. He thinks he has five more minutes to swing. The truth is, I get five more minutes to watch him play."

Catch my meaning? Like the Queen Mary, we are making our future now, and "now" can never be recaptured. Fame and fortune, career and corporation, are good goals but not the most important ones. When we are forced—*and we will be*—to let go and adapt to a new way of living and being, will we have built the resources and cherished the precious moments and people to find grace in the new moment, as well as the opportunity to love and grow in a new way?

Over and above our jobs, over and above our "image," which is so important today in a world without substance, over and above our fashion statements, this larger truth endures: "Every person who ever came into this world was sent into this world by God to do some special task. Every person is, as it has been put, a dream of God." That task need not be a task that is great as the world uses the word great. It may be to care for a child, to make someone else happy, to teach someone's mind, to cure someone's body, to bring sunshine into the lives of others across a counter or in an office, to make a home. To make a difference.

The Queen Mary never dreamed it would be anything but a playground for the rich and famous. But when war broke out and courage was called for and service demanded, it came through. We remember that, which is why we have memorial days. The Queen Mary didn't stay stuck in one category. A terrible war intruded but it responded to the moment. And so must we respond to new chapters in our lives. At the time, the Queen Mary, with its hyper-design and forward-looking engineering, didn't realize that it was also being built for future service in a way it didn't expect. So are we.

Let me sum it all up by fittingly recalling a war movie, Steven Spielberg's *Saving Private Ryan*, where a squadron of young soldiers, you recall, is sent on a mission to find one soldier behind enemy lines and bring him home. Most of the young men in the squadron, including the captain, die in the rescue attempt. As he lies dying, the captain's last words to Private Ryan are, "Earn this."

Many years later, Private Ryan, now an old man, visits the grave of his captain. As he kneels at the grave, he says, "Not a day goes by I don't think about what happened....And I just want you to know...I've tried. Tried to live my life the best I could. I hope that's enough. I didn't invent anything. I didn't cure any diseases. I worked a farm. I raised a family. I lived a life. I only hope, in your eyes at least, I earned what you did for me."

A good sentiment for us today on Memorial Day. A hoped-for sentiment for someone tomorrow who will remember us.

48
Fourth of July

I have two stories—both true—to tell you first. On January 13, 1982, an Air Florida flight crashed shortly after takeoff from Washington, D.C. and fell into the icy waters of the Potomac River. Some of you recall that incident. Lenny Skutnik was there and he saw the plane go down. He stood with the other spectators on the riverbank, watching a woman who had survived the crash and was struggling to swim in the cold water. Skutnik plunged into the river and rescued her.

Skutnik had never taken a life-saving course, but he saved the woman's life. He didn't use the proper form or technique when he swam to the woman's side, at least not as professional swim instructors would teach it. He may not have followed the Red Cross lifesaving manual in the method he used to grab the woman and bring her back to the safety of the shore. But he saved her.

My second story. An Italian fisherman named John Napoli was returning with his catch of fish one foggy morning. He piloted his boat beneath the Golden Gate Bridge, into San Francisco harbor. What he saw next horrified him. There were people everywhere in the water. A hospital ship, the Netherlands, had collided with an oil tanker. People were shouting, "Help me! Save me! I'm drowning!"

John Napoli carefully guided his fishing vessel to a cluster of drowning men. Quickly he began to pull them aboard one by one. Soon the small fishing boat was overcrowded. And then John Napoli made one of the hardest decisions of his life. He knew that the lives of those men were far more important than his small fortune of fish. Within minutes he dumped his entire cargo of 2000 pounds of fish, worth thousands of dollars, into the waters of San Francisco Bay. Then he pulled more than seventy people aboard his boat.

It's the Fourth of July week. These two stories set you up for my final story, fittingly enough, from the annals of war. And then we shall draw our conclusions.

It was an unforgettable photo. You know it well. The raising of the flag at Iwo Jima. In fact, if you had to pick ten photographs to tell the story of our country, this one featuring US soldiers lifting up an American flag would be one of them—even if it was a posed re-enactment of the real event.

Iwo Jima is a dot in the Pacific where the United States needed a landing strip for bombers striking Japan during World War II. Some 70,000 marines were sent to take it from a dug-in enemy. "The thing I'll remember forever," recounts retired Major General Fred Hayes, "was the courage and the guts of the kids...and these were young kids." They were kids but also heroes.

There are six flag-raisers in the photo. The four in the front are Ira Hayes, Franklin Sousley, John Bradley, and Harlon Block. The back two are Michael Strank and Rene Gagnon. Strank was hit by a mortar shortly after the photo was taken, and died. He is buried in Arlington cemetery. Block, who had enlisted in the Marine Corps with twelve of his teammates, was also killed by a mortar blast just hours after the flag-raising. Franklin Sousley died at age nineteen on Iwo Jima. Bradly, Hayes, and Gagnon survived and became national heroes within weeks.

What is most amazing is how ordinary each of these flawed heroes was. Mike Strank played the French horn and once slugged a baseball out of Points Stadium in Johnstown, Pennsylvania. Harlon Block was an outgoing daredevil with many friends at Weslaco High School in Texas. Franklin Sousley was a red-haired, freckled-face "Opie Taylor"-type kid raised on a tobacco farm in Kentucky. All that's left of him are a few pictures and two letters he wrote home to his widowed mother. In one he wrote, "Mother, you said you were sick. I want you to stay out of that field and look real pretty when I come home. You can grow a crop of tobacco every summer, but I sure as hell can't grow another mother like you."

Ira Hayes was a Pima Indian from Arizona who was told by his chief to be an "honorable warrior." But he had deep emotional problems with being dubbed a hero and with going on money-raising tours to promote the war effort. He felt he was no hero but rather, that his buddies who died on Iwo Jima were the real heroes. He went back to the reservation but the war and the searing memory of his fallen buddies had taken its toll on him. He turned to alcohol and he died at age thirty-two after a night of drinking.

Rene Gagnon was just a kid from Manchester, New Hampshire, who ended up being the youngest of the survivors. He was the one who carried the flag up Mount Suribachi. And John Bradly was a Navy Corpsman from Wisconsin who "just jumped in to lend a hand," as he put it. He was wounded in both legs and won the Navy Cross for heroism. He returned to his home in the Midwest, became a farmer and businessman, was married for forty-seven years, and had eight children.

So, we have three stories of ordinary people. At the time, Lenny Skutnik was only twenty-eight years old. He was a general office worker who had a wife and two children and lived in a rented house. An ordinary man. For John Napoli, the Italian fisherman, there was something more important to him than profits. He deliberately lost his profits in order to save people. An ordinary man. Then there was that handful of kids on Iwo Jima and a famous image of a flag-raising among the dead bodies of their comrades. Ordinary kids.

And here we contemplate and pray deep within ourselves, for remember this, my people. Freedom—spiritual freedom, personal freedom, national freedom—arises not from programs, not from training, not from manuals; but, as Jesus taught us, from the selfless heart, something we should pray for at this Mass.

When *we* move beyond our own personal concerns to save others; when we put people before profits; when we reach out—even if we have to pay for it with our lives—to raise the flag of decency and truth there is release, newness, spirit, freedom. True freedom.

This Fourth of July you can have all the patriotic speeches you want. You can wave the stars and stripes 'til the cows come home. You can march in parades 'til you drop, but freedom is always won on the one-to-one level of the daily small heroisms of ordinary people—like Lenny Skutnik, John Napoli, Ira, Franklin, John, Harlon, Michael, Rene, and us.

Don't forget *us*.

September 11, 2001

This date, when the World Trade Center in New York City was destroyed by terrorists and the Pentagon was partially destroyed and nearly three thousand innocent people, mostly young, lost their lives, will be forever remembered as a turning point in American history.

The twelve homilies that follow reflect the sense of shock and loss that followed these events. The first two are quite specific and local but since, alas, tragedy will always be with us in one form or another, the thrust and dynamics of these homilies may be helpful and so I have included them. I must add that, although very well received, some few found these first two homilies somewhat too graphic for the children in the congregation.

The remaining ten homilies were preached in the weeks and months that followed September 11, 2001. Although they reflect the aftermath of the tragedy, they can be used on other occasions.

49
America At War

For decades we have seen the horrors of war portrayed in the movies and on television. We have winced as whole villages were burned to the ground, the billowy smoke the only indication that men, women, and children once lived there. We have looked aghast at the continuous black plumes from the Nazi gas chambers, and sat in horror to watch the footage of the bombings of Britain, Poland, France, Germany, the Netherlands. Cities, towns, hamlets, great castles, museums, cathedrals—all up in smoke. In fascination we watched the death-dealing mushroom clouds rise over Japan. We checked out the photographs in *Life* magazine of the massive mounds of human skulls in the Cambodian killing fields.

And eventually we all began to watch those horrors with a certain detachment, even those who lost loved ones in the wars, as Hollywood turned carnage into entertainment and killings into box office, mass exterminations into discussion panels and unspeakable horrors into cash receipts. So we flipped the pages of *People* magazine to see what Madonna was doing. And, in a way, no wonder. All those things, those terrible, terrible unmentionable things, were "over there" in Europe and Africa and Asia and South America. We were never bombed. We were never invaded. Our skies never saw war smoke, war ash, explosions. Our cities were never wiped out. Our family members' body parts were never scattered among the debris.

So we tightened our belts, used our ration stamps, bought our bonds, mourned our dead soldiers who died "over there." But in our land, we were free of the personal horrors of war and could never quite resonate with the wild language and metaphors and desperate prose of our allies who walked stone-eyed and ash-dusted amid the half-houses and half-bodies of their neighbors.

That is, until this past Tuesday, when the unbelievable happened. America has been violated. America has been terrorized. In the very blue skies of a beautiful day there was sudden black smoke; and where there were two massive towers holding thousands of people—nothing. The halls of Congress were evacuated, leaders were led to bunkers, the Pentagon was crashed into by an airplane and set afire, airlines shut down, and an ocean of tears and dismay flooded the land as people simply couldn't believe what they were seeing on TV. The country was brought to a standstill. It was like a bad movie come true and we're still reeling from its impact. Terror had arrived at our doorstep and we will never be the same; our travel, our security, our innocence will never be the same.

Who among us will ever forget those images of the jets crashing the towers, the fireballs of flame, the towers themselves collapsing before our very eyes, the ash-covered streets, the people jumping to their deaths from high windows, the herds of people walking zombie-like over the bridges, away from suffocating smoke, the reports of brave people killed by falling concrete: 350 firefighters, 200 Port Authority employees, 40 police officers, 700 workers each from various financial companies, 266 people on the airplanes, nearly 200 at the Pentagon. And these—it's so hard to say—are only preliminary figures as New York has ordered more body bags for what is to come. These "preliminary figures" are, of course, people: our parents, spouses, children, lovers, relatives, friends with names, faces, and histories violently and terrifyingly cut short.

One lady, a former parishioner of mine whom I haven't seen in years, called to tell me that her son—her wonderful son—worked on the one-hundredth floor of the Twin Towers. The buildings are no more and she is sick at heart fearing that he is also no more. The people at the Armory, where they stack bodies and what's left of them, have asked her for his dental records and his comb to check the hairs for his DNA so they can measure them against body parts. Not her son's intact body, but whatever bits and pieces they can find. She waits in anguished hope as do thousands of others, pitifully holding up photographs of their loved ones pleading, "Have you seen my husband? Have you seen my daughter? Have you seen my father? Have you seen my niece? Have you seen my friend?"

They, and indeed some of us here today, being so close to New York and who have family and friends who worked in lower Manhattan fear, and rightly so, that the body count, as they continue to dig out from under the still-smoldering debris and continually collapsing buildings, will exceed that of the Civil War. Like the psalmist of old we cry out, "My heart is in anguish within me, the terrors of death have fallen upon me. Fear and trembling come upon me and horror overwhelms me. And I say 'O that I had wings like a dove! I would fly way and be at rest...'"(Ps 55:4–6). But there is no rest. At least, not for a while.

And the chips fell unevenly. A friend of mine who works at the Trade Center decided to take that day off to bring his son to pre-school orientation. He is still badly shaken. On the other hand, another friend's son just started work there last week and he's gone. Another who works on the eighth floor above the fire line escaped. Others did not. My niece and nephew who work and live near the Twin Towers, we finally learned, are safe but countless others are not. Loud lamentations, worthy of the ancient prophets, and funerals at every turn will be our daily companions for a while. We are a nation in shock and grief.

For beyond the excruciating destruction of this past Tuesday, and whose fallout we have yet to fully absorb and catalogue, the real deep-down pain is in the sudden and rude awareness that we are vulnerable. We are not immune from the physical, emotional, and mental rape of terrorism. We are not exempt from massive deaths. Alert as we are, we were not clever enough to prevent this. And, all of a sudden, seeing all of our old reliable grounds of image, wealth, and celebrity cataclysmically revealed for what they are, inadequate shadows, we are forced to look deeper and turn elsewhere for answers.

For other answers I suggest three places to turn. First of all, turn to God. It's a proper instinct. Even the TV stations that put out the most salacious fare and vulgar sitcoms, and which are fighting for the right to use even more explicit language, are saying, "We are suspending our programs in the light of these events. Our thoughts and prayers are with the victims." Our thoughts and prayers? Obviously, even secular TV stations don't have a language equal to the tragedy. When the chips are down, after they do the Ralph Kramden mumble, they too are forced to talk about prayer.

And even though some may not have been to church for a long time or are not even functional believers, I hope they continue to return because we all sense there's got to be something to explain all this, some way to straighten it all out, someone to appeal to, even, if you want, someone to shake a fist at, someone to humbly cry out to. Chastened by tragedy, we turn to God. Now, a people officially at war turn to God. Take heart from St. Paul who knew a thing or two about terror. He wrote:

> We are afflicted in every way, but not crushed; perplexed but not driven to despair; persecuted, but not forsaken; struck down but not destroyed; always carrying in the body the death of Jesus, so that the life of Jesus may also be made visible in our bodies. (2 Cor 4:8–10)

Second, we must turn to our loved ones near and far. Those heartrending cell phone calls, all ending with the soulful last words, "I love you"; the heavy realization that some died before we had a chance to tell them how much they meant to us; the fragility of life pointing out that we all have a limited time to love out loud—all remind us poignantly that indeed we must turn to love those nearest us. Now.

And to those far as well. By this I mean that we—no Christian, no American, no one here—could ever be a part of the shameful behavior of one group of Americans harassing another group of Americans. This intolerance is what started it all to begin with. By this I mean those who vent their anger at the six million American Arabs among us, forcing them to stay inside their homes, picketing their mosques, terrorizing their children, throwing Molotov cocktails at their meeting halls, firebombing their centers.

In this vigilante mentality none of us is safe if all Irish are drunks, all Jews are miserly, all French are promiscuous, all Poles are dumb, all Italian are Mafia. I thought St. Paul settled all that for us when he wrote, some two thousand years ago: "There is neither slave or free, Jew or Gentile, male or female for all have been made one in Christ."

Finally, we must turn to the bereaved. Comfort them. And here let me give you this advice: don't worry about words. As I said to one man who has lost a son, "I usually have no trouble with words. They come easily. But now I find that I'm at a loss at what to say to you in your pain. But if I can't offer words, what I can do is offer you two shoulders to cry on and my simple presence of being here with you in your time of grief." And he said, "That's enough." And it is.

Turn to God, turn to one another, turn to the bereaved.

My friends, we will, all of us together, eventually rebuild New York, our nation, our lives. We are a resilient people: remember we have defeated an oppressive monarch at our beginnings, come through an economic depression and two world wars, brought down the Berlin Wall and defeated communism.

We are a good people: witness the outpouring of help, the long lines of blood donors, the army of volunteers, the everyday heroes beyond counting. Hopefully, we will rebuild on love and justice. Here, today, in church,

in united prayer,

in shared grief,

in common hope,

in mutual support—

is a good place to begin.

50
A Week Later

One of the more poignant pictures from the Ground Zero tragedy is that of a firefighter, grimy and covered with soot, totally exhausted, kneeling against a fallen block with his head in his hands. He seems about to cry. And why not? Three hundred and fifty of his own fire-fighter buddies have been killed or are missing; 200 Port Authority employees, 40 police officers, 700 workers each from the various financial companies, 266 people on the airplanes, nearly 200 at the Pentagon, and more than 7000 still missing. How can one absorb a tragedy of such magnitude? And there were many like him: police-men, emergency personnel, volunteers—all overwhelmed by the emo-tional and physical magnitude of the tragedy.

This morning I want to focus on two groups in particular who are concerned with this tragedy. The first group I would like to mention is often forgotten and taken for granted. These are those carrying the heavy spiritual and emotional burdens of so many deaths, particular-ly the deaths of the young who were so prominent. I am talking about your priests—not just those like the Franciscan priest Father Mychal Judge, the fire department chaplain, who died heroically administer-ing the sacraments to the victims—but also those everyday priests you know who are dealing with untold numbers of their townspeople and parishioners affected by the tragedy.

And those numbers, which are legion, follow the commuter lines to and from New York. The geography of terrorism, if you will, is quite apparent in our Jersey communities. For example, Father Toborosky from Basking Ridge in North Jersey with ten dead parish members, and Monsignor. Masiello in Westfield with eight members, to Father Hughes from Rumson with a half-dozen members, Monsignor Rebeck from Holmdel with five members, Father Griswold from Colts Neck with seven members, Monsignor Lowrey from Red Bank with six, and Father Stas with five. So far.

Worst of all, there is Father John Dobrowsky from St. Mary's in Middletown, where I was once an associate pastor. Every day Father John looks teary-eyed and stunned at the seventy names—yes, seventy names—twenty-six members of his parish and forty-four relatives and friends of parishioners lost in last week's terrorist attack. That is, also, so far. How does a priest handle that?

Ruptured, there are gaping holes in our neighborhoods. The fabric of our communities has been torn apart as spouses and parents, Little League and football coaches, volunteers, card partners, car pool sharers, dinner companions, vacation friends, buddies, and neighbors are no more. The ripple effect is wide indeed. Some have to be buried. The priest will be there. Others, vaporized, have to be honored at memorial Masses. The priest will be there. Family members, neighbors, and friends who are in shock must be comforted around the clock. The priest will be there.

And it is the priests who are there every moment to listen: "He was my dad; he was my hero." "She was a good daughter, always considerate, our mainstay. What will we do now?" "We were friends. We grew up together. We've known each other since the fourth grade." And try to find words of comfort, if there are any to be found. And try not to break down, for there are others awaiting their ministrations.

The shortage of priests has nearly stretched these pastors physically, spiritually, and emotionally to the breaking point. They too, like their parishioners, also have to sit there in stony silence as the list of the missing is read aloud in their churches. And the list keeps getting longer and longer. Those with schools visit the classrooms to try to comfort the children. They ask how many know someone who has disappeared in the Trade Center, and most hands go up. And then, what do you say to children? How do you maintain control in front of those innocent, searching eyes? They tirelessly counsel people late into the night. The phone keeps ringing. It's been non-stop for the priests. I just wanted to remind you of that.

What is so hard, as I've indicated, is that the vast majority of the victims are so young, in their twenties, thirties, and forties. And their peers are stunned. Let me share, if I may, my own personal encounter. I just buried a young man I knew as a lad growing up, twenty-six-year-old Swede Chevalier. Miraculously, his intact but charred body from one of the towers was identified. The family asked me to preside at the funeral, and I did. To encourage them, somewhere in my homily, I reminded them of St. Paul's words:

> We are afflicted in every way, but not crushed; perplexed but not driven to despair; persecuted, but not forsaken; struck down but not destroyed; always carrying in the body the death of Jesus, so that the life of Jesus may also be made visible in our bodies. (2 Cor 4:8–10)

"Struck down but not destroyed." These words came home in a most unusual way. Let me tell you about it. Several nights before the funeral, Elaine, the boy's mother, had a vivid dream. She revealed that there were three figures in that dream: first, there was her son Swede, twenty-six-year-old Swede, looking quite happy. Then there was an archangel at his side. It is very significant who the archangel was. It wasn't Gabriel, the announcer, or Michael, the warrior. It was Raphael, the protector and guide of young men. Then, last but not least, their dog, Holly, was in the dream, a yellow lab who had died a few months before.

Thus, her dream as she told it to me. She had no notion, but what she described was right out of the Bible, the Book of Tobit, which is the story of a good but fussy and self-righteous father who sends his son, Tobias, to seek his fortune and a bride. Tobit, the father, is worried that his son, the same age as Swede, is inexperienced and wishes he had a guide to go with him. Lo and behold, in answer to his prayers, a certain man, who passes himself off as Azariah but who is really the archangel Raphael in disguise, comes and offers his services, promising that he will be with, protect, guide, and bring to safety Tobit's son. Which, by the end of the story, he does. And Tobias' dog, says the Bible, ran out of the house and joined them.

There they are, the three figures in the mother's dream: the family dog, an archangel whose speciality is young men, and a happy son. Quite a biblical story. Quite a peaceful sight. Quite a significant dream. Quite a sign from God that all is well, that, in St. Paul's words, Swede, like so many others, was struck down by terrorist madness but not destroyed.

I told the people in church her dream. And then I said to them,

Remember Swede. Remember him as your son: handsome, confident, hardworking, honest. Remember him as your blood brother. Remember him as your fraternity brother. Remember him as your best friend. Remember him as one who made a difference. Remember him as a good listener, a gentle person, a witty young man. Finally, remember him, not in the hell of terrorist fire—that was only momentary—but as he is, in the heaven of peace and joy, with his angelic guide and his faithful dog.

Parenthetically, I had to add, that a dog should be in heaven is, of course, no surprise to dog-owners; they are more surprised that people are there. But that's another story.

Not unexpectedly, there were a lot of young people in church, mostly all in their twenties. They were numb, I could tell, even as they cried and hugged each other. And they are the second group I want to talk about. There is nothing—nothing—in their young experience to prepare them for this. They have been protected all their lives. They have been raised in affluence and privilege. They take their spring breaks in the tropical islands. For them the Persian Gulf War is something that happened in elementary school, the Korean and Vietnam wars are but a chapter in a textbook, and World War II is the stuff of blockbuster movies, bestsellers, and an HBO series.

They have never known war and scattered bodies. They have always known peace. They have never met death, except for the remote deaths of their grandparents. And certainly, they don't die. Not when you're twenty or thirty years old. Until twelve days ago. How could it be? I could see it in their eyes. So, as I concluded my homily, I spoke specifically to them as I now speak to you, offering the same message. I said,

I see a lot of young people here, each with your own personal memories and stories about Swede. Many of you, I suspect, have come a distance. How fine, how decent, how noble of you. You buoy my faith in the next generation. I thank you for that.

But, as I end, I want to charge you with something. I want to challenge you to gradually move beyond your personal grief and momentary sorrow. I want you to take this life, what you knew and loved of Swede, and use it to motivate yourselves to become more than you think, more than would have been without him. I pray that you will not have your lives shortened but live them out to their fullest allotted years and when you are old, I want you to look back on this sorrowful day as an event that made a difference to you.

You may remember that in Steven Spielberg's movie, *Saving Private Ryan*, a squadron of young soldiers is sent on a mission to find one soldier behind enemy lines and bring him home. Most of the young men in the squadron, including the captain, die in the rescue attempt. As he lies dying, the captain's last words to Private Ryan are, "Earn this."

Many years later, Private Ryan, now an old man, visits the grave of his captain. As he kneels at the grave, he says, "Not a day goes by I don't think about what happened....And I just want you to know...I've tried. Tried to live my life the best I could. I hope that's enough. I didn't invent anything. I didn't cure any diseases. I worked a farm. I raised a family. I lived a life. I only hope, in your eyes at least, I earned what you did for me."

Young men and women, the best tribute you can give your friend is to earn what he has meant to you.

And so now I say the same to you. Earn what the deaths of so many have meant to you. Give support to the young. And say a prayer for your priests.

51
Faith: Coming Home

Twenty-seventh Sunday in Ordinary Time, Cycle C
Luke 17:5-10

As you know, the churches were overflowing on the Sunday following the World Trade Center disaster. People came in great numbers, with shaken lives and shattered hopes, praying anxiously the prayer of the apostles in today's gospel: "Increase our faith." It was an understandable and earnest request, and a distressed and stunned people were right to make it.

But I don't think they realized what they were really praying for, that their request wasn't primarily what it sounded like on the surface. Yes, of course, they would like to have a firmer faith in God, that is, believe God exists even though there are as many good reasons to believe God doesn't exist—such as the loss of all those innocent lives. (At certain times in their lives, most people waver between the two.)

But I think the issue goes beyond the mere question of God's existence. I think that when people pray, "Increase my faith," deep down, they subconsciously mean, "Give me a sense of home." For faith, when you come right down to it, means home—home because there, more than anywhere else, we crave to experience two things. Those two essential things are care and comfort.

A case in point. In last weekend's Sunday New York *Times* (September 30, 2001), there was a long article on the singles' scene after the World Trade Center tragedy. It starts off with the story of a young single woman, once happy to be single, living unencumbered the full cultural and social life of the city, suddenly having second thoughts. The article reports, "In the aftermath of September 11, like so many single men and women, she has re-examined the meaning of being uncoupled." The young woman is quoted as saying, "[The disaster] made me realize for the first time in my life that I was alone....I've always loved being single, but during the crisis, I hated it." She realized that in this time of terrible trauma, she desperately needed someone to care for her, someone to comfort her.

Another single said, "I'm a serial dater. I love dating. I'd go out on maybe three dates a week." But in the wake of recent events, this woman said she's had less interest in sitting at a dinner table with someone she doesn't know, only to discover that his favorite Godfather movie was Part III. "I have less time for the superficialities," she said. "This has made me understand the value of belonging to someone. Feeling your own despair was just too much to bear."

Some went to a friend's house for care and comfort so as not to be alone. As one head of a matchmaking company that has seen a jump in business observed, "This is a wake-up call; people are asking themselves, 'Am I where I want to be?'" For some swinging bachelors, marriage is starting to look good. One-night stands don't seem to cut it. There has to be a stable person in your life to give care and comfort in good times and in bad. Some singles literally went back to their parents' home during the tragedy because "home" represented the one stable thing in a shifting world, a place where they could get care and comfort.

The obvious message of the article is that, in times of tragedy, the human need to connect with someone is enormously powerful. That's why people went to church. Even those long absent came back because they felt a need for larger home, a need to connect with faith people, not their usual secular acquaintances. One lady I know angrily left the church years ago, after her husband left her for someone else. Over the years she got married again, and flirted with one religion or another, finally declaring herself independent. But the Sunday after September 11, she was back in her old church, with tears streaming down her cheeks. All she simply said was, "I needed to come home again."

I submit that "home again" is what faith is all about. It is where those stable, fundamental human needs for care and comfort are met, where the cry, "increase my faith," means, in reality, increase my belief that there is someone who will never tire in caring for me, never cease to comfort me, someone who is home to me.

But why do I keep coming back to care and comfort as the ingredients of faith? Because care implies meaning. It translates this way: care for me because I mean something. My life has meaning. What I do and suffer have meaning. What happens to me has meaning even though I don't understand what's going on. That I exist at all has meaning. In a word, caring for me tells me that I count. And I want to count, I need to count. I'm not an insect among several million others, here today and stepped on tomorrow. Care validates me as a unique human being; it validates all that I stand for. So we are praying, "Care for me and my lost ones. Although their lives have been cut so short, they counted for me. Make them count for you." That's why care is so important.

And comfort implies worth. If you comfort me that says I am worthy of your notice. I am worthy of your caress. I am worthy of your lap, your hug, your soothing words. Beneath all my limitations and stupidities and sins and the dumb things I've done, I am worthy. I am worthy; comfort tells me that. So comfort me now as I tremble in my fears, as I mourn my loved ones, family members or people I knew. They too were worthy. And that, I think, is essentially what brought people back home to church. In their stress and shock they may have thought they were looking for faith, but what they were really looking for was faith as an increased awareness of care and comfort, of meaning and worth. So they came home to find it.

By their presence at church, they were saying, in so many ways, "Increase my instinct that ultimately there is someone who deeply and sincerely, without stint, cares for me and my friends; that there is someone who comforts me in my perplexity and sorrow just because I am me, someone who will make it 'all right.' And that someone, that Someone who I want to believe gives care and comfort unconditionally, is written with a large capital 'S.' That is why I came home to church."

That is the faith they were seeking. Not an intellectual faith in some remote deity, but a heartfelt, homebound faith in the kind of God who could say, "Come to me all of you who labor and are burdened and I will refresh you. Take my yoke upon you for I am meek and humble of heart and you will find rest." "Not one sparrow falls without your Father knowing it. You are worth more than many sparrows."

Press care and comfort together and you get faith. Press faith and home together and you get church. That's what the singles were seeking. That's what all the people who flocked to church were seeking. When they prayed, like the apostles, "Increase my faith," they were really praying, "Increase my sense that, in all this unspeakable tragedy and loss, in all this horror and lingering pain, care and comfort will be the last words."

If they were familiar with St. Paul they might have mouthed his famous words when he was searching for care and comfort:

Who will separate us from the love of Christ? Trial or distress or persecution or hunger or nakedness or danger or the sword? As Scripture says, "We are being slain all the day long." Yet in all this, we are more than conquerors because of him who loved us. For I am certain that neither death nor life, neither angels or principalities, neither the present or the future, nor powers nor height nor depth nor any other creature will be able to separate us from the love of God that comes to us in Christ Jesus our Lord.

That's what they were after. Let me close with a modern version of Paul's words. It's a true story from a young man who writes:

The locker room was silent as a tomb as my hockey teammates and I peeled off our gear. We'd lost the game 12-0. I was the goalie. How could I have let the other team score twelve goals? I was totally disgusted with myself. Leaving the locker room, I faced the gauntlet of parents and friends lining the hall. I couldn't look any of them in the eye.

Then I felt a hand on my shoulder. It was the mother of a teammate. "Good game," she said. "No it wasn't," I replied. "We lost." She took me by the shoulders and looked me straight in the eye. "Listen, Jay, I know you feel terrible right now. But I want to tell you what Tim Wakefield, a Red Sox pitcher, said once when his team had just gotten crushed by the Giants. He said his parents always told him, 'No matter what happens, three things are for sure. Tomorrow, God will still love you, we will still love you, and the sun will rise again.' Why don't you go on home and think about that."

I can't say her words took away all the sting, but it did put our defeat in perspective. My parents tried to comfort me in the car on the way home. Before bed, I knelt and said a prayer. In the morning, I woke to bright sunlight streaming in my window. I was home.

I hope that is the meaning you find here: that those of you who come all the time will stay; that those of you who have returned will stay. This is your home.

52

Cured on the Way

Twenty-eighth Sunday in Ordinary Time, Cycle C
Luke 17:11–19

This is a beloved and familiar gospel, this oft-told story of the ten lepers. But I want to invite you to see it in a new light. I want to suggest to you this morning that this timely gospel has something profound to say to us, especially at this moment in our history. And it does so in three ways, for it's a gospel that speaks of loss, of time, and of gratitude. Let's examine each of these ways.

First, concerning loss. I don't know how these lepers contracted it, but leprosy was common enough in those days. Whatever the cause, the disease represented a terrible loss in their lives. Loss of health, mobility, livelihood, and perhaps worst of all, the loss of community. For they were now cut off, segregated from the rest of society. Shunned. Pariahs.

These lepers of our story represent any one of us with loss in our lives: loss of health, loss of a job, loss of a marriage, loss of trust, loss of dignity, loss of self-esteem, and, especially these days, the loss of loved ones such as those who died in the World Trade Center disaster. Lately, we can also add the loss of security as the fear of bombs and bacteria grips us. Yes, we know loss.

Second, this gospel speaks of time. This is most intriguing, most significant. Recall the gospel text: "Jesus, Master, have pity on us!" And when Jesus saw them, he said, "Go show yourselves to the priests." And as they were going they were cleansed. Did you notice it? As they were going they were cleansed. The weren't healed instantly on the spot; they were healed later on, on the way.

I wonder when they first began to notice the healing? How far they had gotten? Did they simply at one point notice that the skin had cleared up, the spots had disappeared? Was it sudden or was it gradual? I don't know. All I do know is that they were cured, not right away, but on the way, on their life journey. All I do know is that in fact this is how it happens for most of us.

Oh yes, some people with the leprosy of depression or sadness, the loss of their loved ones, the drying up of faith, the slavery of addiction to drugs or alcohol or sex, at their wits' end over a sick or wayward or difficult child—some, I say, cry out, "Jesus, Master, have pity on us!" And he does! Right away. They find immediate healing. Some do. Some few. Very few. But not most of us, isn't that true? Most of us, I am afraid, continue to plod on with our lives like those lepers, tread our life's journey, deeply wounded, crying out again and again, "Jesus, Master, have pity on us!" until we're tired of it, until we wonder if anyone is listening, until we wonder if we'll ever find peace.

But, emboldened by this gospel, I want to offer this hope, the promise the gospel holds out to you; that, almost unconsciously, quite imperceptibly along the way, on your journey, just like these lepers, healing does happen, will happen, in strange and different ways.

I think, for example, about a young man named David who knew loss from day one. Dave's mother was an alcoholic. Not only did her condition cause her to neglect her children, she also was cruel and abusive while drunk. She beat and burned Dave, and forced him to live in their cold, dark, dirty garage. She treated him like a slave, and only fed him when he could perform his endless list of chores to her satisfaction. That didn't happen often. It was a rare day when Dave came to school clean, or dressed in adequate clothing. And when his second-grade teacher tried to intervene on Dave's behalf, his mother chose to punish him by changing his name to "It." She never called him anything else but "It," and she forbade the other children from calling him by name. Could anyone suffer more loss, and at such an early age?

Dave remembers the start of his healing with total clarity. He was in the fifth grade. A few courageous teachers, the principal, and the school nurse convinced the child protective services to step in and remove Dave from his home. That day, as the authorities came to take him to his new life, the whole staff of Dave's school lined up to give him a hug. He had never been hugged before. He had never known love like that before, and he didn't know if he ever would again.

Twenty years later, Dave Pelzer stood before his old teachers at Thomas Edison Elementary School to thank them for what they did. Today, Dave Pelzer is a speaker who spreads his message of inspiration and hope to thousands of people. He was in fact honored with the Outstanding Young Person of the World award. He was also chosen to carry the torch in one stretch of the Olympic Torch Relay. He has risen above the horror and pain of his abusive childhood, his painful losses, to make a success out of his life. But one thing is sure. It didn't happen all at once. It took time to go from an abusive childhood to a caring adult. He was healed along the way and out of his loss found a gain.

On Sunday, March 18, 1979, in Aspen, Colorado, a twin-engine light plane crashed shortly after takeoff. At that moment, Mrs. Stephanie Ambrose May lost her husband, John Edward, her son, David Edward, her daughter, Karla Emily, and her son-in-law, Richard Owen Snyder. Mrs. May kept a diary for the next two months in which she recorded her feelings, her emotions. I want to read an excerpt for you, her entries for May 7 and 8:

> My burden is heavy, but I don't walk alone. My pain is unrelenting, but I thank God for every moment that he blessed me with. I pray that my life will be used for his glory, that I might carry my burden with Christian dignity, and that out of my devastation, may his kingdom become apparent to someone lost and in pain. I must climb to a different plane and search for a different life. I cannot replace or compare my loss. It is my loss. I am not strong. I am not brave. I am a Christian with a burden to carry and a message to share. I have been severely tested, but my faith has survived....I have walked in hell, but now I walk with God in peace. John Edward, David, Karla, and Richard are in God's hands. I am in God's arms and his love surrounds me. This rose will bloom again.

Indeed it will. In time.

These stories tell us that over time healing takes place. The scars will always remain. There will always be bad moments when we break down and cry over our losses but the difference is that these losses will no longer be the center of our lives. They will render us wounded heal-ers bent on the good we can do, which arises out of our tragedies. Like the mothers who lost children to drunken drivers: who can know the loss of a child except those who have been there? But some have got-ten together, as you know, and formed MADD, Mothers Against Drunk Driving, to work hard to see that other mothers do not suffer their loss. Will they ever forget their children? No. But that grief is no longer central: saving other lives now is. That's what I mean. It will take time. Healing will happen along the way, bringing us to another, deeper stage of our lives.

Finally, this gospel presents us with an opportunity for gratitude. The lepers came back—at least one did—to give thanks. My message is that if all goes well on the spiritual journey, we will have learned to give thanks from the ashes of our losses: thanks for the acceptance, the forgiveness, the patience, and the growth we have experienced as a result of these losses.

And, let me add, thanks can arise from the ashes of our current loss-es. Here I'm thinking of all those recently interviewed on TV who, frightened and burdened with a new sense of vulnerability, are admit-ting that they are taking a second look at their marriages, spouses, children, family, friends, and their religious lives. And they are sud-denly realizing not only how precious and important these are but also how foolish they have been to have neglected the things that real-ly matter. They're saying "thanks" for the chance to change their lifestyles. Yes, we can learn to give thanks for our losses.

In this regard, let me close with a powerful cinematic scene.

Nearly thirty years ago, you might recall, there was a great movie called *Little Big Man*, starring Dustin Hoffman. Toward the end of that movie, there is a very touching scene in which an Indian named Old Lodge Skins, who has lost his physical health, is going blind. He knows he is dying, and he begins to pray to God. This is what he prays: "O Lord God, I thank you for having made me a human being, I thank you for giving me life and for giving me eyes to see and enjoy your world. But most of all, Lord, I thank you for my sickness and my blindness because I have learned more from these than from my health and from my sight."

And that, I think, would be the ultimate reason why we would show gratitude for our losses and what they did for us.

So, this familiar gospel of the ten lepers is quite contemporary, isn't it? It talks about loss, about time, and about gratitude. We just have to walk through the steps. And eventually we will. Healing will come but, like the gospel, not now but "on the way."

The thing to learn from this gospel is that there are new and different opportunities ahead: new charities beyond the tears, new hope beyond the losses, new spiritual growth beyond the despair. And when we find them, as we shall, then like the leper and Old Lodge Skins, we shall give thanks.

53

Testimony Among the Ruins

Thirty-third Sunday in Ordinary Time, Cycle C
Luke 21:5–19

Theme: testimony in hard times

Nation will rise against nation, and kingdom against kingdom. There will be powerful earthquakes, famines and plagues from place to place, and awesome sights and mighty signs will come from the sky.

Such unnerving words from today's gospel. In the past, to be truthful, we considered such words fringe talk from another age for people who lived on the constant edge of war, famine, disease, and poverty in hovels, tents, and caves in other parts of the uncivilized world. No need to pay attention to the nut brigade who run around with signs saying the end is near or those insignificant people in strange lands, wearing strange clothes and funny hats and speaking in strange languages.

Until now. Now the words are uncomfortably close, uncomfortably true, uncomfortably ours. Nation *is* rising against nation as terrorists level the mighty buildings of our nation's greatest city and strike at the military headquarters in our capital. Famine stalks Rwanda and Sierra Leone; anthrax has already taken six lives and infected more than thirty others as it creeps toward us all from Trenton to Washington and New York. The threat of smallpox worries us. There are awesome sights in the sky as our planes rain down bombs on Afghanistan and the Afghanis return the fire, while at home, planes fall to earth. Suddenly, the apocalyptic scenario of the gospel is brought home.

Suddenly, it's all too true, all too real, all too *here*. And here, once again, stands Jesus. And what does he say in the midst of all of this? Go back to the gospel. He says that we will be seized by loss, persecuted by terror, laid low by infection, and cowered by fear. But, he says, carefully and soberly, "It will lead to your giving testimony," his exact words in today's gospel. "It will lead to your giving testimony."

Indeed, Jesus is right. If we are to survive, it is time to use our Christian lives to give testimony—testimony that will cost us, to be sure. This testimony demands that we have a wider view of the world, of our brothers and sisters who are kept out of sight, out of mind, by a consumerist system which, like the casinos that have neither clocks nor windows, screens out the cry of the poor and keeps us focused on our own narcissistic wants.

For example, take oil, a subject much on the national mind. As Christians, we must reflect on the fact that, although Americans make up only four percent of the world's population, we use twenty-five percent of the world's oil supply—that's burning nineteen million barrels of oil a day—with nineteen percent of that oil being used for our cars and SUVs. As you know, we get that oil from Saudi Arabia with whom we have contracted billions of dollars worth of lucrative arms sales. But we also know that Saudi Arabia finances Osama bin Laden's network—the network that killed so many of our loved ones at the Twin Towers and the Pentagon—and that it finances other radical Islamic organizations. We know Saudi Arabia sends money to the Taliban, and that it has a repressive monarchy in power which denies basic human rights to its people.

Knowing all this, we turn the other way. Why? Because our lifestyles demand oil—and I haven't even mentioned the thirty million gallons that are spilled annually in this country, greatly affecting wildlife, land, and water. We have become addicted to oil. Jesus asks: is it time to give testimony by changing our lifestyles of waste and luxury? Then, too, you may have seen the United Nations report issued just two weeks ago which mentioned things I never think of, or like to hear, for that matter. It said that, right now, worldwide, two billion people lack sufficient food and water. And while the world's wealth totals some $30 trillion, half the world lives on $2 a day or less. I find that hard to comprehend, but it's true.

In another recent report that disturbs me, UNICEF says that malnutrition kills between six and seven million children every year, making malnutrition more lethal than any disease since the bubonic plague; and, in what further surprised me, UNICEF estimates that more than thirteen million children right here in the United States—one out of four children under the age of twelve—cannot get enough to eat. It's hard listening to those figures and then reading another survey issued last month which shows that the number of obese American adults has now increased to forty million, and that the number of American children who are obese has increased even more so. Something's wrong. Millions of children are dying of starvation and we're going to fat farms.

There's more, I'm afraid. We have homes and beds to sleep in, but right now there are an estimated twenty-seven million refugees worldwide, displaced from their homelands, many living in United Nations camps. That bit of news comes while we keep vying to see who can build a bigger house than Bill Gates's house. Again, the United Nations statistics forcefully remind us that we Americans use nearly one third of the earth's total resources and produce almost half of its hazardous waste. An average North American consumes five times as much as an average Mexican, ten times as much as an average Chinese, and thirty times as much as the average person in India. The world's average per capita consumption of water is 7,700 cubic meters a year. In desert places like Jordan it is 200 cubic meters; in America, the average consumption of water is 110,000 cubic meters per year. Our yearly waste alone would fill a convoy of garbage trucks long enough to wrap around the earth six times. Jesus is clearly asking, is it time to give testimony by at least being aware of the world's hungry, and to scale back our overfed lifestyles?

I don't know about you, but I don't particularly like hearing all this. It's too challenging and pointed and makes me, with my comfortable lifestyle, feel uneasy. But Jesus is like that, forcing us to see Lazarus outside the walls of our isolated lives. The irony is, you know, that we are an enormously good and generous people. Look, for example, at what the Marshall Plan did to rehabilitate a battered Europe after World War II. Look at the awesome heroism, the tremendous outpouring of care and concern for the victims of the World Trade Center disaster. As I said, we are an extraordinarily open, giving, and sensitive people. We have proven that. I think the gospel is saying that we just need to be reawakened, look around us in a wider sweep, and act.

Thus this war we're engaged in right now, like this gospel itself, becomes a moral wake-up call. It says that we can no longer live in a national casino and not see the needs of people in other countries which, unmet, are the seeding ground of envy, hate, revolution, and violence. Those are the words of the Holy Father. And our own United States bishops, who overwhelmingly support the right of the United States to use military force against international terrorism, also said that our response must be part of a broader foreign policy that alleviates poverty, stops human rights abuses, and helps end violence; that we still need to address the conditions of poverty and injustice that are exploited by terrorists. All this basically says that we can no longer be isolationist but need to deal with other nations for reasons other than self-serving ends or bottom-line profit. We need a global view of mercy and justice that goes with our label as Catholics, a word that means an ecumenical, worldwide people of Jesus.

We need to have a deep sense of being connected to all human beings and to the environment, a sense of how our lifestyles affect the planet and the world. We must acquire a new urgency that says our wonderful gifts must be shared with many others; our freedoms must become globally commonplace; our housing, food, and clothing must be scaled down so that the poor and needy of the world may share in some of our bounty. Our charity, our tithing, must be more widespread and deliberate. Most of all, we must let go of the accepted symbols of success measured by consumption and waste. Simply put, we must live more simply. This gospel is saying that this is the testimony we must give: our priorities must be changed, our lifestyles reordered, our values realigned according to the gospel, and our sensitivity deepened to other people on the planet.

"It will lead to your giving testimony," said Jesus—"it" being trauma, terrorism, fear, war, and all the rest of what we're going through right now. These are nervous times, apocalyptic times, but listen to Jesus' hopeful warning. It's not a time to wallow in fright. It's not a time to retreat. But it *is* a time to give testimony.

54

Remember Me

Feast of Christ the King, Cycle C
Luke 23:35–43

Charlie Brown is leaning against a tree, talking to Lucy. She asks, "What do you think security is, Charlie Brown?" Charlie answers, "Security is sleeping in the back seat of a car when you're a little kid, and you've been somewhere with your mom and dad, and it's night. You don't have to worry about anything. Your mom and dad are in the front seat and they're doing all the worrying. They take care of everything." Lucy smiles and says, "That's real neat." Charlie Brown, who never seems to know when to stop, gets a serious look on his face and says, "But it doesn't last. Suddenly you're grown up and it can never be that way again. Suddenly, it's all over, and you'll never get to sleep in the back seat again. Never!" Lucy gets a frightened look on her face and asks, "Never?" And Charlie Brown replies, "Never!" As they stand there, sensing the terrible loneliness, Lucy reaches over and says, "Hold my hand, Charlie Brown."

A bittersweet comic strip that registers so true today. We'll never get to sleep in the back seat anymore. Never. Our old securities have been shattered. War abroad with a difficult enemy, war at home with biological terror stalking our steps, the resurrected fear of nuclear war, checkpoints, baggage searches, latex gloves, air marshals, long lines. We are learning the uncomfortable stance of always looking over our shoulders. We've suddenly become a nation of Lucys: "Hold my hand, Charlie Brown."

The thief on the cross must have felt this way. The clouds were darkening. Blood had already been spilled. The crowd was ugly. There was nowhere to turn. The old securities were gone. There was, however, someone in the middle of the crucified men who seemed, in his terrible suffering, to have a center, a grace, a majesty. The thief wanted, in his despair and fright and loneliness, to reach out to him, pleading like a wounded Lucy, "Hold my hand, Jesus." But, of course, fixed to the cross, he could not. So he did the next best thing. He turned to his fellow prisoner and cried out from the depths of his black heart, "Jesus, remember me...." And Jesus said he would.

This feast of Christ the King is grounded in those words. Strip away all the elegant metaphors, all the medieval trappings, all the golden crowns and, beneath it all, behind this royal feast, is a man reigning from the cross who said he would remember us. But, like the Good Thief, we have to ask. Like the Good Thief we have to first realize that the jig is up, that our old certainties of stocks and bonds, insurance and medical plans, big cars and big spending, rotating spouses and competitive consumption no longer hold—if they ever did. Our salvation is elsewhere. And in that admission, in that moment of truth dawning on us all as we face stressful times, we recognize what really counts, *who* really counts, and we cry out, "Jesus, remember me."

That cry is a recognition of Jesus' kingship, his amazing love that can overcome all things, even death: "This day you will be alive with me in paradise." That cry, which we collectively make on this feast, is grounded in hope. That's why, I think, especially these days, we are drawn back, again and again, to the throne of Calvary, to this unsightly king of ours, because, repentant and chastened, we need to hold his hand or at least whisper, "Remember me."

When I say this I am thinking of W. P. Kinsella, the author behind that terrific movie *Field of Dreams*, one of my favorites. Well, over the last ten years he has made a few pilgrimages to the baseball diamond constructed for the film. He says that he is always amazed to still find a constant flow of visitors. He writes:

Each time it hits me: this is a truly happy place. The visitors seem to put all their dark impulses aside when they get there. I found out about an estranged son who drove from Denver to New Jersey to reconcile with his father, then brought him to the field so they could share a game of catch.

There are love stories, too. One couple from New York came to the field to get married, and they've returned to celebrate their anniversaries. I'm still trying to grasp all this. Maybe this place tells us something about pilgrimage. Maybe these places we visit are ways to get at something that's not really concrete at all, but a place inside ourselves. We need to fill a void, to counter a loss, to seek through outward manifestation some inner peace that's lacking. Pilgrims come to the Field of Dreams in search of wonder, innocence, simplicity, a respite from the chaos in their lives.

I suggest that Calvary is our field of dreams, and that this feast of Christ the King is a way of reminding us we ought to be paying homage to the one whose mercy is wide, whose forgiveness is legendary, whose love transcends time and terror. This feast takes us back to Calvary and to three men on a cross. One dribbles into despair, one talks to God, and one turns in hope from his cross to that man in the middle and wants to hold his hand.

So too today. Some are dribbling away their lives in fear and despair during these scary times. But others, as all Jesus' followers should, talk to God in hope from their crosses, being sorry for their sins, promising to live better lives, and calling up the humility to ask Jesus to hold their hands—or at least to remember them.

The intent of this feast is to reassure us that Christ is in charge, Christ *is* king, Christ *will* remember us; that Christ, among the terror and the tears, *will* have the last word and make good the final promise. And that final promise is paradise.

55

"Go, Thief!"

First Sunday of Advent, Cycle A
Matthew 24:37–44

Theme: setting priorities

One will be taken and the other one will be left....you do not know on what day your Lord is coming....if the owner of the house had known in what part of the night the thief was coming, he would have stayed awake.

Jesus uses strange and unsettling metaphors in today's rather frightening gospel. You know, about one being snatched away, the other remaining. And in trying to convey the suddenness of all this snatching, he even goes so far as to compare God to a thief. God, he says, like a thief, breaks in unexpectedly. His intent, no doubt about it, is to steal. What can Jesus possibly mean by such a bizarre comparison? If God is an opportune thief, then what does God go about stealing? Let me share three stories that answer that question.

A woman in my former parish called me one day crying so hard I could hardly understand her. I eventually made out her tragic words, "I've been robbed! Someone has come in and stolen all of my family heirlooms! The silver, the china! All the things that my mother accumulated and gave to me. Gone!" I rushed over to her house, to find her overcome with grief. I knew how much these things meant to her, how she treasured them, was proud of them, lovingly recalled them as an inheritance from her parents. "This thing could kill her," said one of the parishioners who knew the woman. I was worried about her.

And yet, about six months later, we were talking, and I was shocked to hear her say, "In one sense the burglary was one of the best things that has happened to me. I didn't realize it, but I had become tied down to those things. I was afraid to leave the house for fear this might happen. I spent half my day polishing that silver, keeping up all that old china. That was really stupid when you think about it. Life ought to be more. I thought I would die after the burglary. But I've come to the conclusion that I may be better off without all that stuff." And when I heard her words I began to get an insight into today's gospel that I never understood before and I began to realize that Jesus' metaphor was not so strange after all. Clearly God had broken into that lady's home and stolen her possessions which God knew had slowly wound up possessing her.

Though initially traumatized, now she is free to live life more fully and piously.

My second story is similar and strikes the same note. It's about the great Russian novelist, Fyodor Dostoevsky, who recounted the time he was arrested by the czar and sentenced to die. Now, the czar used to play a horribly sadistic psychological trick on people who rebelled against his regime by blindfolding them and standing them in front of a firing squad. They heard gunshots go off but felt nothing, then slowly realized the guns were loaded with blanks. But the emotional trauma that went with the process of dying, without actually experiencing death, had, as you can imagine, a transforming effect on people.

It certainly had an incredible effect on Dostoevsky. He wrote about waking up the morning of his mock execution with the full assurance that this would be the last day of his life. As he ate his last meal, he savored every bite. Every breath of air he took was taken with an awareness of how precious it was. Every face he saw that day he studied with intensity. He wanted every experience etched on his mind.

As they marched him into the courtyard, he felt the sun beating down on him and he appreciated the warmth of the sun as never before. Everything around him seemed to have a magical quality to it. He was seeing the world as he had never been able to see it before. All his senses were heightened. He was fully alive!

After his captors removed his blindfold and he realized he had not been shot, everything about him changed. He became grateful to people he had previously hated. He became thankful for everything about life, but especially for life itself. Dostoevsky claims that it was this experience that made him a novelist and raised his sensitivities. God the thief had broken in and stolen his complacency so he could see life anew and do something with it.

My final story.

One day a very wealthy city man took his pampered son on a trip to the country, supposedly to visit a relative. In actuality, however, what the father had in mind was to show his son the constricted way poor country folks live. They stayed the weekend in the home of a relative who was a very poor and humble farmer. At the end of the trip, as they were en route back home, the father cleared his throat and asked his son, "Well, son, what did you think of the trip?"

The son replied thoughtfully, "Very nice, Dad." Then the father asked. "Did you notice how they lived?" The son replied, "Yes."

The father, who should have quit while he was ahead, continued, "What did you learn?" The son responded, "Well, I learned that we have one dog in our house, but they have four. Also, I know we have a fountain in our garden filled with all kinds of goldfish, but they have a whole trout stream that goes on and on. And, you know, Dad, we have those fancy imported lamps in our garden, but they have stars! And while our garden goes to the edge of our neighbor's fence, they have the whole sky as their backyard!"

At the end of the son's reply, the father was speechless. Then from the quiet the son said softly, "Thanks, Dad, for showing me how poor we really are."

God stole the father's illusions. Not, of course, the child's: he was still too innocent to have any.

Anyway, maybe Jesus is right. God *is* a thief. He's out to steal the suffocations, barriers, and delusions that prevent us from being full human beings, the saints we were called to be. You know: all those fancy imported lamps and never seeing the stars. God wants to break in and run off with all the self-centered preoccupations that prevent us from being kind and compassionate and, most of all, from sharing our time—time shared with our spouses, time with our children, time with our friends, time with the poor and needy, time with God.

Somewhere in the back of your minds it's probably lurking that, in light of September 11, this gospel takes on an eerie relevance. Two men will be at their desks at the World Trade Center. One will be taken, the other remain. Two women will be working at their jobs. One will be taken, the other remain. Like in the days of Noah, the men and women who were taken away did not know that Tuesday would be their last until the flood of terror came and carried them off. That's why Jesus' words are powerful: if they had really known when the thief had planned to come, they would have been prepared.

Through our stories, we have put a different spin on that thief and turned him around. And so we see him not as an agent of deceit and cunning, out to steal our possessions, but as God of kindly warning come to steal our false values and illusions so that in fact we *will* be ready for him. Like Dostoevsky who, after his frightening experience, now savored every breath of fresh air, every human face, every ray of the sun, we too are challenged after September 11 to see anew, savor what really matters, and live the moral life as the best preparation for our summons.

So it would appear that this gospel is no longer a quaint message for the pious folk two thousand years ago. Since September 11, two thousand years later, it speaks to us with a fresh urgency, and says it's time to invite in the Thief.

56

John and Stephen

Second Sunday of Advent, Cycle A
Matthew 3:1–12

Theme: repent

John the Baptist appeared in the wilderness of Judea, proclaiming, "Repent, for the kingdom of heaven has come near....Bear fruit worthy of repentance....for every tree that does not bear good fruit is cut down and thrown into the fire."

Ho hum, we mentally tell John, we've heard it all before. But wait a minute. Stephen King, one of our country's most successful and popular writers, spoke to the young graduates at Vassar College this year—those young folk with the world at their fingertips, those privileged people who will shortly be running the world. And you know what? Still recovering from a serious automobile accident, King, in his own way, sounded very much like John the Baptist in today's gospel but with a modern spin on his words. John the Baptist and Stephen King, it seems, have spanned the centuries and joined forces. Anyway, this is what Stephen King, sounding like John the Baptist, said to the graduates:

What will you do? Well, I'll tell you one thing you're *not* going to do, and that's take it with you. I'm worth I don't exactly know how many millions of dollars—I'm still in the Third World compared to Bill Gates, but on the whole I'm doing OK—and a couple of years ago I found out what "you can't take it with you" means. I found out while I was lying in the ditch at the side of a country road, covered with mud and blood and with the tibia of my right leg poking out the side of my jeans like the branch of a tree taken down in a thunderstorm. I had a MasterCard in my wallet, but when you're lying in the ditch with broken glass in your hair, no one accepts MasterCard....

We all know that life is ephemeral, but on that particular day and in the months that followed, I got a painful but extremely valuable look at life's simple backstage truths. We come in naked and broke. We may be dressed when we go out, but we're just as broke. Warren Buffett? Going to go out broke. Bill Gates? Going to go out broke. Tom Hanks? Going out broke. Steve King? Broke. Not a crying dime. And how long in between?

How long have you got to be in the chips?...Just the blink of an eye. Yet for a short period, let's say forty years, but the merest blink in the larger course of things, you and your contemporaries will wield enormous power....Of all the power which will shortly come into your hands gradually at first, but then with a speed that will take your breath away, the greatest is undoubtedly the power of compassion, the ability to give. We have enormous resources in this country, resources you yourselves will soon command but they are only yours on loan. Only yours to give for a short while....

Not that long ago, we would have dismissed first-century John and twenty-first-century Stephen as full of rhetoric, if not something else. But since the World Trade Center disaster on September 11, the crash of American Airlines flight 794 on November 12, the fear of terrorism, and the wars in Afghanistan and in Israel, we're not so ready to do that, are we? The Advent theme of repentance, of making ready for a savior through the work of compassion, as King puts it, comes closer to home. In our brief time on earth, as he so dramatically put it, it's up to us to make ready the Lord's coming in grace and love. The message is, repent, in the sense of getting rid of self-measurement and self-centeredness. Use the power of compassion. Take the time God has given you to daily prepare for a savior by kindly deeds.

For an example of how it's done quite simply, listen to this recollection of Archbishop Desmond Tutu of his early life as a poor child in

South Africa. He recalled the day his mother met the man who was to became Archbishop Trevor Huddleston, one of the great opponents of apartheid in South Africa. The young Desmond Tutu remembered in particular the way in which the tall, slim English priest spoke to his mother. His quiet demeanor, and the way that he graciously lifted his hat and inquired after her health, just as he inquired after everyone whom he met, white or black, impressed the child. Tutu said this experience shaped his understanding of faith and life, and his sense of vocation.

There it is. In one simple act a man goes against the ethos of his society and treats another person as a fellow human, a child of God. A boy watches and remembers. Trevor Huddleston sowed the seed that meant another life was changed, a life that has brought about a radical change and the restoration of hope in South Africa today. That's it; simple acts that pull us out of ourselves and into compassion.

John and Stephen, as we heard, have both spoken of time running out and so, once more, we have been warned. If we heed the warning and begin to bear good fruit, then after our time runs out and as our new life in God begins, we would dearly want said over us the words of that moving eulogy transmitted worldwide during the funeral service for the New York City fire department chaplain, Franciscan Father Mychal Judge. This heroic priest, you recall, was killed while administering the last rites to a dying firefighter at the World Trade Center. In tribute to this fallen hero, the eulogist beautifully pointed out that at his final moments, Father Mychal Judge was where the action was, praying, talking to God, and serving his fellow man. The eulogist then added wistfully, "Can anyone think of a better way to die?"

On this second Sunday of Advent in the year 2001, John the Baptist of yesterday and Stephen King of today together ask the same question in a different way: "Can anyone think of a better way to live?"

57

Good News

Third Sunday of Advent, Cycle A
Matthew 11:2–11

Theme: good news in bad times

"Go and tell John what you hear and see: the blind receive their sight, the lame walk, the lepers are cleansed, the deaf hear, the dead are raised, and the poor have good news brought to them."

Remember: when Jesus spoke those words he knew, like everyone else in the area, that John the Baptist was languishing in prison. He had heard the rumors to that effect. Therefore, Jesus knew that, alone and depressed, wondering if it paid to do the right thing after all, since evil seemed to be as flourishing as ever, John needed some positive words, some encouragement, some good news.

In this sense, when you think about it, things are not much different today in this Advent of the year 2001. Many people feel John-like. They feel that, once more, evil seems to be winning. War, the fresh memories of terrorism past, the fear of terrorism to come, a holiday of mourning for many, worrying about opening one's mail, watching Arabs and Israelis kill each other's children, wincing over our *own* children planning a new Columbine-like killing of their peers or a killing of their parent, feeling the pinch of the economy or the blow of the loss of a job. The bad news comes daily and, like John in prison, we have our questions. Are you the one who has come with love and peace as you declared, or shall we look elsewhere?

Right away Jesus sensed John's doubt and depression, so his response to the messengers John sent was essentially this: "Look, go back, sit John down, and tell him some stories." And when they asked, "What stories?" Jesus smiled and said, "You know, look around you: the stories of the blind seeing, the lame walking, the lepers being cleansed, and all that sort of thing. And jazz it up and make the stories interesting. He needs a pick-up. He needs to hold onto faith." So if that was Jesus' approach in today's gospel, so shall it be mine and I too will share some good news with you in the hope of making your personal imprisonments easier.

First, let me relate the true story of an Israeli nuclear chemist named Jacob Gilat who right now is in this country studying at Berkeley. The Jewish Gilat tells the story of a Catholic, a Polish farmer named Alex Roslan, who saved his life. The story goes this way. When the horror began in Poland and Jews were being slaughtered in the very streets of their ghetto, the farmer quietly and bravely rescued two small boys, Jacob and his younger brother, Shalom. They were hidden in his house even though his wife was terrified—and rightly so—that they would be found out and be put to death.

The story could end right here and there would be heroism and compassion enough to go around. But there's more. When Jacob and his brother Shalom contracted scarlet fever, they infected Alex's own son, Yurek. Yurek was sent to the hospital in Warsaw and, though only ten years old and having learned compassion from watching his parents, he cunningly took notes on what the doctors did to cure him. He also hid half his medicine so that his parents could take it home to the Jewish boys.

That's incredible and the story, once again, could stop here and gain our admiration. But there's more, for it turns out that even *this* was not enough to help and so, would you believe, Alex and his wife sold their three-room apartment and took a smaller one in order to raise some money to bribe a friendly doctor's staff and smuggle the brothers into a hospital. Shalom died, but Jacob survived to become the scientist with a good news story forever in his heart, a man who, amid all the imprisonments of the Hitler era, experienced good news.

There's a footnote to this story, by the way. A rabbi who was told this story by Jacob was so moved by it that he was determined to seek out other "rescuers in Europe," as he called them. His search found

that there were at least 50,000 non-Jewish rescuers from many countries. He even founded a fund to aid some of them, now living in
poverty. Beyond the camera lens, this sort of quiet good news goes on
all the time today

Then there's a woman named Terri, who took her two small children
and fled an abusive marriage. She moved into an apartment and started a new life for herself. But one day, Terri came home to find that her
key no longer worked in her apartment door. She broke a windowpane
and got in, only to discover that all her possessions were gone.
Everything. The police showed up shortly, but rather than pursuing the
criminal who stole all her stuff, they started to arrest Terri for breaking
and entering. It seemed that Terri's roommate had taken Terri's rent
money but never paid the rent with it. The roommate had been evict-
ed that day by the landlord, and when she moved out, she took all of
Terri's stuff with her.

Terri was in shock. She and her two daughters were now homeless.
They had lost everything they ever owned. Terri took the little cash she
had and bought them dinner. Then she did the only thing she could
think of. She drove to the park to spend the night there. As the girls
fell asleep, Terri noticed other people drifting into the park. They were
homeless, dirty, down and out. Not the kind of people Terri would
ever associate with. She was frightened, very frightened.

The next morning, Terri found a phone in the park. She called her
boss desperately explained her plight, and asked him for an advance
on that week's paycheck. As she fiddled with the phone, a dirty,
unshaven "bum" walked up. He was one of the homeless she had eyed
with suspicion. Hesitantly, he said, "Ma'am, please excuse the intrusion, but…well…I couldn't help but overhear the situation you are in,
and, well…me and the fellas took up a collection for you and your little girls. It's not very much, but maybe it'll help a little." And he
pressed a small wad of cash into her hand. Terri began to cry as she
realized that these men, whom she had discounted, were showing her
a love she was not capable of. Terri returned the money with a big hug.

But the story, like all good news, goes on. Later that day, when
Terri's boss gave her an advance, she bought a bunch of groceries and
drove to the park. She and her daughters laid out a feast for the home-

less men. They spent the afternoon talking, laughing, and sharing their stories. As Terri later said, "As long as I live, I will never forget that day, when God showed me what true generosity and giving meant. When he showed me love comes from the most unexpected places, in the most unlikely way. Those old men will live in my heart and memories forever, as the richest people I ever knew, because they had enough love to share with a mother and her two daughters, who would never have given *them* the time of day."

That, too, is a good news story for those in the prison of doubt, hurt, and despair. There *are* merciful farmers and compassionate bums in the world. There are quietly heroic people in this world taking the sting out of evil, many of them, I sense, sitting here right now. These people are prophets and messengers, who go before the Lord preparing his way. There are none greater.

Now, having shared those bits of good news to let you know there's a lot of it around, a final thought. Not a story, but good news, very good news, nevertheless. So, let's leave Alex and Terri and focus on *you.* The good news here is how much you are loved by God, how our head-over-heels-in-love God cherishes you. That's a good way to end. To get this point across, I will take advantage of these pre-Christmas times and your anticipation, knowing that you have Christmas shopping and agendas and lists still very much on your minds. And I can easily picture you right now in my mind's eye, stalking the malls, walking the aisles, spying-out the sales, inspecting the stores—all of you searching for that extra special gift. I know you. You are secretly stashing away a few dollars a month to buy him some lizard-skin boots; you are staring at a thousand rings to find her the best diamond; you will stay up all night Christmas Eve, assembling the new bicycle. And so it goes. So it goes.

But my question, my big question is this: *why* do you do it? Why do you do it? Well, we all know why. The answer is obvious. You do all this so that eyes will pop and jaws will drop. You do all this to hear those words of disbelief: "You did this for me?" And you, choked up, will reply with your heart, "Do you like it? Yes, I did it all for you."

And so, in these nine days before Christmas, friends, if you're wondering about the best news of all, that God loves you, let me put this to you: the next time a sunrise steals your breath away, a meadow of flowers awes your soul, a spouse's sacrifice drops your jaw, a child's hug warms your heart, a stranger's kindness blows your mind, a neighbor's charity leaves you speechless—remain that way. Say nothing, and listen as heaven whispers, "Do you like it? I did it just for you."

58

Saint Joseph

Fourth Sunday of Advent, Cycle A
Matthew 1:18–24

"Now the birth of Jesus the Messiah took place in this way." Thus begins Matthew's account. And this account, unlike that of Luke, sees the event from the eyes of Joseph, not Mary.

Joseph. His name is mentioned four times in a few verses in today's gospel, and yet we know so little about him. But what we do know forms our solemn reflection for this Sunday before Christmas. And whatever else we can say about Joseph, three things initially stand out about this man: he was perplexed, he was marginal, and he was a loser.

Joseph was perplexed. His fiancée was pregnant by another man, as far as he could tell. He was torn between his trust in her and what seemed like the obvious facts. He was afraid to take her as his wife, as the angel noted. Between his knowledge of Mary's condition and that dream of his, he spent tortured days and sleepless nights. There was so much he didn't understand.

Joseph was marginal. He comes and goes quickly in the gospel stories. Gone and forgotten. There is not even one recorded word of his. Everyone else has something to say: the angel, Mary, the shepherds, Herod, the Magi. But not Joseph. Silence. The spotlight, literally and figuratively, shines on Jesus and Mary. He's not even the child's real father. He's a stepdad. The manger scene often puts him in the shadows. Like the Lone Ranger, everyone asks, who was that masked man? We really don't know.

Finally, Joseph was a loser, to put it mildly. He had to fall in love with a mystic, someone claimed by a higher power. He had to struggle with doubts and desperately search for answers. He lost his wife to

God, as it were. Then he, the so-called great family man, lost his only son and had to go looking for him down the alleys of Jerusalem. Finally, he lost his life somewhere between that search for Jesus and Jesus' start of his public ministry. He was gone. Deceased. His left his wife a widow and his son fatherless. Not a great track record. Joseph the loser.

And yet, in this particular Advent of the year 2001, laced with memories of terrorism and death, it is this Joseph who, of all the characters who appear in the Nativity story, speaks to many, resonates with many, identifies with many. Let us look.

We said that Joseph was perplexed, and we also are perplexed. There is so much we don't understand in today's world: the ramifications of human cloning, why other people hate us, why September 11 happened, why families break up, why children kill children, why parents divorce, why a child is on drugs. Why, in short, is there so much evil? But notice: Joseph, who was also perplexed, didn't just stand there paralyzed. His perplexity did not stop him from doing what he could. He led his pregnant wife on a long caravan journey to Bethlehem, found a place for her to have a baby, fled with his family to Egypt like the von Trapp family fleeing the Nazis, supported them by his handiwork, and taught his son a trade.

The point is, in spite of so much he didn't understand, he did what he could to make this world a better place. He did his duty, simply, faithfully, loyally, dependably. To that extent, Joseph speaks to everyone who, at the beginning of this new century, is perplexed by it all, and he says, do what you can do to be caring, compassionate, and helpful. Stay loyal and faithful to your beliefs and convictions. Do your duty. *You* make this world a better place.

We said he was marginal but, remember, this man also had dreams—just like another marginal person of the twentieth century who proclaimed, "I have a dream." As such Joseph speaks to today's hopeless, today's marginal. Not just those shunted aside because of the color of their skin or their nationality but the slow, the unpopular, the unattractive, the disappointed, the poor, the hurting, those considered on the fringes of Nerdville, beyond the social pale—anyone who desperately dreams that things could be better. Joseph speaks to them all.

He reminds them to cherish and hold on to their dreams. Have faith, he would say. Look: Mary of Nazareth became queen of heaven; Jesus, the infant in danger of death, became Savior. And he himself, dreamer that he was, eventually emerged from the shadows so that the whole world now knows him as *Saint* Joseph. So have faith in God. Remember Joseph. Cherish your dreams.

Finally, we said he was a loser, a man who knew loss. He speaks deeply to all others who are losers, who also have suffered loss. He knows, for example, that this Christmas will be hard on the thousands upon thousands who have lost their jobs in the ripple effect from September 11, who will experience a leaner holiday, smaller meals, fewer presents, and perhaps feelings of failure, of desperation. He knows this Christmas will also be a blue one for those who have lost family members and friends in the World Trade Center disaster, especially those with no closure or without any other family members or friends to help them cope. With sorrow he sees that there will be empty places at the festive table, empty spaces under the tree, empty beds, empty hearts, perhaps a photograph with a vigil candle on the coffee table. It is so unbearably sad.

Joseph, who almost lost a wife and did at one time lose a son, knows the feeling. But, again, he also knew that God would have the last word, that God in time could make loss the very condition of compassion, service, and growth. He knew that, although scars would remain and grief would now and then openly assert itself, loss could be the seeding place of quiet greatness.

So, in this Advent of the year of the Lord 2001, Matthew has presented us with a role model, a man for our seasons. He asks, in effect, are you, like Joseph, perplexed? marginalized? hurting over losses? Let Joseph's steadfastness and example be yours, for he is the kind who often might have the occasion to utter this ancient Gallic prayer. Listen as I close with it.

As the rain hides the stars,
as the autumn mist hides the hills,
as the clouds veil the blue of the sky,
so the dark happenings of my life hide
the shining of Thy face from me.

Yet if I may hold Thy hand in the darkness,
it is enough.
Even though I may stumble in my going,
Thou dost not fall;
Thou dost not fall.

59

Christmas Storytime

Luke 2:1–14

A kindly, ninety-year-old grandmother found buying presents for family and friends a bit much one Christmas, so she wrote out checks to put in their Christmas cards. In each card she carefully wrote, "Buy your own present," and then sent them off. After the Christmas festivities were over, she found the checks under a pile of papers on her desk—which meant that everyone on her gift list had received a beautiful Christmas card from her with "Buy your own present" written inside, but without the checks! I'm sure that was a Christmas they will long remember.

On this Christmas Day, 2001, I start off with a smile because, as you know, it's a different kind of a Christmas, this year, isn't it? Who would have thought this time last year, for example, that the date of September 11 would be seared into the national consciousness? That words such as police, firefighters, Ground Zero, Taliban, anthrax, terror, Afghanistan, words hitherto unknown or unattended to, would become national buzzwords? Who would have thought that, for so many, this Christmas would carry gaping holes, deep emptiness, a visit to the gravesite, and an empty place around the festive table?

The way we all deal with these tragedies, whether we realize it or not, the way humankind has *always* dealt with tragedies, from time immemorial, is to turn to storytelling. We instinctively turn to storytelling as a way of coping, a way of reassuring ourselves and others that we are still alive and that the world goes on. That is why we tell stories of the deceased at funerals. We use stories to mesh emotion and intellect, heart and mind, in the face of a world turned upside down.

I might add that children especially need stories. They spend hours, sometimes alone, watching graphic images of destruction. Unlike adults, children process grief by talking out loud. Our tendency is to silence or distract them, which means the children end up processing their emotions alone. But we need to give them the opportunity to tell their stories and, above all, to listen to stories of hope and renewal. That's why we have to carve out space, in all of the hectic comings and goings of these days, to be with our children and story them.

And surely, at this season, beyond the manufactured TV stories, we must tell the deeper good news stories of the Nativity we celebrate: of a perplexed Mary and a bewildered Joseph, of wicked kings and crafty Magi, of mean innkeepers and sweet-singing angels—and, most of all, about this baby, this Jesus, this Son of God, who would make all things new again and whose love would always be the last word no matter how bad things got. We must also tell those derivative stories that sound the same good news of redemption and hope and the power of love, and draw their inspiration from the Christ Child.

There is, for example, a story from long ago, of a black man walking along Forty-second Street in New York, from the railroad station to his hotel, carrying a heavy suitcase and a heavier valise. Suddenly, a hand took hold of the valise and a pleasant voice said, "Pretty heavy, brother! Suppose you let me take one. I'm going your way." The black man resisted but finally allowed the young white man to assist him in carrying his burden, and for several blocks they walked along, chatting together like cronies. "And *that*," said Booker T. Washington years afterward, "was the first time I ever saw Theodore Roosevelt."

We don't have to spell out the meaning or the deeper significance of one man help carrying another's burden. The story speaks for itself.

Then there's that marvelous story about a certain statue in a town square in Eastern Europe. It's not what you would ever expect to find in a town square because it's not a statue in honor of a war hero or a prime minister or a famous athlete or even a rock star. Rather, the statue is a tribute to beauty in the midst of horror, and here's its story.

One day during the war in Sarajevo, a bomb was dropped on a bakery where twenty-two people were waiting in line to buy bread. All twenty-two people were killed. A citizen of Sarajevo, a man named Vedran Smialiavic, decided that he wanted to do something to mark the death of these innocent victims. But, he said to himself, "I am a simple man, what can I do?"

Before the war, Smialiavic had played in the Sarajevo orchestra, but once the war started everyone was afraid to venture out just to hear music. With no music to perform, he walked the streets near his home and tried to find things to keep himself busy. But when he heard about the bakery bombing, Smialiavic came up with an answer to his question. He dressed up in his tuxedo and took his cello and a chair and marched to the site. He sat there amid the debris for twenty-two days, one for each of the victims of the bombing, and played his favorite piece of music, Albinoni's *Adagio in G*. He braved the artillery fire and ducked the snipers' bullets and went on playing his cello.

So, the statue in the town square is a statue of Vedran Smialiavic sitting on his chair playing his cello. People often bring flowers to put around the base of the statue, always twenty-two flowers to honor those twenty-two people. He's a hero because, little man that he was, he made a difference doing what he could do. His fame is that he made beautiful music among the rubble. He gave people hope.

Does this remind you of a tiny infant born in a stable, lying on a bed of straw, being heavenly music among the earth's rubble? The story of Vedran Smialiavic, like the Christmas story, challenges and becomes a story to live by. It's the kind of story that asks you to imagine yourself all dressed up in a tux or evening gown, taking your cello and playing, say, at Ground Zero. Or anywhere for that matter: as a Christian, you have the mission of making beautiful music wherever there is rubble.

"Merry Christmas!" said the small boy as he handed over his Christmas present to his mother. Earlier that Christmas Eve, he had shyly presented himself to a department store clerk. "I would like to buy my mom some pajamas," he said bravely. "Very nice," said the clerk, "but first I'll need to know more about your mother. Tell me, is she short or tall?" To which the boy replied, "She's perfect." Whereupon the clerk wrapped a nifty size medium for him. A few days later, mom returned the nifty size medium pajamas and exchanged them for a size extra large.

We smile, but this story is also a variation of the Christmas story, and its kernel of truth is this: *could we not learn to see as that child?* Not a fat lady, not a loser, not a bum, not a nerd, not a sinner, but someone who, as God's image and likeness, is perfect? Is this what Jesus meant when he said, "Unless you become like a little child you cannot enter the kingdom of heaven"? Isn't this the way God sees *us*? Isn't this what the Christmas story is really all about with its helter-skelter mix of elegant Magi, bottom-of-the-pit shepherds, stinking animals and heavenly angels? With that motley crew around the manger, is *anyone* excluded from the love of God materialized in this Child?

Looking over this vast congregation tonight, I can't think of anyone. Merry Christmas!

60

The Divine Absence

Feast of the Baptism of the Lord, Cycle A
Isaiah 42:1–4, 6–7

Theme: the problem of suffering

A bruised reed he will not break, and a dimly burning wick he will not quench.

There is a scene in the play called *Ma Rainey's Black Bottom,* written by August Wilson, in which some African-American jazz musicians are shown rehearsing in a Chicago recording studio. At some point they take a break from their rehearsal and they begin to tell stories. One of them tells the story about a cousin of his, a minister whose sister in Atlanta was desperately ill and so he took a train to visit her. The train stopped in a little Georgia town to take on water, and the minister got off the train to use the bathroom. He went into the station and was told that colored people couldn't use the bathroom inside; they had to use the outhouse.

So the minister went to the outhouse and while he was there, the train left the station. There's the minister standing on a railroad plat-form in south Georgia—no train, no friends. Across the tracks there's a group of hostile, young white men, and not wanting trouble, the minister simply starts walking up the railroad tracks. The group of men follow him. They surround him. They demand to know who he is and what he's doing. He tells them, "I am a minister." He shows them his Bible, he shows them his cross, he tells them his sister in Atlanta is sick and he's been left behind by the train. No matter: dance for us, they say...dance...why don't you dance for us?

254

Someone pulls out a pistol and begins to fire at the ground, and they make him dance. The musician who's telling the story says, "Can you imagine that? Can you believe they did that to a man of God?" One of the other musicians says, "What *I* can't believe is that if he were a man of God, why did God let them do it to him? If he was God's own man why didn't God bring fire down from heaven and destroy those crackers? That's what I want to know."

Ah, there it is. That's what *we'd* like to know. Why didn't God step in and nuke those creeps? Why, in fact, does God seem so indifferent to any suffering in this world? Why does he allow rampant injustice? At times, truth to tell, he seems like such an impotent God, an insensitive God. All this misery, innocent children abused, tortured, dying, and God does nothing. Cancer, September 11, war, death; the evil prosper and the wicked climb to the top. The rich get richer and the poor get poorer. The list is endless. In the face of so much unfairness there are times we'd like to throttle God, write him off, shake him up, shout at him, if the thought weren't so blasphemous and we weren't so scared. Yet at times we are angry with God, or at the very least mightily perplexed, profoundly disappointed, and painfully hurt. Some God. Some divine justice.

I must tell you here in church and quite up front, I have no answers to the misery and unfairness of life and God's terrible silence. I can only offer these two considerations.

First, we say that all we want from God is simple justice. Bring down the dictators, imprison the embezzlers, give payback time to the murderers and cheats, the rapists and drug dealers. But be careful what you pray for. Do we, you and I, *really* want God's absolute justice? Here and now? Think again, because that justice would also come *our* way as well. Are we ready for that—to be judged strictly, fairly, right down the line? Do we want our every sin weighed, our every failing punished, our every connivance, lie, and impurity exposed and punishment meted out? Are second chances to be denied, repentance foreshortened, mercy withheld? Is this what we really want when we cry out for justice?

Could it also be that God is giving others the same chances as ourselves? Is God that forbearing? Maybe so, because there is today's

Scripture with its cryptic description about a *servant*-God saying of him, "He *shall* bring forth justice to the nations..." but notice: "*not* crying out, *not* shouting, *not* making his voice heard in the street. A bruised reed he shall not break and a smoldering wick he shall not quench." We just don't understand. What is this? We *want* God to cry out and shout and make his voice heard in the street—can't he see all the pain?—but he doesn't. Instead he shows an exquisite sensitivity, an unwillingness to break a bruised reed or snuff out a smoldering wick as long as there is the hope of life. So then, does the God of the Bible have an inexplicable soft spot that seems to let the world's suffering go on in the hopes that the wick of human decency and compassion will flame again?

Then there is the charge against God that he is indifferent, absent and aloof from human suffering, and so why should he care? But there are powerful hints that he cares a lot because somehow God actually seems to suffer along with us. It seems that God is *not* abstracted from our hurts; not apart, looking like some impotent spectator above it all; not distant from human suffering but right in the middle of it. Think. We are created in God's own image and likeness and if we suffer, does our Image and Likeness suffer also? Then too, we just celebrated God's coming into our very flesh in the incarnation. Yes, he took on our full human condition, and therefore, he mysteriously suffers like us and with us like any passionate lover. Like a mother who echoes in her heart every hurt of her child, God sympathizes with us and throbs with our pain.

A sense of what I'm trying to convey comes from a passage in Elie Wiesel's harrowing book *Night*, the story of life and death in a Nazi concentration camp. In one scene, in a reprisal for some misdemeanor, the Nazis decided to teach a lesson by hanging three people, including a young boy. Elie Wiesel describes the terrible scene:

> The SS seemed more preoccupied, more disturbed than usual. To hang a young boy in front of thousands of spectators was no light matter. The head of the camp read the verdict. All eyes were on the child. He was lividly pale, almost calm, biting his lips. The gallows threw its shadow over him....
>
> The three victims mounted together onto the chairs. The three

necks were placed at the same moment within the nooses. "Long live liberty!" cried the two adults. But the child was silent.

"Where is God? Where is he?" someone behind me asked. The two adults were no longer alive. But the third rope was still moving....Behind me, I heard the same man asking: "Where is God now?" And I heard a voice within me answer him: "Where is he? Here he is. He is hanging here on this gallows."

Can that be? Is God somehow not *apart* from human suffering but a part *of* it, still groaning with the pains of giving birth to a people who will do his will? Is it really true what faith says: *God* in a stinking manger, *God* crying out sorrowfully in Gethsemane, "Father let this pass me by," and in near despair, asking on Calvary our oft-asked question, "My God, my God,why have you forsaken me?" Is this *God* who is hurting, bleeding, suffering, and dying? Is this *God* on the gallows of human existence? Then we have to ask, if, like any lover, he suffered our agony, cried, and died with us, is his resurrection the signal, the hint, the ultimate response to our questions of life's unfairness? I don't know.

There is a story about the ancient rabbi Baal Shem-Tov and it goes like this:

One day, the rabbi and his students were standing on a hill when they noticed foreign troops invading their town. From their vantage point on the hill they were able to see all the horror and violence of the attack. The rabbi looked up to Heaven and cried out, "Oh, if only I were God." A student asked, "But, Master, if you were God, what would you do differently?" The rabbi answered him, "If I were God, I would do nothing differently. But if I were God, I would understand."

We are not God. We do not understand. All that we're left with is an enigmatic description of a God who is reluctant to break bruised reeds or quench smoldering wicks, a God incarnate in Jesus Christ who in his suffering made an heroic final act of faith in his Father, "Father, into your hands I commend my spirit," and received on behalf of us all a final act of vindication, the resurrection.

This will have to do for now.

Notes

1. Spirituality

This introductory homily is one of the very few where I have used substantially another's work. The thoughts and paragraphs come from Ronald Rohlheiser's splendid work, *The Holy Longing: The Search for a Christian Spirituality* (New York: Doubleday, 1999). The many comments from the people and the unusual requests for copies of this homily only serve to confirm my conviction that people are indeed hungry for spirituality and capable of challenging thoughts. The story about the robin comes from my retelling of a retelling by Flora Cooke.

4. The Desert Fathers

People were intrigued by the stories of the Desert Fathers and even more surprised to hear about them. Perhaps we should mine that rich source more often.

5. What We Might Remember

The Bob Stringer story comes from "Making Wrong Right," by Patrick Rogers, Bob Stewart, and Jerry Mitchell (*People*, September 7, 1998). Caryll Houselander's words are from her book, *The Reed of God* (Collegeville, MN: Christian Classics, 1994). People who do not know her work were fascinated with this quote and asked for its source.

6. Good Pope John

People loved this homily and it's good to keep alive the memory of a great man while still making an Advent point.

11. Jesus Among the Beasts

This homily is one of those that obviously calls for passion in its opening paragraphs!

12. The Transfiguration

The mall story comes from Bass Mitchell of Hot Springs, Virginia.

14. Remember the Past

For these thoughts and their development I am indebted to Walter Burghardt, SJ.

17. Forgiveness Around the Campfire

The immediate situation behind this homily is the bombing of the federal building in Oklahoma City and the subsequent arrest, trial, and execution of Timothy McVeigh. The homilist, alas, will always have a current example to update this homily.

18. No Options

I have appropriated the inspiration and the story at the end of this homily from William Willimon.

20. The Holy Shadow

I am indebted to master storyteller John Shea for this story. It's from his book, *Elijah at the Wedding Feast and Other Tales: Stories of the Human Spirit* (Chicago, IL: ACTA Publications, 1999).

23. The Mote in the Eye and Other Jokes

The thrust of this homily comes from William Willimon. The Douglas Adams account comes from Father Joe Nolan's homily service, *Good News* (New Berlin, WI: Liturgical Publications, Inc., 25 February 2001).

25. The Seventy-Two

The Brennan Manning story is modified and condensed from his book, *The Wisdom of Accepted Tenderness* (Denville, NJ: Dimension Books, 1979). Thanks to his words, this was a very powerful homily.

26. Come Apart and Rest

The quotation is from Christian de la Huerta and Lam Kam Chuen, *Coming Out Spirituality: The Next Step* (New York: Jeremy Tarcher, 1999). The Brennan Manning quotation is from his book, *Abba's Child* (Colorado Springs, CO: Navpress, 1994). The story of Sister José Hobday is from *Parabola*, (volume IV, number 4, November 1979).

30. A Cloud of Witnesses

The inspiration and words for the current Christian martyrs comes from my modification of the words found in *Celebration*, 19 August 2001, by Patricia Datchuck Sanchez. The wonderful story comes from that master storyteller, Edward Hays, *A Pilgrim's Almanac: Reflections for Each Day of the Year* (Leavenworth, KS: Forest of Peace Publishing, 1989).

24. Why I Am A Christian
The TV interview is from Donald Shelby, "The Lord's House and Ours." This moving homily received a good response.

26. When the Miracles Stop
I've used the story of Carly in another book. It's from Anne Donovan, "The Painful Effort to Believe," by Anne Donovan (*America*, 19 September 1998). The story of the unbelieving Jesuit is from John L'Heureux in *The Expert of God* (New York: Penguin Books, 1990).

34. Vocation
The recruiter story comes from Patricia Datchuk Sanchez, "Discipleship, a dear and daily cost" (*Celebration*, September 1998). The Chiune Sugihara story is from Stephen Aeterburn, *The Power Book* (Nashville, TN: Thomas Nelson Publishing, 1996).

35. Spiritual Blindness
The original story, "Paradise Squandered," by Dale Van Atta, can be found in the May 1997 issue of *Reader's Digest*. I am indebted to Wilke Au for the reference to the rabbi story in his book, *The Enduring Heart: Spirituality for the Long Haul* (Mahwah, NJ: Paulist Press, 2000).

37. The Rich Young Man
The clever "liturgy" is from *101 Things to Do With a Dull Church*, by Martin Wroe, Adrian Reith, Nicak MacIvor, and Simon Parke (Downers Grove, IL: InterVarsity Press, 1994). The Millard Fuller story is quoted in an article by Michael G. Mauldin, "God's Contractor" (*Christianity Today*, 24 June 1999). The Oscar Meyer story is from an article by Chuck Collins, "Giving Back" (*Fast Company*, December 1999).

39. Justice and Charity
I am indebted to Father Joe Nolan's homily service, *Good News* (21 October 2001; see note 23) for a summary of the movie, *Family Man*.

43. Money
This homily was very well received. People seldom hear about this critical subject beyond an appeal.

45. Christ the King
The Gandhi story is from *A Second Helping of Chicken Soup for the Soul*,

by Jack Canfield and Mark Victor Hansen (Deerfield Beach, FL: Health Communications, 1995). The Father Luli story comes from *Priest* (April 2000).

45. Christ the King

The W.P. Kinsella account is modified from "Joy in Dyersville" (*Attache*, July 1998).

46. Mother's Day

The Alicia Sferrino story comes from "A Second Gift of Life," by Michael Bowker (*Reader's Digest*, April 1997). Applause for this one.

51. Faith: Coming Home

The boy's story, by Jared Wilhem of Mason, Ohio, can be found in *Guideposts*, September 2001.

52. Cured on the Way

The David Pelzer story is modified and summarized from its original telling in *Chicken Soup for the Soul*, fourth edition, by Jack Canfield and Mark Victor Hansen (Deerfield Beach, FL: Health Comm., 1995).

55. Go, Thief!

I adapted the story of the lady and the burglar from William Willimon, in *Pulpit Resource* (Logos Productions, 2 December 2001). The story of the father and his son is adapted from "The Lesson," reprinted in *Vanguard*.

56. John and Stephen

Stephen King, "Scaring You to Action," is excerpted from a speech delivered at Vassar College, 20 May 2001, found on Beliefnet.com.

57. Good News

The Jewish rescue story can be found in full in *America* (15 October 1994) by Charles A. Cerami. The ending to this homily, "I did it all for you," is modified from a source attributed to Max Lucado in *The Great House of God* (Waco, TX: Word Publishing, 1997).

58. St. Joseph

Not an especially great homily, but for my part of the country, only fifty miles from the World Trade Center, memories and wounds are still fresh, and so a simple nod to Joseph in his various roles was in order.

59. Epiphany
The *Wall Street Journal* article referred to was written by Ted Roberts. The story of the Goat's Hair Monk, which I have slightly modified, comes from that wonderful storyteller, Edward Hays, in his book, *The Ladder* (Leavenworth, KS: Forest of Peace Publishing, 1999).

60. The Divine Absence
Every once in a while the preacher needs to tackle a difficult subject that really can't be tackled in ten minutes. But just raising the issue, however unsatisfactorily settled, shows empathy for one of life's profound and perennial issues: the mystery of suffering. It lets the people know that everyone, including the preacher, struggles with the questions surrounding this mystery. This is the kind of a homily where, even before you preach it, you know you will lose some people and perplex others. Still, as I said, you have to toss it out there every so often. The Ma Rainey synopsis comes from preacher Tom Long who in turn was quoted by William Willimon in *Pulpit Resource*, January 2002.

Other Books by William J. Bausch

Best of Bausch CD-ROM
Containing over 400 homilies and stories by Bausch. Editable and printable.
User-friendly.
1-58595-113-7, $129.95 (A-97)

Breaking Trust
A Priest Looks at the Scandal of
Sexual Abuse
1-58595-234-6, 112pp, $10.95 (X-68)

Brave New Church
From Turmoil to Trust
1-58595-135-8, 312 pp, $16.95 (J-85)

The Word: In and Out of Season
1-58595-003-3, 304 pp, $16.95 (J-44)

The Yellow Brick Road
A Storyteller's Approach
to the Spiritual Journey
0-89622-991-2, 320 pp, $14.95 (J-35)

Catholics in Crisis?
0-89622-965-3, 240 pp, $14.95 (J-13)

A World of Stories for Preachers
and Teachers
0-89622-919-X, 534 pp, $29.95 (B-92)

The Parish of the Next Millennium
0-89622-719-7, 304 pp, $16.95 (M-93)

Storytelling the Word
Homilies and How to Write Them
0-89622-687-5, 304 pp, $14.95 (M-64)

While You Were Gone
A Handbook for Returning Catholics
0-89622-575-5, 112 pp, $7.95 (B-91)

More Telling Stories,
Compelling Stories
0-89622-534-8, 200 pp, $9.95 (C-92)

Telling Stories, Compelling Stories
0-89622-456-2, 200 pp, $12.95 (C-44)

Timely Homilies
0-89622-426-0, 176 pp, $9.95 (C-27)

Pilgrim Church
0-89622-395-7, 480 pp, $24.95 (B-52)

Becoming a Man
0-89622-357-4, 324 pp, $19.95 (W-19)

A New Look at the Sacraments
0-89622-174-1, 300 pp, $14.95 (B-48)

Storytelling: Imagination and Faith
0-89622-199-7, 232 pp, $12.95 (B-12)

TWENTY-THIRD PUBLICATIONS

185 WILLOW STREET • PO BOX 180 • MYSTIC, CT 06355
TEL: 1-800-321-0411 • FAX: 1-800-572-0788
E-MAIL: ttpubs@aol.com • www.twentythirdpublications.com